The
Last
Primitive
Peoples

The
Last
Primitive
Peoples

Robert Brain

Crown Publishers,Inc.
New York

87191

First published in the U.S.A., 1976, by Crown Publishers,
Inc.

Produced by Walter Parrish International Limited, London
Designed by Stephen Chapman

Set in Apollo 645 12 on 13 pt.

Typeset by Photoprint Plates Ltd, Rayleigh, Essex.
Colour origination by Colour Reproductions Ltd,
Billericay, Essex. Colour printing by Balding and Mansell
Ltd, Wisbech, Cambridgeshire. Black and white printing,
and binding, by The Pitman Press Ltd, Bath, Avon.

Printed and bound in Great Britain

Library of Congress Cataloging in Publication Data

Brain, Robert.
    The last primitive peoples.

    Bibliography: p.
    Includes index.
    1. Ethnology. I. Title.
GN378.B7   301.2   76-7230
ISBN 0-517-51872-4

Contents

Introduction

In the world of the anthropologist, the 'primitive' is now merging into the 'civilized'. For many observers today, primitive systems can be found in industrial England, the closed communities of America and isolated self-contained villages of the Mediterranean. At the same time we are no longer nervous of applying the epithet 'civilised' to the cultures of Polynesia, Africa and pre-Columbian America. We have begun to realise that the differences between Us and Them are more apparent than real—we can find a savage under a dinner jacket and a gentleman under a vivid coat of paint and feathers. For this reason, anthropology, the study of the primitive, is not only concerned with tattooed islanders but the man in plus-fours and dyed moustaches. It matters little whether he deals with the suburb or the jungle, modern dancing or a ritual orgy, the cures and charms of a New Guinea witchdoctor or the work of a contemporary psychoanalyst.

I have set out in this book to list and describe many of the 'peoples' of the world—concentrating specially on those which many of us in developed, Western countries have tended to dismiss as more or less primitive, and to certain others which we might just as well call primitive in some ways if we consider the word in a fresh light. For convenience, I have divided the world into broad cultural zones—perhaps rather arbitrarily in cases, and the way in which each is broken down varies from section to section. Maps are included too, not to serve as an exhaustive source of information in their own right, but to clarify the text. Only names mentioned in the text have been given.

Today most people would agree that the dividing line between primitive and non-primitive is certainly not a simple racial one. There is no easy way of classifying people into hard-and-fast categories by races, linguistic units, tribes, or even ethnic groups. Race is notoriously a very fluid concept; languages can be adopted or lost by people of widely different cultures; and well-demarcated tribes may be less so on close inspection. There are many problems of this kind to be faced in any attempt to make sense of the kaleidoscopic picture presented by the peoples of the world. Race, language and culture rarely coincide with any degree of perfection and all classifications made by the scholar must be arbitrary and shifting. A good example of the possible permutations are the nomadic Fulani of West Africa, a group of pastoral people who live an extremely simple existence across the savannah lands from the Atlantic coast to the Cameroon. Despite a degree of Negro admixture they must be classified racially as Caucasians and are probably of North African, Mediterranean stock; they stand out clearly from their shorter, blacker, stockier Negro neighbours. Nevertheless they speak a Negro language and

6

must be classified linguistically with the neighbouring farmers. On cultural criteria—way of life, social differentiation, religion—they are very different from both Negro and Caucasian groups; as simple cattle-herders they are technologically far more primitive than the Negroes who live near them.

Scientists have shown that there is no way of defining 'primitive' and 'civilised' through the attribution of physical factors—brain-size, blood groups, colour. Unfortunately the differences between, say, Negroes and Caucasians are not so clear-cut as some people would have us believe. Moreover in most caste systems—India was an example—separation and economic differentiation of particular groups are justified by the attribution of physical differences which on close examination do not exist. Take another example: for hundreds of years the Japanese have discriminated against a pariah group—a 'primitive' caste—known as the Eta or Burakumin. In Japanese cities the segregation of the Eta has been justified on racial grounds—there is a commonly shared myth that these people are descendants of a different race, a 'less human' race, than the stock which fathered the Japanese as a whole. Yet this group is quite indistinguishable in any physical sense from the population at large. The Japanese and the Eta are so similar that—like the German Jews in a similar situation—the Eta were in the past forced to wear special insignia and clothes in order to make them identifiable. Notions of racial inferiority and primitivity are invented to justify the economic and social degradation of a human group. In such cases sub-groups within a community are treated with contempt and often become scapegoats on whom the ills of the majority are projected. Gypsies in England, Untouchables in India, the Jews in Germany have all been accused of contaminating the way of life of the majority groups by their primitive blood and their primitive ways. In some cases it even seems a psychological need to set apart a group to loath or despise inside a community.

Throughout history persons of different cultures have considered themselves as different from each other as dogs from cats. It is common for people of a relatively self-contained community to think of those along the road, over the river or behind the mountain as 'not quite human' and therefore legitimate targets for their scorn, their slave razzias and their cannibalism. Fantastic prejudices are encouraged about the physical conditions or habits of these strangers—the Japanese Eta were supposed to have tails, some African peoples say their neighbours walk on their heads or eat their children or marry their daughters; to the English, the French were traditionally all snail-eaters and adulterers. Treating foreigners as somewhat less moral, less human than ourselves was taken to an extreme in the 18th and 19th centuries when Europeans conquered countless diverse ethnic groups all over the world. They discovered the noble savage in his jungle and on his island, but as time went by and these people were not immediately amenable to their demands for land and labour they became filthy primitive wretches, stereotypes expressing only the white man's need to believe in his own superiority. Thus we have the creation of a myth that one sector of humanity—the white Anglo-Saxon race—was civilised while the rest were primitive; this myth served to justify the depredations of the colonialists, the wars of their soldiers, the proselytizing of their missionaries and the exploitation of their traders.

What about language? In India it is language which determines whether a person belongs to the mainstream of Hindu civilisation or to a Classified ('primitive') tribe. In South America, being 'civilised' (which implies belonging to Hispanic rather than Indian culture) depends on very simple criteria—whether or not you speak a native language, wear native clothes or practice Indian customs. In Australia, until recently, a language test existed to screen migrants arriving in White Australia. In South Africa, more realistically, language is not considered a sufficient guide for the racist policies of the government and birth and race are used as criteria in classifying Bantu, Coloured and White.

The word 'primitive' has been used in a less pejorative sense to describe the kind of peoples thought to be living in a prior state. However, as a term to describe in this sense the peoples studied by anthropologists, whatever their way of life, it is wrong. No society exists today which is 'earlier' than any other. It is not correct, for example, to consider the Bushmen of the South African Kalahari, or the Australian Aborigines, as either survivals of our distant past or a contemporary example of the infancy of human society. These ideas imply that if a simple hunting band were left to itself it would eventually evolve into a fully-fledged European-like civilisation.

Some anthropologists classify the peoples of the world purely on cultural criteria, as pastoralists, hunters and gatherers, farmers, peasants, members of industrial society. While this kind of classification has a more objective basis it is of very limited use in attempting to describe the thousands of diverse societies scattered throughout the world, and such a classification has an in-built grading system from the more primitive technologically—the hunters and gatherers and nomads—to the more advanced—the farmers and members of industrial societies. Unfortunately the amount of food stored or energy harnessed does not always correspond with levels of civilisation. Great civilisations have been based on agriculture in some parts of the world, while other farming communities have remained at a low cultural level. Many nomadic groups have greater cultural traditions, in art and poetry, say, than their settled neighbours.

However, as far as the traditional dichotomy between civilised (implying usually the bearers of Western culture) and primitive (the rest) is concerned, the notions of 'industrial' and 'pre-industrial' have played a great part. 'They, the primitive' have included in the past groups of people living outside the international market economy, usually in self-contained, self-sufficient communities, a prey to the economic greed and political aspirations of the civilised. May we suggest that the term 'civilised' implies a devotion to technological progress and an invaluable capacity for analytical thought? And that the term 'primitive' implies a magic-oriented attitude to the world where the sun goes round the earth and each person lives in a subjective, personal universe? Apart from the fact that most men have brains capable of roughly the same amount of intellectual activity, are we in fact any more rational and scientific than a Pacific Islander or an African hunter? For most of us, indeed, the sun still does go round the earth, whatever the books say, and most of the equipment that makes our civilised world function does so as if by magic. A Polynesian Islander understands and can explain the whole of his cultural equipment—he is a universal man. Can you or I explain the functioning of a videotape recorder or even a firework, much less *make* them? Both civilised and primitive men use personal fetishes, magical gestures and ritual avoidances to help him through life. The argument that primitives are technically backward, hence *deprived,* no longer holds water today. We no longer hold very confidently to the old Western beliefs in the inevitable progress of mankind through our control over the material world, having learnt that such control does not necessarily help in cultural or moral progress or in obtaining a better quality of life.

In the same way, almost all the many definitions of the primitive disintegrate on close examination. Primitive society is marked by the importance of the family in ordering social, religious and political affairs—yet on closer inspection we find that all societies have extra-kin ties, institutionalised friendships and impersonal alliances. Primitive society is fetish-ridden, inspired by a religion of fear based on ideas of pollution and taboo, while civilised religions have discarded useless mumbo jumbo, prolonged ritual and magical abracadabra—yet a close look at an ordinary Christian rite may persuade us to change our minds, while the new waves of oriental mysticism in the West may provoke doubts about our confident and rational approach to the supernatural. Primitive society, say the economists, is simply organised, without classes, rich or poor, the ruled and the rulers—yet a glance at the literature shows this to be manifestly untrue. There are many examples of small-scale societies based on primitive techniques where the principles of market competition apply and where there are specialised roles, the rich and the poor, masters and slaves.

So what are we left with? Little more than the fact that many primitive groups live in backward ecological niches and practice a simple way of life. Thus the Bushmen of the Kalahari have been pushed by their more aggressive neighbours into the harsh world of the semi-desert where they eke out a 'primitive' existence. Are primitive societies always isolated cultures? Most of the peoples studied by anthropologists might be classified as marginal cultures and it is true that in isolated communities certain elements seem to develop which we have begun to think of as primitive. Society often grows rigid and static; conservative traditional values are encouraged and change is rejected. Even a specific physical type may develop with a certain amount of in-breeding in closed groups. In fact the first, and most famous, primitive societies to be studied in detail by trained anthropologists were good examples of such isolated societies—island groups or communities of hunters pushed into harsh, unprized ecological zones. At the same time the isolation and uniqueness of these groups was often exaggerated by these scientific reporters intent on describing the neatly-structured society of a primitive community. In fact no society is self-sufficient: Polynesian Islanders travel hundreds of miles in dangerous seas to trade yams and fish hooks. The Trobrianders do the same merely to establish social contacts with neighbouring islanders who speak different languages and practice a very different way of life.

Thus science, history, common sense all fail to provide us with a satisfactory definition of the primitive. We know that all primitives are not aggressive, fetish-ridden, isolated from cultural mainstreams, 'coloured', communist or even technologically backward. As far as I am concerned, the only common feature of primitive societies is that they are small-scale communities where social relations are of the personal, face-to-face kind where everyone knows everyone else and shares the same values. In this society the sick and the unfortunate are able to depend on friendly neighbours, people share supplies and tools in need, the village idiot remains in the village and is not sent off to an institution, the old are loved and cared for. Relations in these communities are solitary and personal, sometimes because they are isolated from other groups. In some cases a feeling of solidarity is encouraged by creating a sentiment of enmity or friendly rivalry with a neighbouring village.

This approach allows us to look in a new way at many diverse groups, even those who nominally belong to our own civilised industrial society. Few would deny the label 'primitive', if used in this sense, to the closed, traditional and conservative Amish groups and the isolated farming Appalachian communities. It is also an epithet which can be applied to the closed, traditionalist groups in the higher echelons of our own society—in fact anthropologists in the 1970s often find more exotic material to analyse in the upperclass suburban communities of our large cities or among closed professional groups such as the Scottish bar, than in the highlands of distant New Guinea. If we must use the term 'primitive' let us use it, therefore, in this wider, less-prejudiced sense and apply it to small groups of people bearing the same traditions, ideals and symbolic systems, relatively closed communities sharing common values and a sense of personal solidarity against the outside world.

This book, if it has achieved anything, has revealed the great heterogeneity of peoples and cultures throughout the world. Small groups have survived, proud of their traditions and determined not to be assimilated into the ways of the great majority. The prestige of the West does not shine so brightly as it did and many peoples have come to question the view—once held blindly—that the West represents Civilisation and that its bearers are God's chosen people. Some of us are beginning to suspect that primitive peoples in the African bush and the South American pampas may be enjoying a better life-style than ours. We have discovered to our surprise that simple societies often have cosmologies and thought systems as complex and abstract as our own. Artists have long looked to primitive sculpture for inspiration. Educationalists have acquired new ideas about child-rearing and sexual behaviour. Psychologists and doctors are taking seriously the once-despised and primitive techniques of 'witch-doctors' and 'magicians' in curing the sick and the insane.

There is a serious danger that all these small communities will be merged into a neutral, monotonous grey culture based on Euro-American, Pan-Russian or Chinese conformist ideas. Once we tried to convert the world to Western ways through the propaganda of capitalism and the proselytisation of the Church. Today we are beginning to appreciate that the uniformity that may well result from economic and cultural conformity is undesirable and even dangerous. For this reason the heterogeneity of human cultures, the exotic worlds of the primitive community, are things to be prized and enjoyed, not despised and discouraged.

Melanesia

Melanesia is a geographical entity—the people who live there are politically, and racially diverse. Nevertheless the general ethos of the area is markedly similar. The name means literally 'island of the blacks', and the area consists of a great crescent of islands to the north and north-east of Australia, stretching from the west end of New Guinea to the New Hebrides and New Caledonia. It includes the Solomons, the Santa Cruz Islands, the Loyalty Islands and Fiji; the western outliers of New Guinea such as Waigeo, Japen and the Schouten group; eastern outliers such as the Louisiade Archipelago, the d'Entrecasteaux group, and the Bismarck group. The last-named is dominated by New Britain, New Ireland and the Admiralties, of which Manus is the largest. Most of the groups are racially Melanesian, although Tikopia, Ontong Java, Rennel and Bellona are racially Polynesian outliers.

New Guinea is the second largest island in the world. Its length is equivalent to the distance from London to Moscow, and its main physical feature is a range of mountains which runs the whole length of the island with peaks sometimes exceeding 15,000 feet. The west end of New Guinea has long been in contact with some of the Indonesian sultanates and was nominally incorporated into the Dutch East Indian Empire. New Guinea was politically divided in colonial times between the Dutch and Australians. Today, the former Australian protectorate is independent—including Papua—while Indonesia has the western half (West Irian). The inhabitants of West Irian, although they are mostly Melanesian in racial type, speak languages related to those of Indonesia and the Philippines. Their cultures too show Indonesian traits such as double descent (descent traced on both sides of the family) and the institutionalized exchange of women and goods.

After New Guinea the main Melanesian Island is Fiji, a country of dense jungle and sparse savannah, palm-fringed villages and large towns, wild pigs in the forest and lobster thermidor in the tourist hotels. Although the indigenous inhabitants are definitely Melanesian in race, their culture resembles very much the stratified societies of Polynesia with their emphases on rank, taboo and mana.

Throughout the Fijian islands there is a diversity of customs, however, and a diversity of physical appearance: Fijians, Lauans, Tongans, people from the Rotuman group (said to be Polynesian and the former inhabitants of Ocean Island),

12

the Banabans who were transferred to a Fijian Island after the Japanese had overrun their homes, all these groups have their own characteristics. There are also Polynesians originally from Vaitupu, who bought for themselves a neighbouring island in the Fiji group. Then in this miniature melting-pot there are over a quarter of a million Indians, Hindu descendants of those who opted to stay after their period of indentured labour expired. There is a Moslem minority, too. Many Indians grow sugar and rice on land they lease from the Fijians, and in some towns all the stores are owned by Gujarati Indians. Indeed, they are now beginning to outnumber the indigenous Fijians. In the towns Fiji's bankers, on the other hand, are Chinese. On the whole, Fiji has managed to establish a harmonious inter-racial society, but depending on quite a high degree of racial exclusiveness.

What do we mean by 'Melanesian' race? This is a problem, despite the fact that there is a great deal of homogeneity. Melanesians have frizzy hair and a much darker skin colour than Polynesians and Indonesians, a fact which led them to be regarded once as simply an eastern branch of the Negroid Africa stock. Speculations regarding their relationship with Africans began, indeed, when the Spanish explorer Oritz de Retus coined the name Nueva Guinea, because the natives bore such a striking resemblance to the Negroes of the West African coast. However, recent investigations, particularly into blood-group frequencies, show that the physical components of the two peoples are very different. Moreover, fully African traits, such as woolly, spiral hair and everted lips are not found in Melanesia. As with many racial histories, we have to consider the population as the result of hundreds of years of mixing of different groups, with Africa possibly playing a part in it; archaeology shows that the Melanesian island groups have been populated by small groups over a long period of time with few signs of any deliberately large-scale immigration. It is wrong, therefore, to try to class Melanesians as 'Negroid', 'Australoid', 'Papuan' or 'Palaeo-Melanesian'. Nor is it exact to attempt a three-fold division, such as Melanesian and Papuan plus Negrito, the latter covering the smaller peoples in the interior of some of the larger islands. The variations are much more complex.

We have already mentioned several islands which have more in common racially with Polynesia than with Melanesia. Another interesting variation is the Aiome pygmies of New Guinea, who number some eight to ten thousand. They are not Melanesian, but rather an isolated and differentiated people whose very existence was unknown a generation ago. They live in the mountains and valleys of the New Guinea highlands, at the foot of the Schrader Range, seventy miles west of Madang. Their average height is four feet two inches. Their skin colour is yellowish brown;

Fijian women at work in the village of Maru near Suva, Fiji.

their hair is frizzy and rather abundant on face and body and their noses short, broad and fat. They grow root crops and keep pigs like their Melanesian neighbours, but they differ in that their huts are scattered over the cultivated slopes and the women are secluded to such an extent that they are hardly ever seen by strangers. It has been thought that such small people may be related to the Negritoes, who survive in Malaya, the Andaman Islands and Luzon, but there is no concerted opinion as to the exact anthropological status of the Aiome, who may have developed their special physical traits through years of isolation in their present habitat.

The language situation in Melanesia is even more diverse than the racial one. In some parts, particularly West Irian, where there have long been contacts with the Indonesian people, Austronesian languages are spoken, related to those of Indonesia and the Philippines. The other languages are called either Papuan or simply non-Austronesian, because of their complexity. The majority of the 'Papuan' languages are on the island of New Guinea and the islands east and west of it. To the east, the Rossel islanders in the Louisiade Archipelago speak a Papuan language and so do several communities in New Britain, New Ireland and Bougainville. Four Papuan languages have been described for the Solomon Islands.

Over three million Melanesians live on the small islands or in the interior valleys and mountains of this vast island group. A very aggressive individualism maintains the ideal of equality and is often associated with war and head-hunting, together with bird-symbolism. Justly or not, Melanesians are famed for their head-hunting and their great feather masks. Unlike other cultural zones where vast empires and confederations developed, grouping large congeries or tribes of primitive peoples—such as the Yoruba and Ashanti nations in Africa and the Iroquois confederation or the Aztec empire in northern America—New Guinea for example remained particularly fragmented into small communities and groups of

A single-outrigger canoe from eastern New Guinea, with bow
and stern ornaments of a type once used for war expeditions.

villages. Recurrent warfare never resulted in the hegemony of one tribe or the
creation of large states. As a result, throughout this enormous island we have the
typically primitive situation of peoples living in small groups, in intimate, dyadic
relations. Fellow-villagers, neighbours, even enemies were parents or people
known to you. Long-distance trading between members of different tribes were
always carried out in the same idiom, trading partners being converted into
fictional kin or ritual friends. While this intimate situation also existed in Africa,
there most villages had some kind of tie with a more comprehensive state apparatus
and owed fealty to a distant overlord.

In New Guinea political leaders—'Big Men'—were chosen from among the
temporarily influential men of the village. Big Men have acquired influence
through their own abilities; they are powerful and wealthy men, alert to all
economic opportunities. They are the focus of an economic system and their status,
like that of any wealthy capitalist in Europe or America, depends on their
shrewdness and material possessions. They are helped in their transactions by
younger men who are attracted to their service by prestige. The Big Men may also
be the priests of a village; in mythology, they are credited with the ability to make
gardens fertile, and their earthly representatives are considered to possess 'mana' (a
type of sacredness), as well as skill, and wealth. They use their ritual powers when
trading voyages are undertaken. They are also thought to be powerful sorcerers,
causing drought, disease and famine.

As we have already seen, this area cannot easily be divided into large 'cultural
zones' based on language units, political spheres of influence or types of economy.
Equally, the distinction between island, coastal and mountain groups is not helpful
in this case. New Guinea is a vast conglomerate of peoples speaking hundreds of
different languages, existing in small communities, many of which have been
visited by administrators or studied by anthropologists only in very recent times.
Few, if any, comprehensive studies are available, therefore.

Nevertheless, there are cultural traits which, although not universal
throughout this enormous island, combine to give the whole zone a prevailing
ethos, and perhaps the most useful approach is to look at certain of these 'themes' in
some detail—they include ritual aggression found in perennial warfare and
headhunting; a fondness of body decoration and art in general; and a passion for
ceremonial trading and exchange.

Dani tribespeople beside a salt spring in West Irian. Salt is an important trading resource in New Guinea. String netbags for carrying food are worn over the back of women's heads.

Headhunters and warriors

The 'Big Men' of the local communities were traditionally battle-leaders in the wars and headhunting parties for which Melanesia has a considerable reputation. In some parts of New Guinea today a constant state of warfare can be said to exist between communities, often of the same culture and language. The Dani, for example, are divided into some dozen alliances all of which are potential enemies of the others. Warfare, however, is not the out-and-out destruction of whole groups, but a rather ceremonial affair. There are two kinds of battles—the first is more of a ritual and would only last a day or two, preceded, accompanied and concluded with magical ceremonies. Then there follows a period of fierce fighting in which as many as twenty clashes take place. At the end of a day, the members of each side sit down on their own edge of the no-man's-land and roundly abuse their foes. This kind of battle is more in the way of a stylised, aggresive dance; informal raids, on the other hand, are attempts to take lives and are usually instigated in order to avenge a death.

Dani raids, in function, resemble headhunting. Throughout Melanesia, the men of a tribe may 'indulge' in periodic raids to capture enemy neighbours, rape the women and bring home heads. The Asmat, who live in almost complete isolation on the south-west coast of New Guinea, have chosen the praying-mantis as their headhunting 'totem'. They have watched the female insect bite off the head of the male directly after or during mating, and they use this as a symbolic explanation and even justification for their headhunting, which has important ritual and sexual undertones. Among the Asmat, it is the women who actively encourage and incite the men to hunt heads, shaming their husbands in public should the family collection of skulls be too small!

Almost every large Asmat festivity or public ritual presupposes a headhunting raid. Festivities, occurring at regular intervals and generally lasting for weeks or even months, are organised when a man's house is built, when an ancestral pole is

16

OPPOSITE:
Mekeo dancers in south-east New Guinea. In such communities, such dances provide an opportunity to demonstrate tribal solidarity and individual excellence.

Asmat warriors painted and carrying symbolically decorated spears prepare for a dawn raid. Headhunting may be undertaken to preserve territorial boundaries.

carved, when masks are woven. On each occasion, the spirits of the dead come back to the community of the living and, reviving the memory of the dead, also encourage a spirit of vengeance; headhunting is practised to get even with and satisfy these spirits. However, the main motive of Asmat headhunting seems to be to safeguard village territory and the fertility of the sago farms; and, since the ancestors are seen as the protectors of the tribe's economic resources, the complex rituals prior to a raid involve sacrifices to the ancestors.

The raid proper takes place at dawn and is composed of a group of archers, spearmen and shield-bearers. The leaders are the elders, and the warriors the strong men of middle age. Arriving by canoe in a neighbouring village, the enemy may be killed and decapitated (only the head and thigh being taken home) or made captive. On the return journey, victims are beheaded at confluences of rivers or at river bends, and after the festive home-coming, raid celebrations are begun. A head is also a source of individual prestige; the procuring of a head (the victim's name must be known) helping to secure for the Asmat man a status on earth and in the realm of the spirits. The man with 'heads' is the ideal of perfect manliness; a man with no heads is 'nothingness'.

These wars and headhunting were put down by colonial powers whose governments have been involved in horrific whole-sale world wars—wars that slaughter thousands and thousands in a day. In New Guinea, ceremonial wars and head-taking, which hardly claim more than a few score men each year, are part and parcel of the people's way of life. It is in a large measure true, that a group's health and happiness depend on the aggressive pursuit of its traditional enemies.

A seated figure from the Santa Cruz Islands, said to represent the shark spirit, 'Men-ar-ta-lu'.

Headhunting was part of a complex and sacred ceremonial, at least in most cases; warfare heightened the people's sense of obligation to their ghosts and ancestors since, until the ghost of a murdered man is avenged, both people and their food crops are believed to suffer. The 'pacification' also affects rituals; the offering of a cannibal victim in some ceremonies is no longer possible, since the person eaten had to be taken from among the enemy. How are the people meant to react— replace the human victim with a pig? But everyone knows that a pig is a pig and a man is a man . . .

Art

The peoples of the low hills and flat lands of the Sepik River area are renowned for their art, of which there is a good deal in European and American museums. Most of this art is produced for the male initiation cults, when young boys pass through a series of ceremonies, each of which use many carved and painted objects to symbolize complex ideas involving the fundamental values and beliefs of the Sepik peoples. These great ceremonies, with their displays and parades, have the air of a great secular festival and everyone enjoys themselves—except possibly the initiates, who get a beating at the price of enjoying the display.

The last stage of the initiation rites is the most sacred of a not very obviously religious ceremony. At this time, carvings which are shown to the initiates are painted, along with the flat panels used to line the initiation chamber, and other decorations. The painting phase begins when all the initiators purify themselves from past sexual contacts—and they must observe a total taboo on sex until the painting is finished. The designs, in earth colours, are those used by their ancestors, and the paint, associated with ancestral symbolism, acquires a supernatural power and is rubbed on the initiates.

The most spectacular sight of the public ceremonies is the wearing of huge feather head-dresses carried by adult men. The feathers are the breast plumage of small birds, and tens of thousands are needed to make the largest of them. The feathers are made into a design on a light cane framework and surmounted by a 'mast' of pith twenty-five feet high on which further feathers are stuck.

A Kawelka man from northern New Guinea. His intricate feather headdress and striking white paint and nasal septum pierced with a bone are all part of a ceremonial obligation. Apart from showing wealth, decorations are executed as competitive demonstrations of skill.

International trade

Although the Melanesian communities could easily be self-sufficient, at least as far as food is concerned, trading and exchange is a universal and very favourite pastime. Intricate trading networks link mountain tribes with the coast and mainlanders with islanders, and throughout the islands, manufacturing centres of important articles are localized in different geographical areas, so that groups may have to travel over long distances for pots, stone implements, dog teeth, porpoise teeth, pierced stone discs, feathers, belts and other ornaments many of which are used in marriage payments.

Trade, however, though important, is not the only incentive in a complex exchange system, known as the *kula*. The exchange is carried on between members of related communities and also between culturally and linguistically separated

87191

This village, on the east coast of Papua, is built on stilts in shallow water just off a coral beach. Villagers bring their families ashore for medical treatment when visited by travelling clinics.

peoples who inhabit a wide ring of islands, forming a geographically closed circuit. On each island in the ring, a more or less limited number of men take part in the kula, receiving the ornaments, retaining them for a short time and then passing them on. Members of the kula network, therefore, periodically receive an ornamental armband or necklace which then is ceremonially consigned to a further partner at a later date, armbands travelling in one direction, necklaces in the other.

The kula is an example of the way communities succeed in promoting their economies by means other than strict adherence to market principles and the use of a state bureaucracy or elaborate legal codes. An international exchange between distant island groups speaking languages as different from each other as English and Russian is carried on between ritual friends and trading partners who see each other only once a year and sometimes less. Relations between these partners, who exchange ornamental objects as well as trade goods are inherited by sons (if the system is a patrilineal one) or sisters' sons (if the system is matrilineal). An elaborate eonomic and diplomatic system is maintained by traditional means in a face-to-face situation without the need for legal sanctions or written codes. We should not forget, as well, the skill of these primitive navigators in confronting the open seas often for days at a time, and despite often severe conditions arriving at the appointed rendez-vous as 'arranged'.

The basis of the relations between kula friends is reciprocity, but it is a delayed reciprocity, since there can never be a direct exchange, from hand to hand. An armband is handed over, but a man must wait until his friend makes a return visit before he receives a complementary necklace. It is gift exchange between friends, not commerce between traders, since the equivalence of the objects exchanged is never discussed, bargained about or computed. Nevertheless, of course, there is always much longing and sighing for the best ornaments and each of the more famous bands and necklaces has a personal name and provenance; as they circulate around the kula cycle, their appearance always creates a sensation. All the friends of a man with a specially wonderful necklace in hand will compete for it and try to obtain it by blandishments, promises of the gift of a pig, axe-blades or food.

The exchange exists for the sake of the exchange. Here is a world where not only food and manufactured goods (trade goods), but ornaments, customs, songs, art motifs and all kinds of other cultural influences travel from island to distant

The Trobrianders are expert wood carvers and make hunting and fishing spears, as well as the domestic and decorative items used both in exchange ceremonies and in daily life.

island. It is a ceremonial exchange between friends which finds elaboration in myth and in the rituals embellishing canoe buildings and feasts associated with the kula. The magic made when a group leaves on an expedition is aimed at success in the exchange and is directed at the partner's emotions—it aims to make him soft, unsteady in his mind, eager to hand over to his friend the best kula *gifts*—not the largest and cheapest yams.

The relationship between kula friends and partners is brought out clearly in Malinowski's well-known description of the arrival of a Trobriander expedition in the enemy island of Dobu. There is less intimacy with kula partners the more distant and foreign they are and a Dobuan is separated from a Trobriander on both counts. In Dobu, the Trobriander sailors only disembark from their canoes when they have performed extensive rituals to ensure the success of their visit and have made themselves irresistible to their friends through the use of spells and cosmetics. And whatever the normal state of enmity between the two groups of islanders as a whole, the kula partners always show the utmost friendship.

Arriving in their great canoes after a long journey, the Trobrianders rest for a while before beginning to undo their baskets. The older men murmur their magical formulae and all of them wash in the sea and rub themselves with medicated leaves to make themselves beautiful and attractive to their Dobu partners. They break open coconuts, scraping and medicating them before rubbing their bodies with oil to give their skin a shining appearance. Before arranging their hair, they chant spells over their combs. With a crushed betel nut mixed with lime, they draw red designs on their faces, while others use aromatic resinous stuff and draw ornamental patterns in black. The sweet-smelling mint plant, which has also been chanted over at home before the voyage, is taken out of its little receptacle where it has been preserved in coconut oil. The herb is inserted into the armlets— ornaments they have brought as gifts—while the few drops of oil are smeared over the body and a special magical bundle of trade gifts.

All the magic which is uttered in the canoes before landing in Dobu is personal, beauty magic and the main aim of the spells is to make each man irresistible to his kula friend. In Trobriand myths, there is often a description of an old, ugly and ungainly man transformed into a radiant and charming youth through this kind of magic; the myth is an exaggerated version of what happens every time the beauty magic is spoken on the beach at Dobu. As one Trobriander put it: 'Here, we are ugly; we eat bad fish, bad food; our faces remain ugly. We want to sail to Dobu; we keep our taboos, we don't eat bad food. We wash; we charm the leaves; we charm the coconut; we annoint ourselves; we make our red and black paint; we put on our . . . smelling ointment; we arrive in Dobu, beautiful-looking. Our partner looks at us, sees our faces are beautiful; he throws the ornaments at us . . .'.

The belief in the efficacity of the cosmetic and spells, of course, makes them effective, since the trader—like the modern western woman dependent on Helena Rubinstein and Elizabeth Arden—has the conviction of being beautiful to his friend and the magic provides this assurance, influencing his behaviour and deportment. In the transaction between the two kula partners it is the manner of soliciting which matters most. The beauty magic will make a man's friend and partner hug him and 'take him to his bosom'. In the spells he and his friend are likened to a pair of pigeons and a pair of parrots, birds which symbolise friendship to the Trobrianders. Wearing these preparations, the visitors will sit on their partner's knees and take from their mouths the betel-chewing materials. 'My head is made bright, my face flashes, I have acquired a beautiful shape like that of a chief; I have acquired a shape that is good. I am the only one; my renown stands alone'.

The ferocious Dobuans on shore have a general taboo on strangers which is waived for their trading friends, but the Trobrianders still feel the necessity of bridging this taboo by magic. At certain periods of the year, the visitors are received with a wild show of hostility and fierceness and treated as intruders; this attitude ceases as soon as the visitors have ritually spat around the village. The Trobrianders express their feelings in this situation characteristically: 'The Dobu man is not good as we are. He is fierce, he is a man-eater. When we come to Dobu we fear him, he might kill us. But see! I spit the charmed ginger root and their mind turns. They lay down their spears, they receive us well'. A remarkable example of the achievement of friendly feeling against all odds in the interest of exchange.

The Trobriander canoes are ranged in a low row facing the shore. After the historic moment of tension is over the Dobuans shed their arms and smile welcomingly in their war paint and listen to the leader of the Trobriander group as he harangues them, telling them to give the visitors a large number of valuables and surpass all other islands and past occasions. After this, his own partner blows his conch shell and offers the first gift of valuables to the master of the expedition from the Trobriands. Other blasts then follow and men disengage themselves from the throng on the shore, approaching the canoes with necklaces for their special

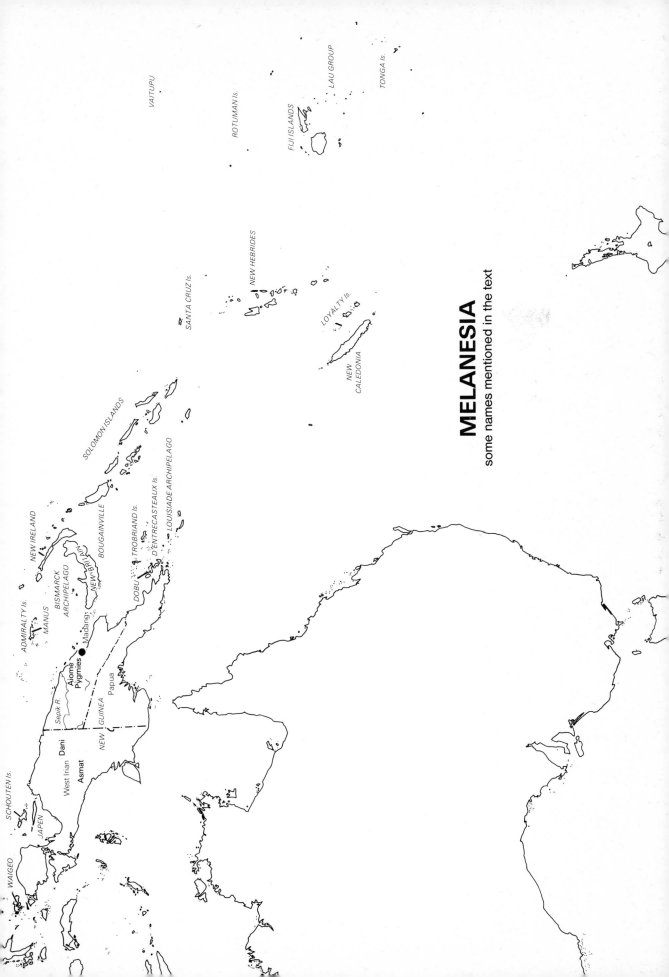

MELANESIA
some names mentioned in the text

The Trobriand fishing village of Kavataria. Trobriand villages are roughly circular in pattern with the dancing area, burial grounds and chief's quarters at the centre.

partners. The necklaces are always carried ceremonially, tied to a stick with the pendant at the bottom. The fleet of canoes then sails around the island stopping in front of each hamlet where the Trobrianders have their partners.

At each stopping-place—where no visitor can eat any local food, yams or coconuts, before he has received all his gifts—the Trobriander continues to try and soften the heart of his partner; he will even feign illness, remaining in his canoe and sending word to his partner that he is suffering from a mortal disease. If this fails, he may have recourse to magic again, magic to seduce the mind of the man on whom it is practiced, magic to make him amenable to persuasion, send him silly and numb all his faculties: in fact the same rites performed when a man is trying to seduce a woman. When the ceremonial exchange is finished the partners meet and chat, exchange food, and trade may take place between visitors and local natives who are not their partners although they must belong to the same community as those with whom the kula is made.

Polynesia and Micronesia

East of the international date-line, in the great empty half of the Pacific Ocean, are scattered the Polynesian groups. They lie in a triangle with Tahiti at the centre and, at the points in the triangle, Hawaii in the north, Easter Island in the east and New Zealand in the south-west, each of these being at least 1200 miles from another inhabited Polynesian neighbour. All, except New Zealand, are built on oceanic volcanoes, rising from the sea-bottom. Then, to the west, are the far-flung islands of Micronesia, which display cultural features of both Polynesia and Melanesia, and which are described at the end of this section.

All the Polynesian islands were discovered and inhabited by man in late prehistoric times. Polynesians are believed to have originated by way of Indonesia, with evidence of some admixture from South America. They are fairly uniform racially. Their skin is whitish to dark brown; they tend to be heavy (and run to fat), with broad, massive faces, a high forehead and straight nose, full but well-defined lips, a rounded jaw-line and black eyes. However, migrations within the island groups have produced people of varying looks: Polynesians in the coastal and swamp areas are taller with finer features, whilst peoples of the mountains are shorter and more stocky—more Melanesian in appearance. In their blood frequencies, the Polynesian (like the North American Indians) differ from almost all other peoples of the Pacific and Asia; thus there can be little doubt that Polynesians in general have ancestors in common. Although in one sense, Polynesian languages are many—five hundred according to some sources—all are part of the Austronesian, formerly known as Malayo-Polynesian, family.

Polynesian culture is quite remarkably uniform for an area composed of such dispersed island groups, though the indigenous culture of New Zealand, because of the more temperate climate, is something of an exception. Chiefs are everywhere sacred and tabooed persons, deriving their sacredness from supposed direct descent from both their earthly ancestors and the gods. Coconut, taro and breadfruit are grown, and pigs, chickens and dogs reared. Fish and other sea life are caught and consumed in abundance, while pigs are usually kept for ceremonial feasts. Polynesian sea-going achievements are renowned; the sailors cover vast distances

The intricate tattooing of this man from western Samoa is part of a vanishing culture only part of which is fostered by the younger generation.

in their large, fast, sail-powered, ocean-going canoes. Voyages were made in large, decorated, outrigger canoes by mariners with detailed knowledge of winds, currents and star positions. Ritual, religious beliefs and myths have elements in common over the whole area. Generally, villages consist of irregularly grouped houses; those of men of rank are usually built on stout posts over a stone platform. Polynesians did not traditionally make pottery, but use basketry and wooden utensils. One element of their rich art is lavish personal tattooing. These are some of the elements of traditional Polynesian life.

Most of us have a mental image of the area, even if it is not generally quite so specific. For many, the ideal, romantic, primitive community is conjured up by the sound of the ukelele or the rhythmic swish of a grass skirt, by the thought of long, white beaches fringed with coconut palms and a community of half-naked hedonists plucking delicious tropical fruit from a shady bough. This stereotype, like most stereotypes, has an element of truth in it. When the whalers and traders sailed up to the island shores in the eighteenth and nineteenth centuries, the people did seem to live in a balmy, carefree world, unashamed of their bodies and their natural passions, with a lifestyle that required the minimum of physical exertion.

But it failed to include many of the less attractive details of Polynesian existence—exploitation by the ruling classes, the occasional violent storms which wiped out the means of subsistence for months at a time, causing starvation and the decimation of the islands' populations. Then came the contribution of the white man, and suffering far more severe and more demoralizing—contagious illnesses

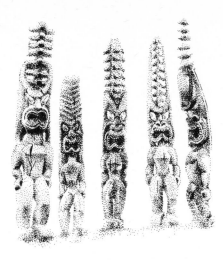

Carved wooden idols representing ancient Hawaiian gods in a temple on the western coast of Hawaii. These were made before European contact.

such as measles and whooping cough, not to mention venereal diseases, firearms, alcohol and tobacco. And so today it is only in the more isolated islands such as Tikopia where a genuine traditional Polynesian culture still survives.

Hawaii, which provides the model for the 'primitive' decor of countless Polynesian restaurants, bars, night-clubs and film sets, no longer exists as a Polynesian culture. The Hawaiian Islands, or 'Sandwich Islands' as Cook named them, stretch in a chain for some four hundred miles across the Tropic of Cancer. Seven islands (Niihau, Kauai, Oahu, Molokai, Lanai, Maui and Hawaii proper) are inhabited and since 1959 this group has been a state of the U.S.A. The ancient Polynesians of Hawaii migrated from south-eastern Asia as long ago as the second century AD, settling in Samoa, Tonga, Tahiti and the Marquesas before arriving in their seventy-foot, double-hulled canoes in Hawaii in the seventh or eighth century. During the next thousand years, the Hawaiians remained undisturbed and developed their own brand of Pacific culture, with a system of taboos as the keystone of their culture, protecting temples, idols, sacred places, priests and fathers of families.

Captain Cook broke Hawaii's isolation at the end of the eighteenth century and from then on we can trace the unchecked retreat of a native culture before western morals, economics and religion; within half a century, Hawaiian culture was virtually extinct, crushed through disease, alcohol, missionary activities, oriental labourers who came to work the island plantations and then the millions of tourists who pour into the islands today. The proud Polynesians seem to have been extra-ordinarily supine in the face of this invasion, making only isolated attempts to resist. The complete physical and cultural assimilation of the Hawaiians to an international world may have had positive results; although many people maintain that they would have done better to eat every sailor, missionary and land-grabber who stepped ashore on their islands. Today the islands are completely Americanized. Language is 99% English; Chinese rituals are in English; only a few scholars and one or two aged Hawaiians speak any Polynesian. Old Hawaiian civilization, 'primitive' Hawaiian culture, has been preserved just for the tourists. The people themselves are devoted to American fashions, American fads and American football.

An early nineteenth century mummified head of a Maori chief, with a tattoo denoting his rank. The feather in his hair symbolizes his warrior status.

At the other end of the Polynesian triangle, the New Zealand Maoris are struggling to preserve as much of their old way of life as possible. Their history in many ways resembles that of the Hawaiians, except that their culture flourishes today and is still recognisably Polynesian. Maori-tanga, an attitude resembling *négritude* in Africa, was a movement instigated by Maoris to express and encourage the values of Maori culture. After a period of withdrawal and rejection, when they were dispossessed of their land and suffered epidemics and a falling birth-rate, there suddenly came an improvement. At the same time there was a parallel loss of confidence in the once-admired white man, his religion and his good intentions. In due course the Maoris regained confidence in themselves, through a re-discovery of their heroic past and the traditional arts and folklore. This renaissance manifested itself in the increasing popularity of tribal gatherings, the erection of buildings for community needs and a general feeling of healthy pride in being Maori.

The Maoris even synthesized a new religion. In 1864, they renounced their conversion to English Christianity and made up their own religion based largely on borrowings from the Old Testament. The Supreme Deity is called Jehovah and the Maoris declare themselves to be one of the lost tribes led into bondage by the Assyrians. Movements like these promised the coming of the Messiah, the resuscitation of the Maori dead and the expulsion of the whites.

While these promises were never fulfilled, the movements served the purpose of reviving Maori pride and a sense of the past, giving them hope for the future. A happy amalgam of indigenous and white culture has been achieved, the Maoris accepting European technology, education and welfare, but they refuse to overstrain their community life in case it should break down altogether. Theirs is a success story, the triumph of 'integration' over 'assimilation', and the Maori picture is certainly a happier one than the scene of total loss recorded for Hawaii.

Let us take a closer look at two of the themes running through the traditional culture of Polynesia.

New Zealand Maori children learning their native dance at school.

Free love?

Strangely enough, facts about the world's most celebrated 'primitive-lovers', past or present, are few and unreliable despite the countless books—both popular and anthropological—which have been written about them. Most sexologists have to rely on traditional lore and legends in describing the Polynesians' delight in sexual adventure, their libidinous behaviour even with complete strangers, the minimal importance they give to the loss of virginity, and their interest in what we would call pornography. Nevertheless, sex does seem to be a relaxed, culturally-sanctioned sport, mostly undisturbed by the longing and pining which we associate with romantic passion. In Samoa, premarital and extramarital passions are the rule—sex is a delightful experience, expertly engaged in, and the Samoan lover composes ardent love songs, calling on the moon, the stars and the sea. Nevertheless, it is never allowed to engross the partners enough to threaten the social order. Polynesians do not 'die of love', or leave their husbands because of a romantic attachment. A Samoan boy declares passionately that he will 'die', if a girl refuses him her favours; but they laugh at stories of romantic love, scoff at fidelity to a wife or mistress and happily believe that a new love affair is the best cure for an unhappy old one. Moreover, the sharing of one's love among several mistresses is never considered out of harmony with declarations of undying love for each and all of them.

Mana and taboo

Anthropologists studying Polynesia have devoted most of their ink to descriptions of the complex Polynesian hierarchical systems, which still survive in isolated pockets, supported by taboos and mana. Mana is a powerful kind of supernatural, impersonal force which, according to Polynesian beliefs, the nobles, princes and kings possess. In Hawaii, the greatest chief—belonging to an unblemished lineage kept pure by incestuous marriages between brother and sister and descended from the gods—had the greatest mana. And while the chiefs had mana, the lower classes had the taboo of defilement and were debarred from contacting their superiors. The system of mana and taboos was the keystone of the old Polynesian culture, since it gave supernatural sanction to a class system and the inequality of the sexes.

A Tahitian woman plaits her daughter's hair. The girl's features suggest mixed racial descent.

In Tahiti, the majority of the people were formerly landless commoners, who supplied all the heavy manual labour, farming for a leisured class—an inter-related group of sacred, chiefly families. Thus, although we might call Tahiti an 'earthly paradise', because of its perfect climate, where planting and harvesting can be done at almost any time of the year with the minimum of work, it may not have been such a paradise for 'workers'. The chief was absolute ruler of an island, or part of an island, and the sacred embodiment of both the land and the people. The ruling families had little direct contact with the commoners, but acted through land-owning sub-chiefs. The situation was described vividly as usual by Captain Cook: 'It is not common for any 2 to eat together, the better sort hardly ever; and the women never upon any account eat with the men, but always by themselves. What can be the reason of so unusual a custom, 'tis hard to say, especially as they are a people, in every other instance, fond of Society, and much so of their women. They were often Asked the reason, but they never gave no other Answer, but that they did it because it was right, and Express'd much dislike at the Custom of Men and Women Eating together of the same Victuals. We have often used all the intreatys we were Masters of to invite the Women to partake of our Victuals at our Tables, but there never was an instance of one of them doing it publick, but they would Often goe 5 or 6 together into the Servants apartments, and there eat very heartily of whatever they could find, nor were they in the least disturbed if any of us came in while they were dining; and it hath sometimes hapned that when a woman was alone in our company she would eat with us, but always took care that her own people should not know what she had donn, so that whatever may be the reasons for this custom, it certainly affects their outward manners more than their Principle.'

It certainly seems odd that the Polynesian girls, who with singular lack of restraint, splashed naked in the water and crowded the sailors on board the ships, should have been so fussy about whom they ate with. Was eating more taboo than sex?

The authority of the ruling-class therefore depended as much on sanctity as on political power and sanctions. Anything in the least connected with a chief became sacred, due to the chief's mana—the land he walked on, any house he entered, any object he touched—and could not henceforth be used by a commoner without elaborate ritual precautions. When travelling the chief was carried on the

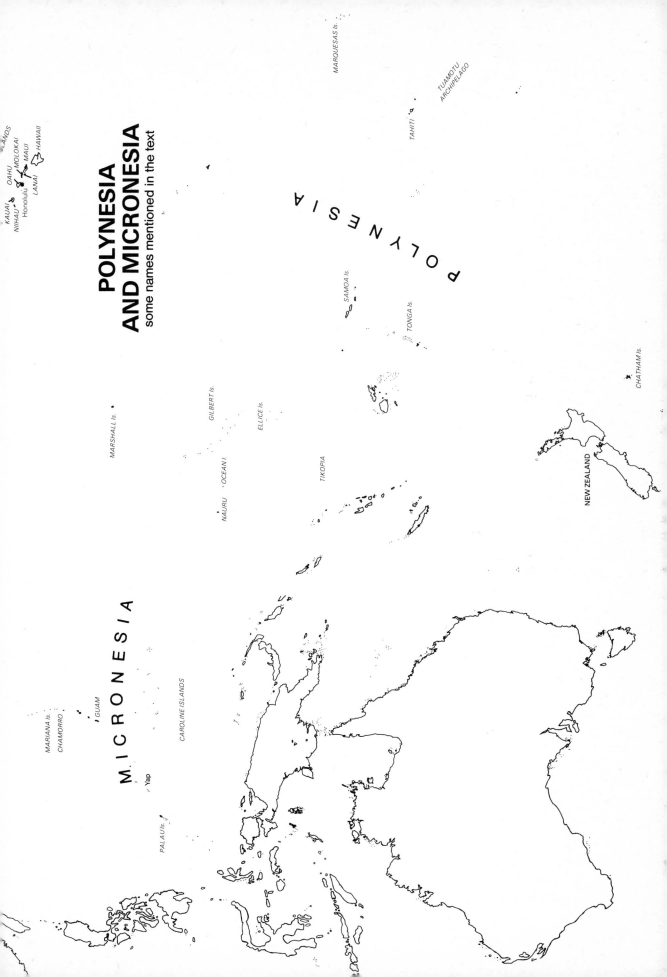

POLYNESIA
AND MICRONESIA
some names mentioned in the text

POLYNESIA

MICRONESIA

HAWAIIAN ISLANDS
KAUAI
NIIHAU
OAHU
Honolulu
MOLOKAI
LANAI
MAUI
HAWAII

MARQUESAS Is.

TUAMOTU
ARCHIPELAGO

TAHITI

SAMOA Is.

TONGA Is.

CHATHAM Is.

NEW ZEALAND

MARSHALL Is.

GILBERT Is.

ELLICE Is.

NAURU
OCEAN I.

TIKOPIA

MARIANA Is.
CHAMORRO

GUAM

CAROLINE ISLANDS

Yap

PALAU Is.

A girl from Tahiti slashes ripe coconuts to extract the white meat used in cooking and cosmetics.

shoulders of sacred bearers. Chiefs had a sacred enclosure with a temple and burial-ground, usually a stone-walled enclosure with a stone platform or pyramid at one end. From this, orders were given to the people and had a magico-religious validity.

Today, this exotic order has passed, probably with few regrets by the majority of the populations. Life was romantic only for the rich and aristocratic; commoners endured hard work, grim sanctions and rigid disciplines.

Closely associated with mana is the notion of taboo. Numerous taboos protected the persons of chiefs, their clothing and possessions. Taboo is a kind of negative sanction, a prohibition whose infringement results in a supernatural penalty. If I break a mirror, I shall have seven years' bad luck—this, in a sense, is a taboo. However, the term, introduced from Polynesia, is employed universally in comparative studies and is used to describe prohibitions (taboos) against performing actions of such danger, that the action recoils upon the violator of the taboo.

Polynesians with political power imposed taboos. The Tongan food controller would tell people what they could and could not eat. Once he had declared a food taboo, it could not be eaten until the next harvest and he could declare any kind of food taboo when it grew scarce. Up till this century the paramount chief in Samoa had four messengers who had the power to taboo the killing of pigs and the use of coconut for feeding animals and poultry. In Tikopia, the chiefs exercised their power of taboo until recently.

Taboos can also be declared individually. It is a widespread custom for men to make their women taboo, and not just in Polynesia. It is on record that, not so very long ago, French sailors when ordered to sail, simply had their local sweethearts

tabooed and when their ship returned, they found things entirely satisfactory: so much for 'free love'! Farmers might place a taboo on their personal crops or property, coupling the food or the object with his name and putting a spell on it.

In Polynesian belief, the parts of the body form a fixed hierarchy with some analogy to the rank system of society: the skeleton is made to play a part in the principle of mana-taboo. The backbone is the most important part of the body and the limbs derive importance from it as a continuation of the backbone. On top of the body is the head—the seat of mana, the seat of a man's vital force. This grading of the skeleton concerned all ranks and could be so important that even architecture was involved, so that people could avoid stepping over another's head: the arrangements of the sleeping-room show this kind of adaptation in the Marquesas Islands. The real significance of this grading, however, was in its association with the rank system—the head of a chief being the most concentrated mana-taboo object. Anything to do with a chief's head was a fearful business. Haircutting involved much of the same behaviour as actual killing and the hands of a person who had cut a chief's hair were afterwards sometimes useless for eating—the barber was in such a state that he had to be fed.

Micronesia

There are two thousand islands in the thousand square miles of Pacific Ocean known as Micronesia. The islands are mostly very small and include the Mariana, Caroline, Marshall and Gilbert archipelagoes and two isolated islands, Nauru and Ocean. Micronesia is more a geographical than an ethnic classification however, and as a cultural term it has only a limited use, due to the heterogeneity of the populations. Nevertheless, Micronesia has more a 'Polynesian' than 'Melanesian' flavour, particularly in the existence of 'aristocracies'—the Yap, for example, had a social structure of nine classes.

The largest single island in the group is Guam—two hundred and twenty-five square miles—while some islets are only a fraction of a square mile. The total population is about 150,000. Migrations to the islands were from two different directions: the first from Indonesia and the second from eastern Melanesia; there were also many internal migrations and European contact has been constantly important since the time Magellan burnt down houses and killed some of the islanders in the seventeenth century. Spanish colonialism and Catholic proselytisation were experienced in the Marianas, where disease and massacres reduced the population of Chamorro from 50,000 to 4,000. Today, the population of

A Caroline Islander cooking reef fish on a coconut-husk fire. Fish and coconuts are two of the main resources in Polynesia.

Chamorro is made up of mixed Spanish-Philippinos, Americans and Japanese; there are no full-blood Chinese and no communities which follow or possess a traditional culture, once based on a matrilineal clan system.

Other Micronesian peoples—the Yap for example—were less disturbed by colonial rule. They have been ruled by both Germans and Japanese, but Yap culture has remained conservative and traditional. The island is forty square miles in area with a population of about 4,000 fishermen and taro growers. Yap men and women belong to two descent groups, one through women and one through men, and these kin groups are ranked according to the type of land controlled. The clan divisions are strict social ones, the lower classes being permanently debarred from landholding. Yap religion is still elaborate and their stone money recalls Melanesian gift-exchange: the stone coins come in varying sizes from a few inches in diameter to over nine feet and may weigh as much as five tons. A four-inch stone might purchase a fat pig, but a five-foot stone might buy a whole village. Throughout Yap, the name, the ownership and history of every large stone is widely known.

Australia

Australians—the word conjures up sun-lovers and surf-riders, or perhaps inhabitants of suburban cultural wastes that begin in Brisbane and end in Perth with vast treeless plains in between. Here the primitive religion of immigrant European groups may be 'sun worship' or the rituals and passions of sport; the primitive groups may be isolated, poor, farming communities in Tasmanian backwoods; the primitive social structures the passionate devotion of 'mates', or the strict division of labour between men and women. The two last Australian traits have been analysed in a book I have written on the anthropology of friendship.

Throughout Australian life we have a relationship between the sexes which has more than a little in common with societies habitually regarded as primitive. Women are relegated to womanly—mostly domestic—roles, and cultural values are based on masculine ethics. Consequently, relationships between the sexes, between brother and sister, between husband and wife are often not close: the conversation between an Australian man and woman may often be an embarassing, if not empty, experience, since their worlds are so different. Go to an Australian country-dance and you will often find patterns similar to an African ritual—the men cluster around the beer cans indulging in masculine play and chat, while the women are invisibly divided off from this sphere, herded into their female zones to talk their female talk. African men drink with men, eat with men and discourse on men's things—in an Australian bar or 'hotel', a woman who wishes to enter this sacred male precinct has either to work behind the bar or use a dark, smelly hole known as the 'Ladies' Lounge'.

In many ways, the Australian men's institution of 'mateship' is a mine of material for the anthropologist interested in symbolic behaviour. In Australia's past—among tramps, gold-miners and stockriders, and today—in the armed forces, in country towns and between members of powerful clubs of former soldiers, the 'china plate', the mate, may be more important than a wife. Mateship involves mutual regard and trust, which may develop into a passionate relationship—with the idea, almost, of a holy grail binding man to man in

One traditional Australian image: white Australian sheepbreeders with distinctive wide-brim hats at a Sydney Sheep Show.

friendship. The chief article of faith is that mates should 'stick together'; it was and is the one law which the good Australian should never break and has, even, in a strange way become bred into the way of thinking and behaving of the large majority of Australians, whose values are based on the miner's and stock-rider's ideal of friendship. It should be remarked that, while it is certainly true that the male-male bond is much more highly valued than any male-female tie, it would be wrong to give the love of a man for his mate—a relationship which provides many touching and curious stories—any homosexual imperative.

But this is only half the story. These Australians are white Australians, and the racial homogeneity of the population has been maintained as far as possible by the famous White Australia Policy. We must not however lose sight of the indigenous population of Australia, the Aborigines. I myself am a Tasmanian of 'mixed' European ancestry with the possibility of an invisible drop of genuine Tasmanian blood in my make-up. Precise racial origins are difficult to assess in these cases particularly as many of us in Tasmania are haunted by the spectre of convict ancestors from industrial England and revolutionary Ireland. The predominantly British character of the Australian population was radically diluted after World War II with the arrival of enormous numbers of immigrants from central and southern Europe. One of the underlying motives behind the encouragement of this Latin and Slav migration was to build up 'white' population resources against threatened invasions by yellow hordes from further north.

Today attitudes to the 'yellow bastards' and the 'abos' are changing and the sense of isolation, 12,000 miles distant from Britain the Mother Country, is fast disappearing. More respect is being paid the original Australians as well—in fact the recent decision to give substantial pensions to all Australians with any aboriginal blood has persuaded many families to bring out skeletons from their ancestral cupboards.

Nevertheless, to the ordinary Australian, it is the black Australian who is the primitive, living in mysterious primitive worlds outside the sight and ken of the dominant white race.

Let us see if the Aborigines are really so unsophisticated.

The Aborigine

To the first English settlers and their descendants, the Aborigines were merely a hindrance, as white cattle-herders and farmers spread along the coast and then inland; the Aborigines, living in the fertile environment of New South Wales, Victoria and Tasmania, suffered shock after shock. They fell back steadily before the white man, refusing to conform, but losing their freedom of movement over their own country. Disease and violent death wiped out all the Tasmanian Aborigines and in Sydney, of the 1500 Aborigines in 1788, only a few hundred remained in 1830, and a few years later even they had disappeared, apart from a few 'tame' and drunken beggars.

Aborigines, as we know them, have been relegated to the more arid central, western and northern areas; but even here they have suffered from European expansion—their water-holes taken over, the totem species hunted out, their wives kidnapped, their children sent to mission schools and their manpower used as labour for the white man. The real tragedy is that, in these zones, the Aborigines can do nothing and yet they have nowhere else to go; tied as they are to their tribal territories by strong spiritual bonds, they are forced into accepting a new role in a white man's world. The Australian Aborigine is intimately attached to his land— he hunts only on his own territory, lands where his tribal ancestors had travelled in the 'Dream Time', the mythical past; and members of each group or horde are bound together by the common belief that spirits exist in that territory until they are incarnated and that, after death, the spirits return to the same territory. Thus, when the whites robbed the Aborigines of their land, they not only parted them from physical resources, but they also wrecked their spiritual past, present and future.

Some Aborigines in Hermannsburg find it hard to accept living in modern houses. Many build additional shacks in their backyards.

In contrast to many other peoples of the world, the Aborigines, scattered over the vast Australian continent, show a basic racial similarity. They have often been spoken of as the most isolated and primitive—in the physical sense—of all peoples. For a long time, they suffered the ignominy of being thought a 'missing link' in human evolution and, in popular fancy, they were even thought to be a different species. In fact, the Aborigine is quite like most 'Caucasians', with his wavy, rather than kinky, hair, his hairy face and body, heavy brow-ridges and the depression at the root of his nose. Nor has the Aborigine been as isolated from other racial groups as was once supposed. The so-called Australoid strain has been reported from other parts of the world: among some of the tribal people of South India, particularly in the Nilgiri Hills, as well as among the Veddas of Ceylon and, possibly, the Hairy Ainu of Japan and isolated peoples of Indonesia and New Guinea.

Some anthropologists have distinguished four major types of Aborigine, the two main groups being the Murrayan and the Carpentarian. The Murrayan, of the more temperate region of south-eastern Australia—the Murray River basin and Gippsland—is said to be more 'Caucasoid' and to be very like the Ainu of Japan. The Carpentarian type in the north is said to have more of the Melanesian-Papuan element and to resemble the Vedda: the Carpentarians show adaptations to desert conditions in their darker skin and taller, more slender, build. The third type, a blend of Murrayan and Carpentarian, is said to exist in the central desert; while the Barrinean, a Negrito-type with frizzy hair resembling the extinct Tasmanians, is distinguished in the Queensland rain forests. More recently, however, anthropologists have tended to discard these racial types and consider the Aborigines as grading into each other. The Tasmanians, as usual, still pose a problem—did they come over as part of the general Aborigine migration, or did they arrive direct from Melanesia? The skulls of Tasmanians are rounder than those of Australians and far more like those of Negritoes.

The first arrivals in Australia probably came in from the north through the Arnhem Land area and Cape York, possibly bringing with them their dingo dog— though among the Tasmanians there was no trace of the dingo on the island. Even after the first migrations, the Aborigines in the north remained in contact with peoples of more northerly islands, particularly Malayan-Indonesian fishermen seeking *bêche-de-mer*. Contact with outsiders, as well as long periods of isolation, may explain the varieties in physical appearance found throughout the continent—differences in height, build, skin and hair colour. The usual estimate for Aboriginal numbers, at the time of first contact with European settlers, is 300,000. Population densities were much higher in coastal, fertile areas, where Aborigines have now become extinct.

The Aboriginal linguistic situation is complex, the different languages varying in structure and vocabulary; nevertheless they are basically one family. There was never a *lingua franca* however—no language whereby a man might make himself understood from one end of the vast continent to the other. An Aborigine learned his own language and the languages of his neighbours with whom he had ritual and trading ties. On the whole, there are various language groups associated with distinct cultures and, apart from individual ties, each tribe keeps to itself. The cultural differences are sometimes marked: for example, a tribe may reckon descent exclusively through the mother, some of its neighbours through the father and some through both, i.e. there are patrilineal tribes, matrilineal tribes and tribes of double descent.

Because of the linguistic and cultural variations within a largely homogeneous area, it is difficult to delimit clear-cut cultural areas. Anthropologists have worked out geographical zones, inhabited by Aborigines, rather than the cultural areas of the type associated with the American Indians. These geographical zones include: the Western Desert, the Kimberleys, the lower River Murray, the Lakes' District, the Great Victorian Desert, Central Australia, Melville and Bathurst Islands, Western and Northern Arnhem Land and Carpentaria.

Although it has been estimated that in the eighteenth century there were five hundred tribal units of between 100 and 1500 members each, it is very difficult today to assess the tribal situation, particularly when we are dealing with isolated and acculturated survivors. In Australia, the word 'tribe' either means a group of people living and moving about together or a people who occupy a recognized

An Aborigine couple in Alice Springs have adopted the European mode of dress.

stretch of country and claim religious and hunting rights over it. These home zones are always reflected in mythology and, through their myths, the people are able to draw charts of their own and adjacent territories. 'Tribe' also refers to people of one language or to people who assume they 'belong' together and regard one another as relatives. The size of the tribe and the extent of its territory depend on the quality and quantity of its natural resources. In north-western South Australià, the middle-eastern part of Western Australia and the central-west of the Northern Territory, territories are large and game and vegetable foods are neither concentrated nor plentiful. On the Lower River Murray in South Australia—along the Coorong and lakes at the river's mouth—such areas are smaller but richer. The same is true along the Northern Territory coasts and rivers: in Arnhem Land, on the Daly River and around Port Keats, and on the islands of Bathurst, Goulburn, Milingimbi and Elcho. Among the tribes with large territories are the Aranda, Bidjandjara, Dieri, Walbiri and Wuradjeri. Smaller tribal territories are—or were—inhabited by the Jaraldi, Dangani, Gorindji, Wogemen, Togeman, Marlgu, Mara, Maung and Jangman.

A Bidjandjara tribesman, one of the few Aborigines living in the Ayers Rock area.

Australian Aborigines lead a simple life of hunting and collecting, using simple techniques: they have a minimum of material goods, do not live in houses, exploit the ever-present fauna and flora. Their primitive—in the sense of technologically backward—way of life do not make them stone-age, however, in an archaeological sense, nor does it make them simple as far as religion and social structures are concerned. We have often wrongly assumed that technical achievement go hand in hand with mental ability, cultural complexity and profound thought. Indeed, there may well be an argument that peoples who have benefited from industrial capitalism and techniques have become 'simple-minded', at least at some social levels—the very highest and the very lowest. The Australian Aboriginal member of a tribe, by the time he grows to adulthood, is informed of the intricacies of his social and religious systems, embodied in a rich and oral poetic literature—and he never leaves the thinking to experts.

The Aranda, for example, now reduced almost to the point of extinction, hunt with boomerangs and spears, the women scouring the land for seeds and bulb-roots, edible fungus, birds, eggs, snakes and the pupae of moths, caterpillars, beetles, flies, honey, ants and burrowing rodents. They are wonderfully observant of nature and have a systematic understanding of their natural world. The appearance of one object, a star, a bird, a flower, becomes through their minute knowledge of the physical world, a sign that rain is coming or that certain fish are rising, or that a certain animal will be plentiful. Yellow flowers of the wattle are a sign that the magpie-geese will be flying along their annual routes, over the giant paper-bark trees from swamp to swamp to eat the lily tubers.

The Groote Eylandt Aborigines—and they are unexceptional—also possess a prodigious reserve of knowledge about the natural environment, particularly the animal and plant species which they depend upon for their food and equipment. The

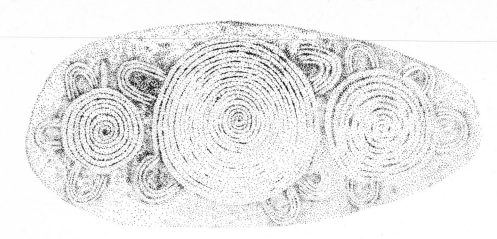

A stone churinga, or sacred object, belonging to an Aranda tribesman of the frog totem in Australia.

Wanindiljangwa of Groote Eylandt—an island in the Gulf of Carpentaria off northern Australia—have inherited a rich body of traditional knowledge about the different kinds of plants and animals around them. On the basis of size, colour, shape and general structure, they can distinguish and separately name no less than 80 types of birds, over 100 sea creatures, more than 120 kinds of trees and plants, some 50 varieties of shellfish and 30 species of land animals. These kinds of animals and plants are further divided into sub-groups. The basic divisions are flying things, which include not only birds, but all insects, flying-foxes, bats and other creatures, that take to the air; sea creatures, land animals, trees and plants. On the whole, they only bother to classify edible or otherwise useful species.

Every Australian Aborigine also has to 'learn' the complicated facts of his kinship system: not the names of a few cousins and aunts, but an elaborate structure of lineages, clans, cross-cousins, and totemic relatives, by which most of his day-to-day life is guided. Australian kinship is a remarkable construct, resembling in many ways a perfect mathematical model. I should like to present some aspects of it here in order to further counteract the image of the simple boomerang-thrower and grub-eater.

The Aborigines are organized into tribes, distinct groups whose members are united by common descent and share a given territory. Within the tribe, there are units which have been called 'local descent groups', smaller than the tribe and to which wives do not belong—women usually marry within the tribe and out of the local descent groups, but in doing so do not relinquish totemic affiliation by leaving their territory. Between the tribe and the local descent group are the clans, most of which are patrilineal and share the same totem. The Aboriginal 'horde' is a different type of grouping again, since it includes the wives and children, unlike the patrilineal clans; it is the local foraging and hunting group.

The clans of the Aborigine are also grouped into moities, a form of dual organization which classifies everyone within the tribe and neighbouring tribes and *all natural phenomena* into two distinct groups—people must marry into the moiety, or half, other than their own. This division into halves provides a simple plan for social and ceremonial purposes and may be organized in different ways— matrilineally, through mothers and sisters, or patrilineally, through men. This aspect of Australian social organization resembles the moieties of the Ojibwa or the South American Indians.

A Walbiri tribesman: the severe scarring on his shoulder is the result of a stone-knife wound in a tribal feud.

Dualism is a phenomenon found often in primitive society, whole communities and even tribal groups being divided into vertical classes separating one group from the next. The moieties are generally named; and, apart from encouraging a sense of friendly or not-so-friendly rivalry, serve many social functions concerning reciprocity, marriage and ritual. The classic anthropological society may be said to be a 'dualist' society with a perfect balance between two halves. The Bororo village, in the Mato Grosso in Brazil, is circular and the two moieties live in opposite halves; the village layout is a reflection of the whole society. Bororo society is divided between men and women, and the universe is classified into male and female things, often based on left and right categories, left representing woman and right man.

This dual structure is not of course confined to primitive societies, and it has been suggested by Lévi-Strauss that our way of behaviour, and even the functioning of the human mind, depend on a constant system of binary oppositions. Throughout the world we have opposed groups—people of the mountains against people of the plains, Oxford against Cambridge, the North versus the South—who fight, engage in boat races, or heartily despise one another, and who yet basically belong to the same culture. Findings by anthropologists concerning the underlying structures of our own societies have often been inspired by attempts to understand the intricate nature of the kinship and social organization of what initially appeared to be very simple and therefore 'primitive' societies.

The Australian kinship system, which I have described very simplistically here, has provided a challenge to the understanding of anthropologists for generations. We still do not have a clear picture of its structure and exact function.

What makes the Australian system unique is the section and sub-section system which further complicates the kinship categories in terms of horizontally conceived classes. It serves to classify people and determine their position vis-à-vis one another—this person is to be avoided, this one must be presented with a certain piece of meat, another is the type of kinswoman who can be married. In the Australian section system, for example, everyone in a tribe belongs from the moment of birth—and even before—to one of four named section groups, membership being traced through the mother but not to *her* section. The sub-section system makes use of eight categories and shows a demarcation between cross-cousins (children of a sibling of different sexes), and also of children of cross-cousins. Cross-cousins have the advantage of being outside a person's clan under either the matrilineal or the patrilineal system and therefore are ideal mates, if you want to marry a close relative.

Consider the Murngin of north-eastern Arnhem Land, also known as the Wulamba. Here we have a patrilineal system, over which the anthropologists are still puzzling. The major units are clans or *mala* and these mala are subdivided into dialect groups—like hordes—known as *mada.* Every clan or dialect group belongs to one or other of two moieties and acknowledges in a general way a common bond with others on its own side of the dual division. Both the clan and the smaller dialect group, the *mala* and the *mada,* are exogamous—i.e. the women marry outside the group—and are associated with local territories, created and given to them by Murngin ancestral and spirit beings. Each has a number of sacred sites and totems associated with a series of myths. Each has special rights to sections of these rites and various sacred patterns and emblems. Within the smaller territories, there are waterholes associated with totemic creatures and children belong to the group associated with this water-hole.

The *mada* and *mala* of one moiety are territorially separate from the *mada* and *mala* of another. Because the members of moieties may not marry, members of the various clans and hordes—the *mada* and *mala*—must seek mates from the other. Because of this a child's parents must belong to different clans and dialect groups, which means that within the elementary family, two dialects are spoken. Generally speaking, as a child grows up he learns his mother's dialect in a basic way and later, gives more emphasis to his father's, his own clan language.

Kinship for the Aborigine is a means of ordering his life, enabling everyone to be identified and slotted into a category. The section and sub-section system offers a short-cut to this. If a visitor, for example, belongs to a certain sub-section, or is allotted one on the basis of what is already known about him, this simplifies his

AUSTRALIA
some names mentioned in the text

MELVILLE I.

Maung

Marlgu

GOULBURN I.

ELCHO

BATHURST I.

Arnhem Land

Murngin

Togeman

PORT KEATS

Wanindiljangwa

Mara

Gulf of Carpentaria

Cape York

Wogemen

Jangman

Gorindji

Walbiri

Walmadjeri

Northern Territory

Queensland

Aranda

Bidjandjara

Western Australia

Western Desert

Dieri

Lake Eyre

Great Victorian Desert

South Australia

New South Wales

Wuradjeri

SYDNEY

Jaraldi

Dangani

Murray R.

Victoria

Gippsland

Tasmania

relationship with other members of the horde. The system, however, becomes complex and necessitates quite a deal of juggling, especially when groups with slightly different systems meet at inter-tribal gatherings or at cattle stations. Discussion can then become quite intricate as people sort out their own systems and reach a working arrangement, usually a compromise. The moieties and sections, in particular, govern the types of preferred marriage. Today, there are problems, since tribes are scattered and in some regions there are simply not enough people in the correct inter-marrying categories. Hence, there has to be a degree of latitude.

Among all Australian Aborigines, relations between kin are expressed by a complex terminology and special behaviour patterns. This may involve complete avoidance, a speech taboo, restraint and respect, special obligations and rights. Or, it may involve a joking relationship—one in which persons concerned can act with comparative freedom. Others involve ritual complementarity. The most wide-spread avoidance phenomenon is between son-in-law and mother-in-law, the two being forbidden to utter each other's name; there is sometimes a complete ban on speech or they have a special 'mother-in-law' language. In some tribes a woman runs and hides when a 'daughter's husband' approaches. Familiarity is considered as bad as incest, and the avoidances symbolize respect and 'friendship'. In 'advanced' Western societies, we avoid strain in the mother-in-law situation by joking, not avoidance.

In Australia, as in many societies where kinship plays a prime role, the relationship between oneself and one's mother's brother is given special significance. In Australia, the uncles play an important part in the initiation ritual of their sister's son or daughter. This is usually explained by their role in providing wives for their nephews, or husbands for their nieces. Marriage is an important part of the kinship and political system, linking social groups into well-tried patterns. All tribes, through marriage, become interconnected—in receiving a wife there is an obligation to repay either at the time or at some future date. In the simplest form, men exchange sisters and women exchange brothers or, in the more complex, the exchange is between moieties.

Two other cultural features shown by the Aborigines, and commonly found in primitive societies; are initiation and totemism. Initiation, or the converting of children into male and female adults through rituals, scarification or education, is a well-nigh universal institution. In Australia, the change of status from child to adult is very elaborate, particularly for boys, and involves blood rites, depilation, cicatrization, circumcision, subincision and other rites, circumcision being

Arnhem Land Aborigine painting a young boy in preparation for a ceremony. Painting derives meaning from magic and religious associations. An artist's attitude is related to his totemic spiritual life.

possibly the most important. Through initiation the Australian Aboriginal youth begins to be acquainted with the religious and mythical lore of the tribe; and from the beginnings of his adulthood he learns the various social and kinship categories which help govern Aboriginal life.

The first initiation rite is usually a simple introduction to a long series of ceremonies and rituals, in which certain religious matters unknown to the boys before, and which are never known to women, are revealed. Among other things he is shown are the various sacred objects associated with totemism and 'Dream Time' myths. Throughout the Great Victorian and Western Deserts, for example, the initiation pattern has—or had—four main stages, the details varying from group to group. In stage one, the novice is taken from the wailing women and fully-initiated men draw blood from their veins, painting the novice with it and drinking some themselves. The novice's nasal septum is then pierced and a tooth in the top row is knocked out. After this he lives in virtual seclusion for about a year with other youths, subject to severe prohibitions. The second phase usually involves a tossing rite and the giving of presents. Then fully initiated men take blood from their arms and fasten feathers down all over their bodies in sacred designs and the initiate witnesses totemic rites. He witnesses ritual dancing and, just before dawn, he is 'smoked' by dancing men and then circumcised. Later, there is his ritual entry into

OPPOSITE:
Aborigine corroboree dancers
with ritual designs painted on
their faces and bodies.

the main camp where he is enthusiastically welcomed by his parents and close relatives. The third stage involves the rite of subincision, when a further cutting of the penis is performed and there is a great deal of blood-letting. As the fourth and last stage, cicatrization takes place, usually about a year after subincision.

Initiation rites are closely associated with totemism. The Australians' close links with nature also imply a close association with the 'Dream Time', the mythical past, and their cosmology depends very much on their relationship with the horde territory. The Aborigine's religion explained such phenomena as the seasons and the working of nature; it explained the origin of their ancestors. Their rock engravings illustrated their beliefs in the 'Dream Time', when their ancestors made human beings from plants, animals and natural features. These then became the totems of modern groups.

We will see later how totems work for American Indians. The Australian Aborigines' system was based on the view that all forms of life share certain vital qualities or attributes. This fundamental similarity was most apparent at the beginning of the world, when people, animals and other creatures had not yet assumed separate shapes or separate physical identities; but the bond between them is still important and is shown in many ways, all related back to the creative period and recounted in the myths. People even claim clan relationships on the basis of their relationship to a totem. In many parts of Australia, before a child is born, its father may find its spirit in a dream or through some revelation; and that spirit becomes associated with the totem which appeared in the dream. Or the child's totem may depend on the place at which its mother first realized she was pregnant, or on a particular food which caused her to vomit at such a time. It is important to remember that totemism not only involves the ritual increase of species on which the Aborigines depend, but serves as a further system of classifying individuals into groups. As such, Australian totemism becomes much more complex.

Totemism may be *individual*—a person becomes related in a personal and individual way to a certain species. Totemism may be *sexual*—each sex having an emblem and the injuring or killing of this emblem or animal is considered equivalent to challenging or attacking the members associated with it. There is moiety totemism, section and sub-section totemism and clan totemism, the various emblems neatly symbolizing membership of units, and those who should, and should not, marry each other. There is also a *local* form of totemism, each member of a territorial grouping sharing an emblem. Sometimes a totem is acquired by an individual, depending on where a child is conceived or born.

Whatever the type of totem or whatever the group it is applied to, there are two major aspects of totemic belief. There may be a *social* emphasis, whereby belonging to groups and the ordering of marriage and relations is emphasized. In this case there is a taboo on eating the totem animal and membership of the totemic group is matrilineal, i.e. traced through women. There may be a *ritual* emphasis. Here, membership is usually traced patrilineally, through men and there is no taboo on eating the totemic animal. In the territory of each tribe, there are sacred sites associated with beings who live in the mythical period. They may be water-holes or rocks or hills, or caves, containing paintings in ochre or blood. Elders are custodians of the myth and ritual connected with the site and perform rites associated with it. The totemic centre of the community is the storehouse where the totem symbols, the *churinga,* are kept. In these objects reside the spirits of the whole group; they are mostly flat, oval pieces of wood or stones carved with symbolic designs. Some have a hole near the end and can be attached to a string and whirled in the air to make the weird noise of the bullroarer. This is used to keep the uninitiated, the women and children, away from the secret rites. The objects are vital and sacred symbols of the Aborigines' ancestors. Their myths form a meaningful symbolic code which is acted out in ceremonies; these enhance the well-being of the tribes by keeping them in touch with the creative 'Dream Time'. The *churinga,* or fetishes, are concrete symbols of this 'Dream Time', and life and strength are conveyed through them.

OPPOSITE:
Ark-shaped Batak houses, and the stone chairs and tables of an ancient King in Ambarita Village, Samosir, North Sumatra.

Indonesia

Indonesians, in the anthropological sense, are not the same necessarily as the citizens of the Republic of Indonesia. The western half of New Guinea, West Irian, is part of the Indonesian republic; although the culture of West Irian shows certain Indonesian traits, the people there are ethnically Melanesian, and they have already been described in the section on Melanesia. On the other hand, the Philippines and Taiwan are often considered to be in the Indonesian cultural area.

Nevertheless, the state of Indonesia, the world's largest island complex, which extends along the equator for some three thousand miles, does contain most of the peoples we call Indonesian—such as the Balinese, the Javanese and at least three hundred groups, locally known as *bangsa*. The term bangsa signifies the tribal, ethnic groups distinguished by name, language and custom, location and social organization; it is more or less a synonym for another term, Proto-Malay, which is used for the indigenous cultures still existing throughout the region in pockets, where there are head-hunters, tattooed village-dwellers and nomads, found particularly in mountain areas.

Indonesians are grouped in the Indonesian-Malay race, also known as Malayo-Polynesian, in company with the peoples of south-west Asia. Indonesians mixed with Africans are also found in Madagascar. The physical type is generally slender and short, with skin colour varying from light to dark brown. The facial features are Mongoloid, implying flatness and the presence of the characteristic eye fold. Hair is black and straight or wavy, and the body and facial hair is sparse. In the Lesser Sunda islands and in the Moluccas, Australoid or Melanesian traits occur, perhaps relics of original peoples. Many thousands of years ago, the islands were probably inhabited by men physically resembling the contemporary Negroid-featured inhabitants of New Guinea and Aboriginal Australia. Hunters of small game and molluscs, they produced crudely chipped tools, developing gardening, probably as early as 15,000 BC. By 8,000 BC, these Australoid peoples had ceased to be dominant in Indonesia, and they survive today as recognisable physical and cultural types only in the eastern parts of Indonesia, New Guinea and Australia.

The modern population of Indonesia derives from a southward migration. Under pressure, probably from the Chinese, the Malayo-Polynesian speaking peoples began moving out of China and south-east Asia along the west coasts of the islands in the Philippines until they reached the western tip of Borneo. Some moved east, spreading into eastern Indonesia; others moved west into Sumatra and from there about 1000 years ago into southern Malaya. These people, combining with Australoid people were the ancestors of the present-day Malay-Indonesians. The recorded history of the island groups is intimately involved with the process of Hinduization that enveloped the mainland as early as the fifth century AD culminating in the powerful fifteenth-century empire of Madjapahit. Later, Islam reached Sumatra and Java from which centres it spread to become the dominant religion throughout the archipelago. The Dutch and the Portuguese were in the area as early as the sixteenth century. Consequently the diversity of historical influences has produced a complex mosaic of cultures and ethnic groups, from those remote bangsa primitive cultures, to international societies overlaid with the civilisations of China, India, Arabia and Europe.

Many attemps have been made to classify the Indonesian peoples into broad cultural types. The most common divides them into Hindu, Islamic and indigenous spheres of influence. The first includes the wet-rice growers of inland Java and Bali and comprises almost half the total population of Indonesia. They are inland villages, sprawling and densely-inhabited settlements, which once formed part of kingdoms of feudal states as we will see in Bali. Throughout this area, the culture is heavily Hindu-biased. Formal etiquette and status distinctions are stressed and the arts—dance, music and drama—are intensively cultivated. The second group includes the Islamic coastal peoples, such as scattered groups like the Malays of Sumatra and Borneo and the Makasarese of the southern Celebes. They all shared in the international spice trade in the years between 1400 and 1900. At nearly every harbour in the archipelago, there grew up a community of heterogeneous composition—Malays, Javanese, Makasarese, Moslem Indians, Arabs and Europeans and Chinese. Islam is everywhere the most unifying element. The immediate rural hinterland is composed of farmers, who are closely associated with coastal fishermen and coconut tenders. Tens of thousands of Arabs have recently migrated to Indonesia intermarrying with Indonesian women. European influence has also been important culturally and racially, although of the 200,000 Europeans, most left for Holland with the Dutch after 1949. The Chinese are of much greater significance. Half of the three million live in Java, with the rest scattered

A wooden figure from the early nineteenth century used in the
Javanese Wayang Golek puppet plays.

throughout the islands, but primarily located in urban areas, where they render
any kind of service that brings profit. They are doctors, priests and storekeepers.
Their situation, economic and political, is a precarious one today.

The third group—the people of the mountainous hinterland—are mostly
pagan and have a wide variety of cultures. Peoples such as the Toradja of the
Celebes, the Redjang of Sumatra and the Dayak of Borneo, have lived in virtual
isolation from the rest of the world, each developing its own distinctive patterns of
life. Many are still engaged in war and head-hunting and are untouched by
Hinduism and Islam. They are on the other hand open to Christian proselytization.
Most of these bangsa peoples are shifting cultivators of dry rice or gardeners of
sago, maize, sweet potatoes. Kinship everywhere plays a more important role than
caste or state institutions.

These types, however, are a very rough guide. Some peoples, such as the Batak,
the Minangkabau and the Ambonese do not fit at all neatly into such a schema.
Moreover, there are groups of agricultureless, nomadic hunters and gatherers such
as the Kubu of eastern Sumatra and the Punan of Central Borneo who are unique.
Until recently, there was doubt as to whether these people actually existed,
because they are very elusive and because, culturally, they merge with their
farming neighbours; they probably only represent poor fragments of these groups.
The Punan are fragmented into small groups completely isolated from each other
and eke out a precarious but self-sufficient existence on the products of the jungle.
'Sea-nomads', boat people known as the Orang/Laut or Moken are found near river
mouths along the western coast of the Malay peninsula as far north as Burma.
Another unusual society is that of the Mentawai Islands of the western coast of
Sumatra. Here, the inhabitants are pagans who have a highly developed sense of
taboo. There is a complete cessation of useful ativity for months at a time when
there is a long taboo period and the men are completely immobilized; the women
obtain all the food and the village is closed to outsiders. These periods of ritual
abstention and inactivity are held on many different occasions: before or after the
building of a new house, the clearing of a field, making a boat, felling a coconut
tree.

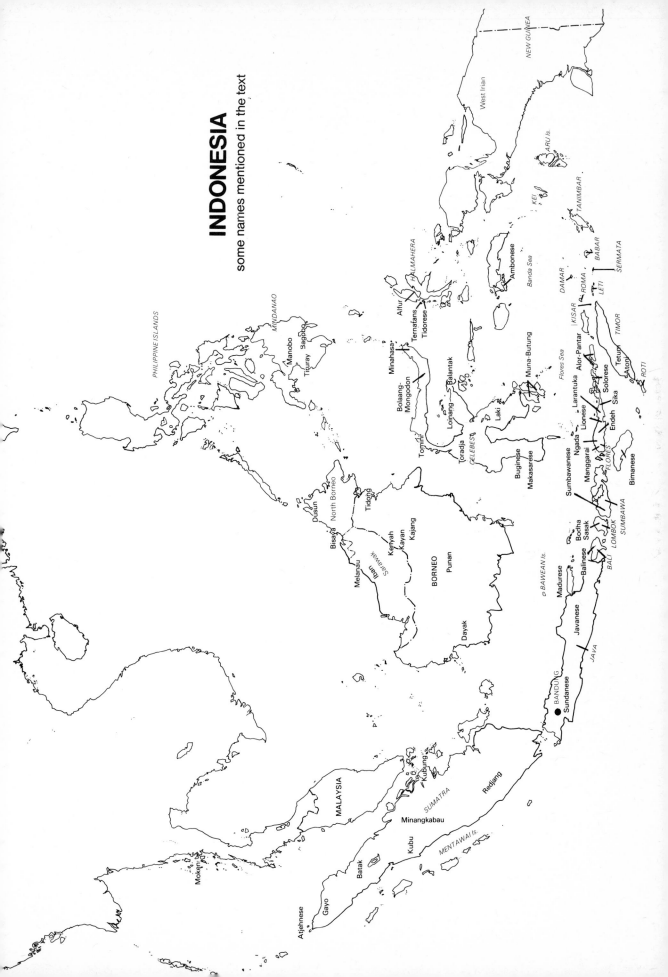

INDONESIA
some names mentioned in the text

Karo Batak girls in Lingga, Sumatra, show off their batik skirts. Formerly rank was identified by colour and adornment; today clothing is uniform.

The Indonesian cultural area is a heterogeneous one, as we can see from the variety of peoples and languages brought together in this section of the book—ranging from the 'Wild Men of Borneo' to the peoples of Java and Malaya with their elaborate state systems. It is impossible to select a representative people from this kaleidoscopic picture of pagans, Christians, Moslems, Hindus and Buddhists, peoples living in roaming bands, mountain villages, and urban settlements; so we will look at the area on a geographical basis. Last of all we will come to Bali and consider it in rather more detail, as it is undergoing many of the changes to which the many other isolated and exotic societies of Indonesia must sooner or later themselves undergo. Moreover, Bali has been well described by anthropologists, travellers and experts on art and dance, and over a long period has resisted the invasion of foreign and more powerful cultures. It remained Hindu in the face of Islamic pressures and today it is attempting to retain elements of its 'ancient' institutions against the pressure of modern political events and the impact of American and Australian tourists.

The Java group

The Javanese comprise more than one half of the Indonesian population of fifty million, and occupy two thirds of the island of Java. However, since the Javanese have migrated to places all over Indonesia and since Java is populated by large numbers of immigrants, it is impossible to estimate their numbers. On the whole,

A Javanese woman spreads rice out to dry; fields are worked by ploughs pulled by bullocks and crops are harvested by women alone.

they are rural Moslem peasants who cultivate irrigated areas beside rivers. The population density of Javanese village areas is the highest in the world and their landholdings the smallest. The Madurese of Madura are related to the Javanese and number over two million. In Western Java live the Sundanese, seventeen million of them, forming the largest ethnic group in Indonesia after the Javanese. Their core territory is the central mountainous area known as Priangan, the capital of which is Bandung. They perform masked dances and the famous hobby-horse, trance dance; they also practice the *pentjak,* the dance of self-defence, found in Moslem cultures throughout the Malay-Indonesia region. The Bawean Islanders, north of Java, number over fifty thousand and are fourteenth century migrants from Madura. South-east, on the islands of Bali, Lombok and Sumbawa live the Balinese, the Bodha and Sasak, the Sumbawanese, Bimanese and Dompu of Sumbawa. The Sasak—the major group on Lombok—are interspersed with Arabs, Buginese fishermen and Chinese and number about one million. Also on Sumbawa is a numerically small population of swidden-farming mountain peoples.

The Flores-Banda group

The Flores-Banda is a general name for the inhabitants of the islands bordering on the Banda and Flores Seas, excluding the southern Celebes. The Sumbanese number more than a quarter of a million and are a homogeneous group. The Florese, from the island of Flores, can be divided into five major ethnic groups: the

Toradja woman combing her hair in the island of Sulawesi in the Celebes. Toradja people have retained their distinctive customs largely due to their isolation.

Manggarai, the Ngada, the Sika, the Endeh and the Larantuka. In all these groups, there is a marked Papuan-Melanesian admixture. In addition, the Lionese, in the mountains of middle Flores, number 100,000; the Solorese, of whom a considerable proportion are Christian, live on the mountain slopes of Solor-Larantuka, where they burn down stretches of forest for their farms. The Alor-Pantar are divided among Moslem coastal peoples and autochtonous mountain dwellers, who have remained pagans, or have recently been converted to Christianity. On Timor and Roti, the eastern Tetum number about 200,000 and along with the Atoni exploit the sandalwood and beeswax of the forests. On these islands there were indigenous Hindu kingdoms; today they are Christians, but still practice their traditional rites. The Rotinese number 70,000 while a few Ndaonese inhabit an island of only nine square kilometres.

Further east in this group, the Southern Moluccas peoples include the island groups of Kisar, Leti, Luang-Sermata, Roma, Damar, Teun, Nila, Serua, Babar, Tanimbar, Kei and Aru. There are hilly and mountainous areas, sheltering a population of 125,000. The Southern Moluccans are of mixed proto-Malay and Papuan stock with Papuan features, generally more noticeable in the east near New Guinea. The area has long been noted for the fierce character of its inhabitants, their head-hunting and cannibalism and their virulent hostility to outsiders. The province of Maluku or Moluccas includes the set of islands east of the Celebes and north of Timor, but the Molucca people proper are concentrated on the island of Ambon. They are racially, geographically and culturally half-way between Malay and Melanesia. Once shifting cultivators, they were for a long time involved in the international spice trade and grew cloves and nutmegs.

In Halmahera we have about thirty ethnic groups in a landscape of high, densely-forested mountains. The Alfurs are pagans of the interior about whom little is known. Some are, or were, nomadic hunters. The peoples of northern Halmahera speak languages apparently unrelated to the great majority of languages spoken throughout Indonesia and the Philippines. These groups include the Ternatans and Tidorese—the two largest groups numbering forty thousand and twenty-six thousand respectively, the Loloda, Tobaru, Galelarese, Tobelorese, Sahu, Pagu and Nodole. The interior tribes of northern Hamahera are generally of Mongoloid physical type while those of the south appear to be Papuan or Melanesian.

The Celebes

Three and a half thousand people live in the mountains of the Celebes, where communications are very bad or non-existent. The Minahasa are totally Christianized and number over half a million. The Bolaang Mongodon, a coastal people, the Tomini, the western Toradja and eastern Toradja number over a 100,000, while the Gorontalo and southern Toradja number more than 300,000. The peoples of the eastern peninsula, the Loinang, Saluan and Balantak, speak languages which are similar to those of the southern Philippines. The Bungku-Laki peoples include the Mori, Laki, Bungku and Maronene. The Makasarese and the Buginese are the dominant people of the southern peninsula, numbering two and three millions respectively.They were formerly fierce seafarers and founded principalities throughout the archipelago. The Makasarese are divided into royal, noble and commoner groups. They inhabit a fertile area devoted to irrigated rice agriculture. On the islands of south-east Celebes live the Muna-Butung, while the Toala are a mountain people from the south-western Celebes, who were once cave-dwellers and made a livelihood from hunting and collecting. They now number less than a hundred.

Sumatra

The major people of northern Sumatra are the Atjehnese, nearly two million strong, who are a product of many centuries of interbreeding between the indigenous population and Bataks, Hindus, Dravidians, Javanese, Arabs and Chinese. The other major peoples are the Gayo, Batak, Minangkabau, Redjang, the Kubu and coastal Malays. The Gayo, who number about fifty thousand, are grouped into independent village states; the Redjang are a product of Javanese, Malay, Minangkabau and Batak mixture and are remarkable for the number of megalithic remains found in their territory. Minor peoples include the Simalur, Banyak, the Niasans, the Mentawaians and the Engganese.

The Batak are a unique people who number about a million and inhabit the Sumatra mountain valleys near Lake Toba and the lowland farmland and towns of eastern Sumatra. They are not Hinduized nor Islamicized to any great extent and lack the hierarchies of rank and title, the complexities of etiquette and the arts, characteristic of the Javanese and Balinese. One-time pagans, they are rapidly becoming Christianized. They are organized in lineages, which play an important

A Dusun woman in Banggi Island, North Borneo.

part, particularly as far as land rights are concerned. The Batak always marry in their mother's lineage, thus perpetuating a marriage exchange between two groups which has continued for centuries. They are also noted for their massive stone statuary and barricaded villages.

The Minangkabau, five million of whom live in the Padang highlands of western Sumatra, are matrilineal, and cultivate swidden rice and wet rice, constructing irrigation canals and ploughing with water-buffalo. They formerly had kings and practice two separate cultural traditions. One is 'masculine' and recognises Moslem law and the legal rights of the patrilineal royal families; the other is 'feminine' and recognises matrilineal customs and the traditions of the local village community. The Minangkabau are well-known traders and some of the more wealthy individuals have been to Mecca or studied in Cairo.

Sections of a Dayak longhouse, raised ten feet above the ground, are joined by a corridor of bamboo. A hundred and sixty families live on this structure.

Borneo

Borneo, including North Borneo, Sarawak and Brunei, presents a complex ethnic picture. The peoples include, in the north, the Dusun (who can be further broken down into separate categories, such as the Rungus Dusun, who number only a few thousand). The Murut—mountain peoples of the interior—are divided into the Idahan Murut and the Kelabitic Murut. The Bisaya inhabit the lower or middle reaches of those rivers in northern Sarawak and western Sabah which flow into Brunei Bay. The Tidong are an Islamicized people found along the Sembakung and Sibuku rivers. Other riverine tribes in Sarawak and Kalimantan are the Kenyah-Kayan-Kajang group. The Melanau live in swampy tidal lands between the mouths

Land Dayaks returning from work in their dry ricefields. They collect forest produce such as rattan, resin and rubber, and carry water in the bamboo pipes on their backs.

of the Rajang and Baram rivers on the central west coast and number 35,000. A large population—almost 300,000—of Iban, another riverine people, practice shifting agriculture in the low hills behind the coast of Sarawak. They are pagans and were formerly head-hunters and feared warriors. They present, anthropologically, a clear example of a bilateral semi-nomadic tribe, which is organized into neither kingdoms, nor tribes, nor lineages. They live in long houses, each of which has a back side composed of a row of apartments for individual families and a front side which is a wide communal verandah. Despite communal living and farming, each family maintains a strict, economic and social independence.

In southern Borneo are found the 'Malays', diverse peoples who have an Islamic religion; various groups of migrants; the Dayaks—a collective name for a great many predominantly non-Moslem ethnic and linguistic groups including the Ngadju, Mąanyan, Lawangan, who live along the large river systems growing rice on swiddens and collecting foreign produce; another group includes the Ot, a generic term for non-Moslem nomads; while the Punan-Penan nomadic group of hunters and gatherers live scattered through the central mountain system.

The Philippines

The flora and fauna of the Philippines belong to the Malay world and the population is usually described as Malay, i.e. they are 'Indonesian' with some admixture of Negrito types. Indian and Islamic influences have long been felt in the Philippines and the early Chinese settlement is evidenced in the million Sino-

An example of tribal sculpture from the Philippines.

Filipinos. After three years of Spanish rule, there are thought to be at least 200,000 Filipinos of mixed Spanish blood who form much of the élite of the country. Originally only Negritoes lived on the islands, groups of small stature with curly hair, dark skin, tinged with yellow, who nowadays live deep in the forest in western Luzon, in the lower mountains of eastern Luzon, in the upland interior of Panay and Negros Islands, and in the north-east of Mindanao. Many of them still hunt with bows and arrows and blowpipes.

The Proto-Malays were the next arrivals and their descendants constitute groups practicing shifting cultivation. They include the Manobo, Bagobo and Tiruray of Mindanao. The Ifugao cultivate rice on remarkable terraces stretching in a great staircase up five thousand feet of mountainside. The Filipinos are more closely related to the people of Malaya than those of Indonesia. As Malays they are rather taller than Indonesians and their hair is straight rather than wavy.

Bali

An aunt of mine, a nursing sister from Sydney, recently sent me a card from Bali, where she had been on a tour with a group of other Australians. She expressed her enthusiasm for the landscape, souvenirs, the friendliness of the people and a 'highly entertaining' visit to a 'tooth-filing ritual' in a native village. My reaction was complex: obviously it is a good thing for Australians to overcome a century-long avoidance relationship with Indonesia and discover other civilizations and countries than those of the Home Country and America; on the other hand, tourism frequently, if not always, spells death to indigenous cultures. A society can disappear in one of two ways: either its members are exterminated through disease and murder—which is what happened after forty years of white rule in Tasmania; or the culture disappears, or is diluted, by the impact of a wider, industrial society. This is what happened to the proud Hawaiians: that grand and elegant civilization, described by Captain Cook in 1778, where all too soon the kings and high priests of the local communities became swamped by a tidal wave of Christianization, Americanization and tourism.

The spoliation of Hawaii began in the eighteenth century. Bali, with a population of about two million, remained curiously isolated from the rest of the world, apart from Java, until the present century. Even Islam and the inter-island

Rangda, the witch in the Barong Dance of Bali. This dance is at the centre of Balinese religious activity and is associated with the death temple.

spice trade seem to have by-passed it, while Dutch colonial government was not introduced until 1908. The Dutch began to introduce reforms in local government, but they never went as far as they did in Java. Nor have cash crops been introduced on a large scale. Consequently, the Balinese provide an ideal tourist attraction. Isolation has not meant cultural inertia and Bali has long been noted for the vigour, sophistication and complexity of its arts—especially its music, dance and drama, but also painting and sculpture. The artistic traditions are Javanese-Hindu, yet Java and Bali are two very different cultures. In Java, practice of the arts is largely confined to court circles and to a few professional dramatic and orchestral troupes; moreover, new artistic creation has slowed down and most efforts go toward the preservation of revered traditional masterpieces. Bali civilization has been formed through an ancient, early Indonesian culture overlayed with several waves of influences from India, then Hinduized Java. After the Islamicization of Java in the fifteenth century, a significant number of Javanese priests, princes and scholars migrated to Bali. In Bali, art is pursued by large numbers of people from all segments of society, even the peasants who farm the irrigated river lands. Their artistic and religious culture include puppet and human plays, deriving partly from Hindu myths, such as the Ramajana and the Mahabharata—classical arts, which are nevertheless practiced every day and night by people from every stratum of society.

In Bali, a communal and public cycle of ritual and display aims at harmonizing the community with the gods. Both art and ritual are centred on temples and the frequent ceremonies, from birth to death (including tooth-filing), associated with them. There are thousands of temples in Bali—each village has at least three or four—and they reflect many different functions and histories. Each temple has a fairly stable congregation, the congregations usually overlapping, since every Balinese belongs to a number of temples. An individual may belong to a temple because it is his father's cult group as well as his father's father's. He will also carry out rites and ceremonies at one or two other temples for his rice-fields, and to several others for personal reasons.

A village temple consists of two, walled-in courtyards, connected by a narrow gate—the first for the orchestra and ceremonial preparations, the second comprises the temple precincts with altars and platforms for offerings. The altars, walls and gates are often elaborately carved and during ceremonies they are decorated with many additional ornamentations—palm leaves, bamboo, coloured cloth banners and streamers. A temple ceremony, unlike the Protestant or Catholic rites 'enjoyed' by most tourists at home, is a gala party for the celebrants and the gods; the latter are invited and entertained by music, processions, dances and offerings of aesthetically prepared food. There may also be a cockfight and a theatrical performance outside the temple. Many village death-ceremonies may include a performance of the dance-drama of the fight between Rangda the witch and Barong, the bearlike dragon, during which some of the performers may fall into spectacular trances and attempt to stab themselves with their *krisses*—all good tourist stuff again.

Life-crisis rites, ceremonies performed at birth, puberty, marriage and death, for example, are further opportunities for artistic performances and displays. The 'teeth-filing' one is the most important; it ceremonially marks the entrance of a child to adulthood—in Australian aboriginal society this is achieved by circumcision and subincision. Cremation is another important ceremony, but it is such an elaborate and expensive affair that it is generally postponed for years after death, the body being buried at death in the village graveyard, and disinterred at the time of cremation. Today, mass cremations are most common in many parts of Bali, poorer commoners sharing the ritual expense at a wealthy man's cremation; or poorer clansmen may share the cremation of a well-off member of their descent group. Wealthy aristocrats are often the focal point for ceremonies, since rites involving nobles involve the participation of thousands of commoners, both skilled and unskilled, as contributors and as spectators. Formerly, the kings maintained communities of craftsmen, although these have declined and are primarily supported by the tourist trade.

There is a set of three temples to which nearly every Balinese belongs and there are thousands of these 'sets' on the island. The first type is the 'origin temple', which represents the ancestral spirits of the present inhabitants of the area, i.e. the first people who settled there. The second is the 'great council' temple, representing all the deities and spirits which contribute to the general well-being of the people and surrounding rice-fields. The third is the 'death' temple, usually placed near the graveyard and at which the local dead and the gods of death are placated.

Bali society is not divided into rigid castes, although there are aristocrats and commoners, the former living in palaces and belonging to high-ranking clans and lineages. Nevertheless, the border between aristocrats and commoners is not very clear; aristocrats are not much richer, and their 'palaces' are not much grander. They are recognised by their titles and through the subservient attitudes of commoners towards them. Before colonial times, ruling kings were the heads of aristocratic kin groups, who maintained permanent or temporary ascendance over certain regions. When the Dutch arrived, there were six kings and countless minor princes in Bali—the six kingdoms now form the present-day governmental districts. Top governmental officials tend to be descendants of kings and the majority of the lower posts are held by aristocrats.

One segment of the aristocracy is composed of Brahman priests, who have enormous prestige. Brahman descent groups were, in the past, closely associated with dominant princes by marriage and ceremonial ties. The priest serves both aristocratic and commoner clients, although they are not connected with any temples (the temple masters of ceremonies are commoners), but with individual families. Every Balinese is tied to a priest; he visits him on special occasions for the holy water which is needed for all ceremonies, but most of his religious needs are met in the temple and by medical healers and spirit mediums.

The village plays second fiddle to temple groups. It is also less important structurally than farming societies, which consist of peasants attached to a small section of wet-rice paddies. Its members, who have constructed and maintained its dams and channels, also belong to a temple congregation. This system of small, farming groups which are very fragmented, is encouraged by the topography of Bali where deep ravines, cut by rivers running rapidly and steeply from the mountains to the sea, corrugate the land and leave very flat areas. Down a single river valley, there may be as many as fifty farming societies using its water, each one fully autonomous. Formerly, these farm societies were used by princes as a means of taxing peasants. At the outlets from the river and in the middle of the paddies, there are the temples where the society holds its rituals and festivals. Certain religious rituals are seasonally performed at the head of each river by the officials of the irrigation office.

OPPOSITE:
Vietnam—preparing sweets for the New Year celebration.

The white bull in which a Brahman priest will be cremated is decorated by a Balinese village craftsman.

How delicate a thing is Balinese culture? Will it survive its contact with the modern world? Balinese social structure is intricate, with its temple associations, ranked title groups, clan structure, farming societies, village associations, musical and dramatic groups, and the remains of its older, feudal states. Plainly, social change, the introduction of commercial plantations and tourists will not lead to further complexity. Balinese society was isolated, but it was never simple. The problem is quite a different one from the degree of complexity. Balinese culture is firmly welded into *local* life; it is not a high culture, as in Java, where social structure, on the other hand, is much simpler. Balinese society is densely populated, highly stratified and composed of multitudes of overlapping groups— but, importantly, relationships are personal (face-to-face) and localized. Taking this into consideration and also the fact that changes are being introduced into Indonesia along traditional channels, there is hope that the fascinating Balinese culture may survive and even be strengthened by modernization.

South-east Asia

South-east Asia has been the venue for such political turmoil and destruction by war that it seems incongruous to look there for primitive peoples, in almost any sense, in our survey. Nevertheless the Vietnamese, the Lao and the Khmer, while playing their parts as nations in the international conflict between the Communists and the West, and suffering the decimation of their populations in many zones, have not allowed their cultural individuality to be submerged. Hundreds of years of culture are not wiped out by the most destructive of wars or the most steam-rolling of ideologies. These major peoples are still distinctive, with distinct language, culture and traditions of which they remain proud. Moreover, throughout South-east Asia there are smaller groups who have remained outside the larger culture zones, usually safely ensconced in isolated river valleys or on mountain slopes. For the majority populations these are *their* primitive peoples, the strange exotic groups of the mountains who have clung to their own dialects, ways of dressing and social structure. South-east Asia is a land of great ethnic complexity—in Burma for example there are between 125 and 140 languages—a complexity which has been studied only in part by anthropologists. It remains to be seen to what extent these pockets of tribal society have been able to survive the recent political revolutions and wars. In South Vietnam for example it was precisely in these tribal areas that guerilla warfare was conducted most effectively, the villages serving as refugee centres and hide-outs for the Vietcong.

In South-east Asia the political frontiers are not always ethnic frontiers, tribal groups frequently straddling two, three or more countries. The Laos-Thailand border, for example, divides in two the large Lao community of the mid-Mekong basin, and the Burma border splits the Shan people into only nominally separate 'national communities'. In Thailand, we have Muong in the north-east, the Shan in the north-west, Lao in the south-east, and the Thais. Nevertheless in each country, there is a majority population—rice cultivators for the most part: the Burmese in Burma, the Thais in Thailand, the Khmer in Cambodia, the Lao in Laos, the Malays of Malaysia, the Vietnamese in Vietnam.

Racially, the people of south-east Asia are grouped in the Indonesian-Malay sub-group of the Mongoloid stock, neither 'Indonesia' nor 'Malay' being used here as political terms. Within this category, we have an unusual degree of variation— the very Mongoloid Yao-Miao (or Meo) peoples, the tall Cambodians who are Malay in type, the Thais with their round heads, prominent cheekbones, short nose and olive skin. The numerous languages of the area may be divided into three widespread families: Sino-Tibetan, Mon Khmer and Austronesian (or Malayo-Polynesian). Most of the scattered languages belong to the first two groups, but languages akin to the Austronesian dialects of the Indonesian island groups are also indigenous to the mainland. Thai and Vietnamese, however, do not appear to fit into any of these language families—like many other smaller 'independent' languages, their classification and historical connexions are still in doubt. Chinese languages such as Hakka, Hokkien and Cantonese are spoken by the largely urban Chinese, but these languages are not indigenous to the region, having been spread there by Chinese migrants.

Speakers of Sino-Tibetan languages are mostly concentrated in the west and north, in Burma, in Yunnan and along the Chinese and Burmese border south into Thailand, Laos and Vietnam. In Burma, they include the Nagas, the Chins and the Garos. The eastern highland group includes the Lutzu, Nakhi, Minchia, Kachin, Kadu, Lolo, Lisu, Lahu, Akha. The Yao-Miao (see also p. 116) are found not only in Kweichow and neighbouring provinces, but also in northern Vietnam, Laos and parts of Thailand. Most of the Hill People (see p. 76) speak one of the Mon-Khmer group of languages, although a few, the Jarai, Rhade and Churu—along with the Chams—speak dialects of the Austronesian, or Malayo-Polynesian, family. Mon Khmer languages are spoken by hillsmen and plainsmen alike, by swidden farmers and rice irrigators. They include the Mon, the Khmer of Cambodia, the Khasi, Khmu, Khua, Lamet, Lawa, Palaung, May, P'u Noi T'in, Wa, Yumbri and Alak, the Bout, Brao, Cao, Cua, Duane, Halang Doan, Katu, Kayong, Loven, Monom, Ngeh, Oy, Paloh, Rengao, Sapuan, Sayan, Sedang, Sek, So, Tau-Oi, Thap and The of the Central Uplands and Chrau, Kil, Lat, Laya, Ma, Mnong, Nop, Pru, Rien, Sop, Sre, Stieng, Tring of the south-east uplands. The Chong, Kui, Pear and Saoch form the south-west upland group.

The Thai-Kadai or Thai-speakers number thirty million and are the largest and most widespread population of the area. They live in valleys and grow wet-rice. The western group include the Ahom, Hkamti, and Chinese and Burmese Shan. In the south there are the Siamese Thai, the Khorat Thai and the Pak Thai. The Central Mekong River groups include the Nua, Lu, Khun, Yuan and Laotian Thai. In the

Miao, or Meo, women gossiping. The colour of a woman's dress often identifies the subgroup—White, Red, Black, or Flowered—to which a Miao belongs.

Central Uplands are the Black, White and Red Thai, the Neua, Phuan and Phuthai, and in the east there are the Chung-Chia, the Chuang, Tung Chia, Tho, Trung Cha and Nung.

Commentators on south-east Asia have frequently felt tempted to avoid the problems of ethnic complexity by dividing the whole zone into two general cultural zones—'highland' and 'lowland'. Lowland south-east Asia would include the coastal and inland plains inhabited by the majority populations where the primary sources of high culture have been India and China. Indian traditions have moulded the civilization of the Thai, the Lao and the Khmer as well as the Cham. Vietnam, on the other hand is an area of Chinese influence. The people of the hills, generally known as *montagnards* or 'hill people' have been cut off from the cultural influences which civilized the plains and, as a result, have retained their individualistic and remote cultures. The people of the plains, throughout south-east Asia, have always considered themselves superior to the Hill People whom they regard as 'primitives' or worse. To the Vietnamese, they are *Moi,* or 'savages', while the Lao call them *Kha* or 'slaves'. The less prejudiced Khmer refer to mountain villagers as *Phnong,* another word for 'Hill People'.

Hill tribes, like the Miao-Yao, Lolo, Karen, stretch from Burma to Thailand, to Laos and Vietnam. For many years there has been a general southern migration, but today, they have either been broken up by war and disturbed political conditions or have retreated further into the mountains, where they practice swidden farming in remote valleys. Tribes living in remote corners, such as the Highland Khmer of the Cambodian-Vietnamese border, have had until recently a closed economy, impervious to outside influences. While the villages vary in size and form, usually due to terrain, houses are usually small and perched on stilts, although there are enormous houses—Mnong for example—built straight on to the ground. Throughout the highland zone, within the tribes a clan system based on descent through men or women is the basic feature of social organization. In religion, they believe in a multiplicity of souls and in the countless *yang*—the totality of the spirits which people their heaven and earth.

A Thai girl making silver bowls.

While it is a convenient device to simplify the cultural themes of a large area, the division into highland and lowland peoples may be deceptive. Similar languages are spoken in both areas. Mnong, Stieng, Bahnar and Sedang are Mon Khmer languages (Cambodian is also one), while others speak Austronesian languages, also spoken by the Cham. Moreover, there has been contact with the plains throughout history. In Cambodia, for example, peddlars sell salt, fancy goods and urns, gongs and bronze pots which serve as important status symbols for the Hill People, who use them in their ceremonial gift exchanges. These objects acquire a huge value with the passing of time and are invested with pedigrees and legends.

Let us examine the ethnic situation in each state.

The Malayan Peninsula

The pre-colonial inhabitants of Malaya were almost all speakers of Austronesian languages, but they were never culturally uniform nor politically unified. Coastal peoples, for example, are Moslem, as against the peoples of the interior who are pagan or Christian. The present ethnic composition is more diverse due primarily to the substantial proportions of Chinese and Indians who were imported as plantation workers from south-east China, southern India and Ceylon. Chinese and Indians are still economically and geographically distinct. The Chinese have been labourers, traders, shopkeepers and are dominant in education and

A Chinese Malay spending an afternoon at a Sabah cockfight. The towel he carries is to rub down his cockerel after a day's combat.

commerce today. They constitute more than three quarters of the population of Singapore and probably outnumber Malays throughout the peninsula. The Indians and Ceylonese have become plantation, mine and railroad workers as well as moneylenders.

Malays have always been predominantly rice cultivators or small-holding rubber growers. They are found mostly as a homogeneous ethnic group on the coast, extending outside Malaysia into Thailand, in the Riau-Lingga archipelago and along the neighbouring coast of eastern Sumatra. There are between four and five million Coastal Malays who represent a distinct cultural group; they should not be confused with 'Malayans', the citizens of Malaya in general.

In the interior, there are pockets of primitive people, shifting cultivators and hunters and gatherers, who do not speak Malay. These are the Senoi, Semang and Jakun. The wooly-haired Semang belong to a racial grouping which has become known as Negrito, related to people of negroid appearance and short stature who have been found in isolated, scattered groups throughout south-east Asia. They include the Aeta of the Philippines, the Kubu of Sumatra, the Toala of the Celebes and the Andamanese (see pp. 67, 63, and 101), whose physical appearance and economy do not differ fundamentally from those of the Semang. The Semang live in Kedah and Perak, scattered in the mountains and valleys. These primitive hunters and gatherers have also been called Proto-Malays, descendants of the early inhabitants of the peninsula. They were driven into the central mountain chain along with the Senoi and the Jakuns, when Malays from Indonesia invaded the country.

The Vietnamese are the majority people in Vietnam. Conical hats are commonly worn by both men and women, who farm the coastal lowlands, and the deltas of the Mekong river.

Vietnam

Vietnam is an hourglass-shaped country with great mountain chains held together by a thin coastal plain uniting two deltas. There are thirty million Vietnamese crowded onto less than 20,000 square miles, living in the fertile deltas and plains, while the mountains contain less than two million persons.

The Vietnamese, known once as the Annamese, are primarily plainsmen occupying the deltas of Tonkin and northern Annam. The Vietnamese in North and South Vietnam probably number about thirty-two million. They represent the great Chinese tradition in south-east Asia, the bulk of the people of the lowlands becoming sinicized during the thousand-year period of Chinese rule; since the tenth century, the Chinese tradition has moved southwards along the coastal plain to the delta of the Mekong River.

Apart from the Vietnamese, there are three main minority groups, which can be collected together in a general way: the minorities of the southern deltas who have inherited the decaying traditions of the ancient kingdoms: the primitive inhabitants of the plateau of south-central Vietnam; and the occupants of the northern mountains whose ethnic and cultural ties span the adjacent frontiers with China and Laos.

About two thirds of the mountain regions of Vietnam are occupied by minority and tribal peoples, who are only marginally integrated with the Vietnamese proper. The border with Laos and Cambodia cuts across mountainous territory occupied primarily by tribal Thai groups, Miao, Yao and various Mon Khmer

SOUTH-EAST ASIA
some names mentioned in the text

peoples such as the Hre, Koho and Bahnar and Austronesian groups such as the Jarai. North Vietnam has more minority peoples than the south; they include Thai-speakers, the Mnong, Miao and Yao. The Mnong are widely dispersed in the highland area of the Red River delta and are related to the Vietnamese; they number about a quarter of a million. The Vietcong have allowed their minority groups a degree of political autonomy.

Burma

The great majority of the population is made up of Burmese, who probably number seventeen million or more. Before the second world war, Indians also constituted a large minority including Bengalis, Tamils, Oriyas, Hindustanis and Gujeratis. Today, they number little over half a million, many having fled the country particularly with the nationalisation of the retail trade. The Chinese provide a smaller and politically less significant minority.

The present boundaries of Burma are largely the result of British efforts in the colonial era to establish a zone of influence distinct from those of the French and Chinese. The mountain regions which now form the international boundary with Bangla Desh, India, China, Laos and Thailand are occupied by peoples who are not Burmese in speech and who differ in other aspects of their culture and include such groups as the Chin, Kachin, Wa, Shan, Karen and Mon. Some of them rivalled the Burmese in the nineteenth century in cultural development and political influence. Recognising this, the colonial government gave such territories as the Shan states and Kayah (Red Kayen) a special administrative status, indirect rule, within which the traditional patterns of leadership were maintained. The tribal peoples were put under a special administrative jurisdiction. In the independent Union of Burma, minority groups were allowed a degree of autonomy, but disagreements as to the arrangements have led to continuous violence and attempts of people, like the Karen, to assert their political and cultural independence. Minority population in Burma is of great magnitude, because the peoples are strategically placed on all borders and, together, form a large proportion of the population. The Karen number over two and a half million and the Shan one million. The former, next to the Miao and Lolo are the largest of the south-east Asian hill tribes, so-called. One group of them, the Padaun, live six hundred miles north-north east of Rangoon in the state of Kayah on the Thailand frontier. Once matrilineal, they have lost much of their former clan structure. They are well-known for the neck rings which their women wear, although younger girls now are refusing to have them, or they remove them after wearing for a few years. Older women cannot take them off,

since after so many years, they are necessary to support the head. If they are removed the head lolls uncontrollably to one side. Removing the neck rings was a normal penalty for adultery, the unfortunate woman spending her life lying down or holding her head in her hands.

Laos

The heterogeneous tribal minorities of the land in the middle, as the country has been called, include about half the population. In Laos the administration speaks of the Lao, the tribal Thai, the Lao Theng, the Lao Xung. The Lao are the politically dominant group and are found primarily in the valley of Mekong and its major tributaries and in northern and eastern Thailand. Most Lao are subsistence growers of wet rice. They are Buddhists. There are princely families, but the villages have no hereditary classes. There are no clans and lineages as among the tribal groups.

The tribal Thai (Nena, Lue, Red, Black and Phu Thai) are found in the higher valleys and also in adjacent parts of north-west Vietnam, south-west China and northern Thailand. The Black Thai are 'typical' in so far as they have preserved much of the traditional way of life prior to the expansions of the Thai-speaking peoples in Indochina. They live in narrow, upland valleys where they cultivate rice, making use of irrigation and terraces and swidden farming and grow opium as a cash crop. Three hereditary classes are known: a princely class which has special land rights and ritual functions; a class of priests; and a commoner class of farmers, artisans and soldiers.

Floating markets in Thailand are an integral part of community life.

Lines between tribal groups are not sharply drawn. Some Lao Theng have become Lao. They are not independent politically, economically or ritually. The 'Lao Theng' is a label applied to a diverse group of people who are descendants of the indigenous proto-Indochinese. They are Mon-Khmer speakers, animist and swidden river farmers and live in autonomous villages. The Lao Xung are mountain-top dwellers related to the Miao-Yao which straddle the border between China and Laos, dependent on swidden rice agriculture and on opium for a cash income.

Thailand

The Thais or Tais entered their present habitation from Yunnan in China in the twelth and thirteenth centuries fighting their way south against the Khmers. They now occupy the immense river plain which leads down to Bangkok, sharing the surrounding foothills with some indigenous mountain tribes.

Thailand is a relatively homogeneous country in terms of language (the people are predominantly Thai-speakers), ethnic origins (Thai) and religion — predominantly Buddhist. The Thai number twenty-six million, the Chinese (who are concentrated in central Thailand) three million, the Burmese, Lao, Cambodian and Vietnamese 45,000; Indians, etc., 7000 and Europeans 6000. Within Thai homogeneity, however, there are important regional and cultural differences. In the hills there are thirty tribes numbering less than 250,000. There is also a large minority (750,000) of Malay Moslems on the peninsula bordering Malaysia.

A Khmer market in Cambodia. Both men and women cover their heads with cloth turbans. Efficient lowland rice farmers, the Khmer produce the crops that bring the country a part of its foreign trade.

Thai-speaking tribal peoples—the Hill Tribes—are concentrated in the north and west and there are two or three hundred very primitive Negrito peoples in the extreme south who speak Mon Khmer languages. The Hill People live in small communities isolated from one another and without much political organization above that of the village. In northern Thailand the hill tribes lead a semi-nomadic way of life, often crossing the borders of Burma and Laos.

Cambodia

The origins of the Khmer of Cambodia are not known. Moreover, their language is not obviously related to those of their neighbours, the Lao, the Vietnamese and Thais; but is grouped with the Mon language of Burma. The Mon Khmer, who enjoyed a period of glory, symbolized by the vast temple of Angkor, number about five million, while minorities and hill tribes comprise less than 60,000. There is also a group of 70,000 Cham-Malays, a rigidly Moslem remnant of the Champa kingdom, who intermarried with the Malay conquerors. The Cham, who are also found in Vietnam, are speakers of Austronesian languages and have long been influenced by Hinduism and Islam. They include the lowland Chams and the upland groups such as the Bih, Churu, Hroy, Jarai, Krung, Noang, Raglai, Rai and Rhade. There are Vietnamese and half a million Chinese immigrant minorities concentrated in Phnom-Penh. The majority dislike the Vietnamese, who are artisans, fishermen and plantation workers; relations with China and the Chinese on the other hand, are good.

South Asia

South Asia, a vast, geographical zone south of the Himalayas and Afghanistan, includes India, Pakistan, Sri Lanka, Bangladesh, Nepal, Sikkim and Bhutan. Hindu, Islamic and Buddhist cultures predominate throughout the region, which contains, besides, a multitude of ethnic groups. These ethnic groups or tribal peoples live outside the general Hindu or Moslem culture; they speak their own languages and are frequently organized into kin groups, such as clans, instead of castes. For a long period they have lived isolated in forests and hills and therefore detached from the mainstream of culture. They constitute 6 or 7% of the total population of India and a varying proportion of the populations of the other countries.

South Asian 'tribals', therefore, are people who live in isolated, localized communities, speak a tribal—i.e. non-national—language and are structurally organized according to long, segmentary principles of grouping, based on descent. When we talk of the Khonds and Bhils of India, we are talking of groups in which membership, rights, or control of resources are based on kinship (real or imagined), and which have a common language and some cultural affinities. Tribals, normally, have a subsistence economic system—slash-and-burn agriculture, hunting and gathering. Now, of course, many are settled farmers living in villages alongside caste Hindus. A caste, on the other hand is a part of society in which groups are interdependent and hierarchically ordered and where one or a few castes control the major resources of society.

As many as thirty million Indians belong to the category of 'Scheduled Tribes', about 450 communities throughout the country, although some of them are sub-tribes of larger groups. The most important numerically are the Gonds of Madhya Pradesh, Maharashtra and Andhra Pradesh, the Santhals of Bihar, Orissa and West Bengal, and the Bhils of Rajasthan. The Gonds and Bhils both number about four million, the Santhals three million. The smallest tribal community which is receiving attention at the national level is the Andamanese, with the strength of less than twenty.

A Manipur man at the Lai Haroaba Festival, a pagan festival held yearly to worship forest deities. The deities are forgotten for the rest of the year, when the Manipur return to their Hindu practice.

In writing about 'tribal groups' we should remember that the major groups of Hindu society are characterized by a hierarchical system divided into elaborate caste groupings. A caste group is hereditary, usually localized and associated with a particular occupation; its members do not marry outside the group. There are complex relationships of superiority and inferiority among caste groups, including restrictions on eating and drinking with one another. At the bottom are the so-called scheduled castes, or 'Untouchables': in India, these amount to 15% of the population. These groups engage in various 'impure' occupations, such as scavenging, sweeping, cattle-herding and leather work. Tribal peoples, who do not fit into this social order, are often considered by Hindus as belonging to this lower caste grouping.

Not all tribal peoples today, however, live outside the Hindu social order. Tribes like the Bhumij, Bhil, etc., can be considered to be incorporated into the Hindu world, having accepted caste structure and they can hardly be differentiated from the neighbouring Hindu peasants. Tribals like the Santal, Oraon, Mundari and Gond are positively related to the Hindu social order, although the bulk of their population has not been included in the framework of the caste system. Tribal communities, like the Mizo and the Naga are only slightly influenced by Hindu culture, while a small group of tribes of the North-Western Frontier Agency are not even aware of the tenets of Hinduism—they eat beef; while their moral constraints and system of pollution do not appear to bear any resemblance to those of the Hindus.

South Asians, whether 'tribal' or not, cannot be easily fitted into any racial category. They are not Caucasoid, Negroid, Mongoloid or Australoid, but a mixture of all of these with, perhaps, the Caucasoid and Australoid strains predominating. Nevertheless, the peoples of the Himalayas have Mongoloid features, while the upper caste groups of the Indo-Gengetic plains are basically 'European' or 'Mediterranean' in appearance. Some of the tribal or semi-tribal populations of middle and southern India have dark skins, flat noses and wavy or even curly hair. The Pashtun (or Pathan), Kashmiris and Sudhi of the north-west are tall with long heads, pale complexions and wavy hair. The Kadar of Cochin, the Andamanese and the Onge of the Andaman Islands, along with the Vedda of Sri Lanka, have negrito characteristics—dark skins, small stature and frizzy hair. The tribes of the jungles of Bihar, Orissa and Madhya Pradesh share certain characteristics with the aborigines of Australia and are sometimes referred to as Proto-Australoid.

This is an area of quite extraordinary linguistic diversity, which reflects the cultural and tribal variety. In India, for example, the most important language group or family is the Indo-Aryan which is part of the Indo-European group of languages. It contains most of the major literary languages of northern India and Pakistan, and includes Sanskrit. A second group is Dravidian, comprising four major literary languages of southern India as well as about eighteen of the unwritten languages used in restricted areas. The third language category, which includes many unwritten languages, is known as Austro-Asiatic, and is spoken in the tribal areas of Orissa, southern Bihar and neighbouring regions; these are genetically connected with the Mon Khmer languages of South-east Asia. A fourth category is the Tibeto-Burmese family of Tibeto-Chinese languages, spoken in the Himalayan belt in the hill regions around Assam. We should not forget two isolated languages—Burushaski, spoken in Pakistan and Kashmir, and Andamanese.

Two typical Afghans, the man on the right a Hazara of Mongol origin. The Hazaras live in high, rather infertile valleys, pasturing sheep and growing wheat and beans.

It is interesting to compare the numbers of languages in each of these groups, and the proportions of the Indian population speaking them.

	No. of languages	Percentage of total Indian population speaking them
Indo-European	574	73.3
Dravidian	153	24.5
Austro-Asiatic	65	1.5
Tibeto-Chinese	226	0.7

In India, the state system since independence has been drawn mainly according to these linguistic criteria; in Pakistan too the four provinces are defined linguistically.

The best way, for our purposes, to look at the peoples of South Asia is to divide the area into six large cultural/geographic zones: the Moslem tribes of nomadic origin in hilly, western Pakistan and Afghanistan; the Himalayan peoples; the non-Indic peoples of the eastern hills of India and Bangladesh; the peoples of North-Western India; the tribal belt of Central India; the small groups of the Western Ghats of the south, including other southern tribal groups and Sri Lanka and the islands of Andaman, Nicobar and Maldive, along with Mauritius.

Western Pakistan and Afghanistan

Pakistan may be divided into five ethnic zones, all of which have managed to maintain their tribal identity to some extent. The Punjab constitutes two thirds of the population; Sindh and the South; the North-West Frontier Pathans—who are divided into a number of large tribes, such as the Durranis and Khaljis on the Afghanistan side and the Yusufaks and Afridis on the Pakistan; the Baluchistan hill tribes including the Brahuis, who are a group of tribes in the south-west, numbering about half a million and speaking a Dravidian-based language—they

OPPOSITE:
In north-west Nepal, goats and
sheep are commonly used as
pack animals, bringing rice and
other food to the area over high
passes.

are fiercely nomadic and despise agriculture; and the Himalayan zone. In Afghanistan, the largest and most important group are the Pathans—the so-called 'true' Afghans; the Ghilrai, neighbours of the Pathans in the south-east, may be partly of Turkish origin. Second in number are the Tajiks found in the north-east and north-central areas: of Iranian stock, they speak Persian; the Hazaras of the central range are Mongol in origin; Turkish groups include the Uzbeks, Turkomans; Nuristanus, called Kafirs (infidels) live in the eastern mountains north of Kabul; a few thousand Wakhi live in the Wakhan Corridor; the Kirghiz roam the Pamirs in the extreme north-east. However, ethnically the boundaries of Pakistan with Afghanistan make little sense and the major peoples merge into their neighbours across the frontiers.

The Himalayan Peoples

These live along a stretch of mountainous territory 1800 miles long from the Hindu Kush to Arunachal Pradesh, which touches the Burmese border. They live in parts of Pakistan and Afghanistan, Asad Kashmir, Indian Kashmir, Ladakh, partly in China, Himachal Pradesh, western Bengal and Bhutan. The whole zone is of great interest, because the valleys and slopes harbour many very isolated and refugee populations.

In the Western Himalayas over 70,000 Kafirs, or 'non-believers', claim to be descended from Alexander's soldiers. They are divided into the Red and Black Kafirs. In Pakistan Kashmir live the Shinas, while the Burusho of the Gilgit river, like the Caucasians, reputedly live to an old age on a health-food diet. They are Moslems and speak a pre-Indo-European language. Balti is a Tibetan-type language spoken by 150,000 Moslems of Tibetan-Punjabi culture. In Kashmir, Moslem peasants live under a Hindu government minority. In the eastern part of Kashmir about 50,000 Buddhists live in Ladakh and are of Tibetan culture. The Bhotiyas, also partly Tibetan in culture, are not Buddhists; they live in the Almora Himalayan district of Uttar Pradesh. In the main valleys of the Indian Himalayas— Kullu and Kangra, for example—there are refugee Hinduised groups, while in the lower Himalayan belt, the bulk of the agricultural population are Paharis, who merge with the Nepalis of Western Nepal; there are over six million of them and they are Hindu in race and culture.

In Nepal, across five hundred miles of the Himalayas, live mixed Hindu, Moslem, Brahman, Rajput and caste groups, with the Tharus forming the most important ethnic element. Above the mid-montane valleys and hills live the

The Himalayas are the home of
this Tamang hillsman.

Bhotiyas, while on the north-eastern edge of the country, there are the related
Sherpas, Tamangs and Lepchas. The Chetris, numerous over central Nepal,
consider themselves as high caste Hindus. They are, however, organized into clans
and divided into middle and peasant classes. They are an intrusive people, the
indigenous groups including the Gurung, Magar and Newar, whose languages
belong to the Tibeto-Burmese group. Chetris and Newar live separately, the Chetris
having always refused to speak the local languages and forced the local people to
speak Nepali. The Gurung, numbering about a quarter of a million, live in several
parts of mid-western Nepal and especially along the southern slopes of Annapurna.
Perhaps the most famous of the Nepalese, along with the Sherpas, are the Gurkhas,
the famous soldiers, who in fact come from several ethnic groups—Hindu,
Thakuris or Chetris and the Gurung, Magar and Tamang. Throughout the mid-
montane area, the variety of people is great, although the Magars are dominant.
Mixed among them are Brahmans, Thakuris and artisan refugees. The Thakali, now
less than five thousand, live in a high valley north-west of Pokhara, where they
once controlled the Tibetan salt trade. The Kirantis of eastern Nepal number half a
million and are subdivided into the Rais and Limbus. The Newars are the well-
known inhabitants of the little Katmandu Valley. They have parallel Buddhist and
Hindu caste structures. The Tamangs are poor and exploited by their neighbours,
the Newars. The Bhotiya groups of Tibetan peoples here include the Sherpas.

In Sikkim, there are Lepchas, Bhots and Nepalese, who constitute three
quarters of the population of Sikkim and in Bhutan, the Bhots or Bhutanese are the
dominant people and their language is the official language of the state.

Common to many Himalayan and some Indian societies is the practice of
polyandry, a system under which a woman is married to two or more men at the
same time. When the husbands in a polyandrous marriage are brothers, the

SOUTH ASIA
some names mentioned in the text

AFGHANISTAN

Tajik

Burusho

Kashmiri

Shina

Hazara

West Punjab

Himachal Pradesh

Ladakh Range

PAKISTAN

Punjab

Himalayas

Bhotiya

Pathan

DELHI

Pahari

Magar

Gurung

NEPAL

Tamang

Chetri

Sherdukpen

Monpa

Bangni

Mishmi

Miju

Brahui

Rajasthan

Uttar Pradesh

Newar

Magar

Sherpa

Lepcha

SIKKIM

Bhot

BHUTAN

Arunuchal Pradesh

Dafla

Adi

Gallong

Naga

Sindhi

Kiranti

Bodo

Santal

Khasi

Manipur

Ahir

Bhil

INDIA

Oraon

Bihar

West Bengal

BANGLA DESH

Mizo

Gujarat

Madhya Pradesh

Munda

Chakma

Bhumij

Ho

Gond

Orissa

Khond

Oriya

Maharasthra

Chenchu

Andhra
Pradesh

Mysore

Yerava

Nayar

Toda

Tamil Nadu

Kerala

Kadar

Tamil

Sinahala

SRI LANKA

Vedda

Andamanese

Onge

NICOBAR Is.

A Gurung woman of the Himalayas, with plate-like earrings of beaten gold and a necklace of coral and turquoise.

practice is called *adelphic* or fraternal polyandry; in this case it frequently happens that any children born are said to belong to the eldest brother. In other instances the role of the father is established by special ceremonies, or the children are said to belong to all of the brothers equally. A related form of marital union, sometimes called a secondary marriage, obtains when a woman cohabits with a man other than her first husband but without having terminated the first marriage by annulment or divorce. Polyandry must be distinguished from the privileged access to a woman by several men—a not uncommon practice and often associated with customs of hospitality. Among the tribes of the high Himalayas, such as the Sherpas, the Bhots and Lepchas, it is common to have more than one husband. The Sherpa believes that a polyandrous union is desirable because it prevents the fragmentation of property and fosters solidarity among brothers. The Tibetans permit any number of younger brothers to share an elder brother's wife. This is also prevalent among the Khasa, the Toda and the Nayar of southern India, who allow more than two younger brothers to share the same woman.

Non-Indic peoples of the eastern hills of India and Bangladesh

In Aruchal Pradesh, about half a million people can be divided into twenty-five tribes including the Monpa and Sherdukpen, who are Buddhist peoples related to the Bhutanese. The rest of the tribes have much in common with the south-east

A Nepalese porter carrying a
load of local basketware to the
neighbouring town.

Asian culture zone and include the Bangni, Aka, Dafla, Apa Tani, Hill Miri,
Gallong, Adi (including the Minyong, Padam, Shimong, Tagin, Rami and Pasi) and,
in the east, the Mishmi and Miju. One and a half million Bodo-speaking peoples live
on the edges of the Assam lowland and include the Bodo, Mikir, Kachari, Riang,
Jamatia and Lalung. Many of these groups of former headhunters are matrilineally
organized.

In the state of Meghalaya in the Shillong Plateau south of the Brahmaputra live
half a million Khasis, speaking a Munda language. The Nagas, perhaps the best-
known of the peoples of the eastern hills, occupy a plateau about four thousand
feet high and number over half a million distributed in twenty tribes, among which
are the Aos, Semas, Konyaks, Tanghkuls, Angamis and Lhotas. The Nagas, like the
rest of the hill peoples, differ fundamentally from the Hindu caste group—
untouched by Hindu civilisation and Buddhism. Christianity has been introduced
in the twentieth century.

Among the former feuding and headhunting Nagas, men and women share
farming tasks, cultivating taro and millet and sweet potato by slash-and-burn
techniques. All live in large, protected villages and in well-built houses often
decorated with elaborate carvings. Some of the hereditary chiefs live in impressive
houses up to 300 feet long, which contain enormous halls lined with skulls of
elephants, buffalo and captured enemies' heads. Head-hunting determined many
of the alliances between Naga groups, the custom being based on the belief that a
part of a man's personality is seated in the skull, even after death. The captor of a
skull thereby acquires this power for himself and periodically feeds his prize with
rice and rice-beer. The Naga also believe in innumerable spirits and in individual
divine guardians. Today more than half are Christian, however, and the
constitution of the Naga state provides for a system of regional representation

Naga girls with bamboo baskets. They retain traditional dress, despite obvious contact with modern society—note the wristwatch.

which involves cooperation between men of formerly hostile villages and even across tribal boundaries. The Naga have acquired a new feeling of ethnic identity in this way.

In the state of Manipur and the territory of Mizoram live Manipuris, Mizos and Chins. The Manipuris are Hindus, while the numerous Chin groups are Mongoloid peoples related to the Nagas. They originated in south-west China in the early centuries of our era. Today, they live in the hills at altitudes of from 4,000 to 7,000 feet. They have mostly been converted to Christianity. The Mizos are homogeneous and separatist and 80% of them are Christian. In the Chittagong Hills in the south-east corner of Bangladesh, 400,000 Buddhist peoples of Mongoloid appearance are distinct from the Bengali; they are the Marma, Chakmas, Mrus and Morung. They are all Buddhists and have links with Burma.

Peoples of North-Western India

In the north-west of India, there are cultural groups which are not classified as tribal by the Indian government, but they have their own distinct identities all the same. They include the Kashmir Pandits, Rajputs, Jats—the dominant agricultural caste numbering eight million and living in patrilineal clans; and eleven million Sikhs, who regard Punjab as their home state, although they are diffused all over India and famed as soldiers, with their own established and formal religion.

In Maharashtra and Gujarat, there is a number of caste groups: the Marathas are an agricultural caste group originally an arm and now forming 40% of the population of the state. The Ahirs are a pastoral caste found in Gujurat; the Rabaris are a gypsy-like group; the Mahar, a large untouchable caste. Baniya is a merchant

Punjabis dancing in the folk festival in Delhi. Their turbans denote the predominant Sikh religion.

caste, while the Jains, numbering three million, are centred in Gujarat. Parsis are descendants of Zoroastrians who fled Persia upon the Moslem invasions during the seventh century, and maintain distinct their ancient priesthood and sacred book. In Madhya Pradesh, in the low plateau, live numerous tribes and peasant groups, de-tribalized castes, bandit castes and elite castes.

The tribal belt of central India

The bulk of India's tribal people live in the central belt, from eastern Rajasthan to Northern Andhra. Eight million of them speak the Munda languages, live in Orissa, southern Bihar and other tribal areas in the east. They include the Santal, Munda, Ho, Savara, Kharia, etc. All of these people are organized into patrilineal totemic clans. The Bhils are a number of large tribes speaking Indo-Aryan languages, related to Gujarati. Other tribes are the Minas of eastern Rajasthan, the Thakurs, the Kolis—both of whom function within the general society as low castes—the Baigas, Gonds, Khonds and Oriyas. We will take a closer look at the last three.

The Gonds, historically and numerically, are the most important group of Indian non-Hindu peoples. They live scattered in the hills from the Vindhya mountains in the north to the region where the Godavari river breaks through the Eastern Ghats, and many Gonds also live in the states of Madhya Pradesh, Maharashtra and Andhra Pradesh. Half the Gonds speak an unwritten Dravidian language, while the rest have adopted Hindi and other Aryan languages. Their total number is over four million. When Gonds live among Hindu castes, they are recognisable by their physical features and different cultural traits.

Gond sculpture: Thákurdeo, the warrior god, shown riding on a horse, carrying a spear in one hand and a sword in the other.

As early as the fifteenth century, several Gond princes were heard of and, in power and status, were equal to many Hindu rajas, as the remains of their forts show. At the same time, the majority of Gond peasants have led lives as shifting cultivators far removed from the centres of higher civilization. Most of them live in the hills where the population is sparse and large stretches of forest separate the different communities. Houses, furniture and other possessions are simple—the only garment of a Gond woman is a cotton sari worn in such a way as to leave legs, shoulders and a greater part of the body bare. Among very isolated tribes, such as the Hill Marias of Bastar, the women do not cover their breasts and the men wear only a small apron-like covering.

Among the Gonds, agriculture is accompanied by innumerable rites—farming is related to the worship of gods and spirits, without whose blessing their millet, maize and beans would not grow. Without castes, the Gonds are organized into elaborate clans and, within the clans, a fundamental egalitarianism functions, presupposing the equality of all Gonds as far as intermarriage and ritual participation is concerned. While the Hindu sees himself as part of a complex society, composed of a large number of interdependent but *different* caste components, the Gond belongs to a separate, homogeneous universe, which theoretically exists separately of any other grouping. Within the Gond clan system, however, there is an elaborate structure, the position of each individual in the system being fixed for ever. This unalterable position extends into the Land of the Dead, where the members of the clan join their ancestors and dwell in the company of the clan god. The Gond believe in a multitude of gods and spirits and seek to gain their support or ward off their wrath by an elaborate system of rites involving the sacrifice of cows, goats and fowl. Hereditary bards are the guardians of the Gond sacred lore. At each major, annual feast they recite the appropriate myths and legends and thereby keep the tradition alive.

Marriage appears to be an irregular affair, the percentage of wives leaving their husbands after an early marriage being very high. The Gonds also take a tolerant view of sexual irregularities and a wife's adultery arises little anger. Widows marry and divorced women continue to remarry without losing the respect of the community. Among the Gonds of Bastar, marriage is more stable and may be related to the institution of youth dormitories. Here the boys and girls enjoy many years of

Pots and jewellery can be bought at this Gond market. The men wear white or coloured turbans, but shirts have become a part of their dress.

sexual liberty, but at the same time learn the moral, cultural and civic values of the group. The organization of these dormitories is in the hands of the young people themselves and no adults are permitted to interfere in their activities.

The Khonds live in the Phulbani District, in the hills of Western Orissa. In their dealings with one another, they are organized, like the Gonds, into local clans, each clan having its own territory and residence in that territory—being a Khond means being a 'brother' or a patrilineal 'clansman' towards the rest of the Khonds living there. Many of the lineage segments of these clans are of different descent, but have assumed a relationship of kinship to fit into the pattern. Between Khond clans, relations of friendliness *or* hostility are institutionalized. Linked friendly clans do not marry, while enemy clans are people who marry your sisters. As in many societies, it is considered right to fight the people they marry and marry the people they fight.

This is explained by the need in most societies to 'marry out', to seek wives in communities outside one's own in order to seek 'fresh blood' and also to establish alliances of mutual interest between groups which may be politically or commercially linked. In cases such as these many men, when marrying into these 'dangerous' communities, are seeking friendly brothers-in-law rather than suitable wives, men who will become trading partners, allies and protectors in a foreign environment. Often the difficult situation of enemies marrying is solved by a ritual bride capture where the friends and relatives of the future spouse ceremonially and with an amount of real violence abduct the bride. Our western custom of carrying the bride over the threshold is thought to be a reflection, if a pale one, of this ritual wife-abduction.

Living in the hills with the Khonds are the Oriyas, who live in villages and are divided into castes—warriors, middle castes and untouchables. The Khonds themselves were, in the past, attached to the Oriya warriors by loose feudal ties. The arrival of the modern administration has weakened the tribal system and at the same time has allowed the Oriya merchant classes to set up business and buy land

Jewellery is a symbol of wealth among the Gond tribal people; these women are wearing traditional silver anklets and several necklaces and bracelets.

among the Khonds. Many of the latter have lost their land and moved to marginal areas in remote valleys or some have migrated to the tea gardens of Assam. Throughout the modern period, the problem has been to protect the Khonds or aim at assimilation. There has been a conflict of opinion over this, ever since the British set foot inside the Khond Hills. Now the Khonds, while cordially disliking the Oriyas, are progressively discarding their own customs and assuming what they think are Oriya customs—taking on the manners and habits of Hindu gentlemen. Like many other tribal peoples in this part of the world, they are becoming 'Sanscritized'.

Southern India, Sri Lanka and the other small islands

The islands of South Asia show no consistent ethnic pattern. Thirty per cent of the population of Sri Lanka is composed of Tamils, centred in the town of Jaffna, including over a million Tamils of Indian origin, brought by the British to work their tea and rubber estates. The main population of the island is made up of Sinahalas, who are Buddhists. Mauritius, 500 miles east of Madagascar in the

A nineteenth century wooden figure for scaring away the 'devils of disease' in the Nicobar Islands.

Indian Ocean, was uninhabited until modern times. Now the population is 66% of Indian origin, with Africans, Creoles and a few French. The aborigine Andamanese of the Andamanese Islands are Negrito types speaking a language that has not yet been classified. Racially and culturally they seem to belong to a remnant Negrito group now living in Malaya and the Philippines. The people of the Nicobars, on the other hand, are definitely of Mongoloid physical type and are similar racially and culturally to peoples of the western coast of Sumatra. They speak a Mon-Khmer language.

In the plains of southern India there are scattered groups of very primitive peoples related to the Vedda of Sri Lanka—the Yerava, Varli and Irular. In the Western Ghats, a range of mountains running parallel to the west coast of Hindustan, we find the Badaga, the Kodagu of Coorg, the Puliyari and the Paniyar. Most famous of all are the Todas of the Nilgairi Hills, who numbered only 765 in 1961, and live on a grassy plateau between 6000 and 8000 feet high on which they graze buffalo. Like many Himalayan peoples, they practice fraternal polyandry, that is, several brothers are married simultaneously to the same woman. Of the Kerala tribes, the Kadar are the best known, along with the Allar, a tribe of honey gatherers, numbering less than 350, and the Kanikar.

The tribal peoples of Southern India, on the whole, inhabit the hill tracts and forest areas situated along the river regions, which until recently remained remote from the high culture of the town and cities. The Chenchu, of the Amrabad hills, are a semi-nomadic people of food gatherers and hunters of the deciduous forests who subsist, or at least subsisted, on wild produce and berries, roots and tubers and a certain amount of wild game. They live in bamboo huts and make leaf-shelters. Recent association with Hindus has not altered their old ways entirely but, without abandoning all their traditional beliefs, the Chenchu have taken over caste rules, such as the taboo on eating beef and the attitude toward 'untouchables'; they have also adopted the use of cooked rice and turmeric for food offerings. The Reddi are another small community who until recently lived like the Chenchu with a primitive economy. They have however succumbed to the linguistic pressure of neighbouring advanced populations and adopted the language of their Hindu neighbours.

In South India there are also heterogeneous groups such as the Syrian Christians, who number 21% of the population of Kerala, practising a faith they claim was introduced by the apostle Thomas in the first century AD. Other minority groups include the Jews, the Tulus, a negroid people called Sidhis—maybe descendants of African slaves, Goanese with a distinct Christian-Portuguese culture and heritage.

An interesting group, found with a general Hindu cultural area are the matrilineal Nayar and Mappila in Malabar and Tuluva. The Nayar are a large Moslem caste cluster, who were once a martial people. At the top of the caste system in Malabar are the royal house and the Brahmans, below them coming a group of relatively high castes who performed personal services for the Brahmans and Nayars—barbers, washermen and schoolmasters. At the bottom are low caste artisans and fishermen and serf castes all lumped together as 'untouchables'.

The Nayars are by far the most numerous of the castes. In former times, the Nayar alone had the right to bear arms and every Nayar youth left his family to join a local military and gymnastic school, where he was for several years instructed in the use of sword, bow and lance. The land-owning hereditary chiefs of districts and villages with their retainers were once exclusively Nayar, but for a long period, landownership has been passing gradually to the Brahmans.

The matrilineally organized Nayar live in a *taravad*—a matriarchal extended family, consisting of a group of related women with their brothers and children. The eldest woman is the titular head, but the house, land and other property is administered by the eldest male for the benefit of the family as a whole. The 'husbands' or mates of the women do not live in the house, nor do they support them. Likewise, the men of a taravad have 'wives' in other households, but their children are supported not by their husbands but by the household where they live. Until recent times the wives frequently had several husbands (often brothers, that is to say a form of fraternal polyandry) and the men, several 'wives'. They were thus both polygonous and polyandrous. Nayar women who have only one mate change mates at will.

Among the Nayar, every girl must be given marriageable status at puberty by the *tali*-tying ceremony. This is a ritual marriage in which a man of the same or higher caste ties a gold ornament round the neck of the girl. For the purpose of the ceremony, the tali-tyer is the husband, but his relations and obligations begin and end with it. Actual mating does not occur until later and then takes place not with the ceremonial husband, but with the Nayar lover the woman invites to her taravad.

The Far East

No great nation, it seems, is without its minority problem. Few people in the West are aware of the heterogeneous nature of the huge Chinese population; the Communists, in forging a new culture, are having to cope with peoples of different racial characteristics and language. Nor is it popular knowledge that about 5% of the Japanese population, in its turn, consists of degraded minorities, who suffer the same fate as the better-known 'Untouchable' castes of southern Asia. Japan resembles South Africa and the United States in the manner that discrimination against indigenous and foreign minorities is condoned.

The major race of China, Japan and Korea—the Mongoloid race—arose in the Far East and slowly overran the east Asian continent. The characteristics of the Mongoloid stock which arose in the Far East possibly as far back as the Ice Age are yellowish skin; coarse, straight, black hair; little beard or body hair; round head and high, flaring cheek-bones; flat face and nose and the upper eyelid epicanthic fold. The classic Mongoloid include such people as the Tungus, and the Samoyeds of Siberia. The American Indians are undoubtedly Mongoloid; this is sometimes, but not always, apparent from their appearance, a 'Red Indian' having superficially little in common with a Chinaman. In fact, however, the hook-nosed plains Indian known to cinema-goers is not typical of the Mongoloid inhabitants of the New World and the agricultural tribes of south-western North America, and South America, do have a very obvious Mongoloid appearance. Owing to its geographical location, racial mixture in China is inevitable; in the west, Mongoloids merge into Caucasoids, with no clearly defined boundary between the two. From north-eastern Asia, the peopling of America (by the Indians) took place; and from the south-east, there have been migrations towards Australia, Indonesia and the islands of the Pacific. Only in the south have the Himalayas prevented a mixture, of Mongoloids of the plateaux and the Caucasoid types of lowland India.

In China, there is a marked physical difference between northern and southern Chinese peoples—the latter resembling more the Indonesian type. The north has been invaded by waves of Tungus, Mongols and Manchus, all of whom have influenced the physical make-up of the populations. Moreover, the northern

In many ways the similarities between lives led in different parts of the world are as striking as the differences: a group of Chinese workers in a steelworks in Wuhan.

Chinese are considerably taller and more slenderly built than those of the south. But despite a general difference between Chinese of the north and south, we cannot mark out the various tribal groups of China according to specific racial characteristics. Traditions, way-of-life (nomadism) and language are the distinguishing characteristics of these Chinese groups.

The Japanese, a nation like the Chinese, cannot of course be called a race, perhaps not even a sub-race. Yet Japan, unlike western Europe and the Americas, even China, has not been subject to great migrations in historic times. For this reason, the Japanese form a relatively homogeneous grouping and share a high number of common physical characteristics. They look alike and share similar blood groups. The Japanese and Koreans are usually classified together as 'Classic Mongoloid': most of their features are similar, particularly the flat face, the epicanthic fold, coarse straight hair and small extremities. Perhaps the Japanese are more robustly built: they have a broad face, slanting eyes, flat nose and rather a wide mouth. The main difference between Japanese and Korean is that the former have more facial and body hair and are usually taller.

The Koreans numbering some forty-five million, feel themselves particularly distinguished as a 'race', and emphasize such cultural elements as dress and language. In fact their language is structurally similar to Japanese but reflects the influence of Chinese culture and contains Manchu and Mongol words. Strategically located between China, Russia and Japan, the Korean peninsula has been a meeting-place and battleground of cultural and national forces—today it is divided into northern and southern cultural and political halves.

The only freak people, from a racial point of view, are the Ainu of Japan, while some other exotic groups and primitive tribes are different because of their language, and cultural and religious traditions. Now I should like to look a little more closely at the Ainu, a physically discrete group whose uniqueness is fast disappearing, and at some other minorities who remain culturally distinct—often classified as primitive by the predominant cultural community—and yet which differ in no physical way from the 'master race'.

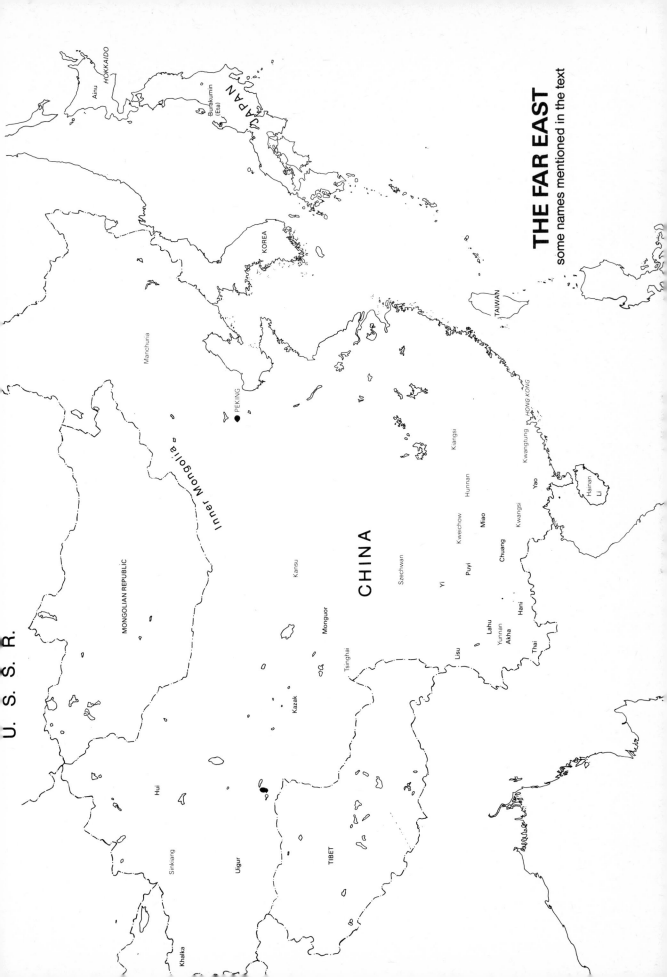

THE FAR EAST
some names mentioned in the text

The Ainu

A 'European' population inhabits the island of Hokkaido in Japan. They are the Ainu—a people who differ considerably from the predominant Mongoloid stock, with their round, brown eyes and abundant body hair. They have been long accepted by anthropologists as a relic group of an ancient Caucasoid stock which was once widespread in Asia and probably in Europe. The Ainu have characteristics in common with Australian aborigines and have also been said to resemble some Russian peasants: for this reason there has been much discussion as to whether they are Caucasoid (that is Europoid) or Australo-Oceanic. Some individuals, considered as 'Ainu', have manifested blue eyes, more pronounced features than the Japanese and differences in finger-print and blood types. It is these tendencies plus a notable increase in the presence of the Mongolian birthmark (which was reported absent in the past among the children of Japanese-Ainu marriages) which have further supported the view that the Ainu are 'White' or 'Caucasoid'. Formerly, the Ainu were great hunters of bear and deer, fishermen who trained dogs to round up fish. Like many extinct peoples of Europe, they had bear ceremonies: a bear cub was tamed and finally sacrificed. Today the number of 'pure' Ainu is less than a hundred and their culture has degenerated to the level of a tourist attraction; in fact, over half a million Japanese and foreigners visit Ainu-land every year in order to buy 'highly prized, authentic, Ainu-made articles'. On the whole, the Japanese consider the Ainu 'primitive' or 'barbarian', treating them with condescension when they attend Ainu Bear Festivals to watch their traditional dances.

Like many minority groups around the world, the Ainu are sadly aware that they are a disappearing people. The battle for survival has been a long and painful business and they have finally lost it; what remains is a general antagonism to the Japanese and memories of long years of injustice. The Ainu have been recorded in history as far back as the eighth century and since that time they are remembered as people of Hokkaido who traded their fish, bear-hides and deer in exchange for Japanese goods such as swords and lacquered containers. During the fifteenth century, large numbers of Japanese migrated to Hokkaido and their cultural influence became so great that Ainu rebellions became common throughout the next two hundred years. Finally, in 1790, they were placed under the direct control of Japanese feudal lords, and enforced acculturation—of the same type recorded in Ireland, America and Africa—proceeded at a smart pace. The Ainu were first forbidden to perform their bear sacrifices, but their reaction was so violent—they believed that all hunting would fail as a result—that the government repealed the

Despite pressure towards full assimilation into the community at large, the Ainu are conscious of their disappearing culture and preserve it through dress and ceremony. The 'Caucasoid' features of this man, outside his reed-walled house in the island of Hokkaido, clearly distinguish him from the Japanese majority.

law. However, assimilation has always been government policy and laws were passed that the Ainu should wear Japanese clothes, adopt Japanese methods of farming and inter-marry with their conquerors. Laws were promulgated to 'civilize' the Ainu—the men were forbidden to wear earrings, girls were not to be tattooed, a woman's house was not to be burnt at her death, spoken and written Japanese were learned by all Ainu, and children were given Japanese names. This policy of assimilation has worked. There are no longer any real Ainu villages, and five million Japanese and Ainu live together on Hokkaido in villages, in valley farms, along estuaries and the seashore. The two races, once so different, are hardly recognisable as such any more.

The Eta

A most curious fact is that, while enforcing the assimilation of the physically 'aberrant' Hairy Ainu, the Japanese have always maintained a complete taboo on any cultural and physical commerce between themselves and a large caste-like

A Japanese 18th-century painting on silk depicting an Ainu family. Here again, one outstanding feature is the bushy beard.

group known as the Eta, or the Burakumin. Japan has discriminated in the past, and continues to discriminate today, against a pariah group that is completely indistinguishable, in any physical sense, from the population as a whole; yet the segregation of this group has always been 'justified' in racial terms. The Eta are a caste group, in so far as they perform certain traditional functions in society—they are leather-workers, butchers and grave-diggers—and over the years, they have become literally 'untouchable'.

Three hundred years of isolation in their own communities has resulted in the Eta developing patterns of social organization, behaviour and speech which differentiated them from the rest of society. The curious thing is that the Ainu, physically distinct from the Japanese, were literally forced to miscegenate. The Eta, Classic Mongoloids like the rest of the Japanese, have been segregated and their segregation justified in racist terms. Throughout the areas where Eta live, there is a commonly-shared myth that these people are descendants of a different race—a 'less human' people than the stock which fathered the Japanese people as a whole. So similar are they that, up till the time of their official emancipation in 1871, they had to be visibly distinguished by special clothes they were forced to wear and by other cultural attributes which made them visible as a caste to 'real' Japanese.

Today, free of these race badges (similar to the badges worn by German Jews), they nevertheless remain a distinguishable segment of the Japanese population and bear the same social stigma as born by some Jews, the American Negro, African caste groups in South Africa and the Scheduled Castes of India. Social practices still serve to keep outcasts sexually and socially apart from Japanese society generally.

Eta—one of the words by which they are known and, formerly, used officially—is a pejorative and offensive term, even worse than 'nigger'. It means 'full of filth', and is now legally banned. Other words referring to these groups include the 'four-legged'; or *hinin,* the 'non-people', the ultimate insult. However,

A Burakumin man working in a Japanese shoe factory. Traditionally outcasts, the Burakumin take pride in maintaining their own identity despite no obvious signs of racial distinctiveness.

throughout Japan, despite legislation to protect these 'special communities' or 'unliberated communities' as they are officially known, most Japanese feel abhorrence at the thought of any intimacy with these pariahs.

In the past, quasi-religious attitudes, as in India, could justify the maintenance of some separate-occupation groups, each of which carried out ritually impure activities. The general theory was that they were an animal-like tribe with 'one dog's bone' or 'a disjointed penis'; it was believed that their skin was different, so that dirt did not stick to their feet when they went barefooted. Another view, linked with almost equally virulent prejudices against Koreans, is that the Eta are descendants of Koreans who came as war captives or as immigrants practising tanning. In fact, Koreans have immigrated to Japan in the past and, with modern discrimination in housing, marriage and employment against them, some Koreans have even married outcasts and themselves become *pariahs*. On the whole, however, the majority of Koreans have formed their own enclaves among Japanese communities and are almost as heartily despised as the Eta.

The fact is that the Eta are genuine Japanese, and the earliest outcast communities recorded are in the Kinki district, the very heartland of Japanese historic culture. Today, they number two million and constitute up to 5% of the population. They are concentrated in the lands surrounding the inland sea and, typically, located on the outskirts of the cities they serve, in the most undesirable sites on river banks, in swamp areas and the northern slopes of hills and mountains. They are no longer confined to traditional roles of butchering, leather-working and grave-digging, but even when they become farmers or factory workers, they remain despised. Even when richer and established, there is never any question of full social acceptance for the Eta.

Like all caste groups, they practice a local and occupation-endogamy. They have been shown to be poorer than the nation at large and, when they manage to find land to farm, they are given the poorer land and even pay higher taxes. Although less than 5% of the total population, the Eta constitute 60% of the unemployed. Like all poor, despised groups, they are in periodic trouble with the police, manifest high delinquency rates, are badly schooled and subject to job discriminations. In Tokyo, the Eta number about 30,000 and are engaged in the footwear industry or as day-labourers and street-sweepers with a large proportion on relief. They are pointed out by non-Eta as drunks (they drink brandy) and eat tripe—a dish repugnant to most Japanese. Many of these patterns, such as offal eating, are maintained by the Eta as symbols of their own in-group solidarity.

The Eta continue to disgust, and even frighten, the Japanese. Why do these attitudes persist, now that the Eta do not wear distinguishing patches of leather on their kimono and have moved out of purely pariah occupations? Most Japanese people today eat meat and there are Japanese butchers, tanners and shoemakers throughout the nation. Discrimination is deep, however, and the reaction on the part of the Eta is shown in hostility towards forms of authority exercised by the majority society. While the Eta may be inconspicuous to outsiders, they insist on remaining conspicuous to themselves. They are proud of their communities and 'being Eta', althouugh the pejorative term 'Eta' has been replaced by Burakumin ('citizens of special communities'). This consciousness of being Burakumin has motivated politically active members to promote their minority interests. Burakumin can be seen defending their interests in demonstrations in front of railway stations and public buildings and are proud of their history of integration struggle. Action in the wider community, courts and schools makes it clear that Burakumin leaders are trying to encourage a historical feeling of 'being Burakumin': and like the Blacks in America, this Japanese minority group now disavow the melting-pot style of integration, preferring the idea of a 'live and let live' pluralism.

Koreans in Japan

The Eta are not the only minority group in Japan. Other small communities and settlements include migrant, marine fisherfolk, wood-workers, hunters, iron-workers, religious quacks and miscellaneous groups. And in addition to Japanese nationals, there are over a million resident foreigners, consisting mostly of Koreans—more than 600,000—who have tended to converge on major industrial and commercial centres. Koreans were much more numerous before World War II; when unemployed and politically militant, they were a constant social problem for the government, despite the fact that Japanese industries favoured cheap Korean labour and contracted hundreds of thousands of Koreans to replace Japanese workers as the war took Japan's labour force to the battlefields. After the war a large proportion were repatriated. The remainder have become a despised group, stereotyped like the Burakumin or Eta, and forced to suffer the same social discrimination. Koreans are a marginal people, systematically refused jobs in major companies, and entrance to many private schools. They are most likely to find work as day-labourers, restaurant employees, construction workers and unskilled factory hands.

Chinese minorities

The minority problem in China has different dimensions. Here, the term 'minority nationality' is used to designate ethnic minority—a community of common origin, bound together by a common language, occupying a continuous area of residence and sharing a sense of group identity in economic and social matters. While the majority *Han* group formerly had the typical attitude of the bearers of a high civilization towards primitive peoples, this has now been changed, at least on the surface. The Chinese administration, since the revolution, has aimed at minimizing group differences; at the same time, the communists have sensibly recognised that the millions of minority peoples can achieve social and cultural progress—at least in the beginning—only in their own accustomed ways. The minority groups, or tribals, are given at least a semblance of self-rule, although as in the U.S.S.R. the ultimate aim is assimilation. Minority governments are set up in conjunction with the party, but as in Russia, the majority group (in this case, the Han) are encouraged to colonize these areas in order eventually to secure a Chinese majority.

A great variety of ethnic groups are distributed over a wide area of China, both in the hinterlands and the border regions. They number roughly 6% of the country's 900 million people and are, on the whole, concentrated in certain regions—Manchuria, Inner Mongolia, Sinkiang, Tsinghai and Kansu, Tibet, Szechwan, Yunnan and Kweichow, Kwangtung and Kiangsi, Taiwan.

On the mainland, non-Han ethnic groups include Koreans, who migrated from Korea to Manchuria; the Manchus of Tungus origin, who have become completely Sinicized; and the Hui, descendants of Turkic-Uigur soldiers and merchants who moved to China more than a thousand years ago. Taiwan has a native population of

A Kachin girl wearing a mantle of silver tassels and discs, in accordance with local custom.

the Malayo-Polynesian group, who number 200,000 and live mainly in the mountains; all, except for the Yami, were once warlike head-hunters—they include the Bunun, Atayal, Ami, Paiwan, Rukai and Yami.

Groups numbering over a million include the Chuang, Uigur, Hui and Chinese Moslems, Yi, Tibetan, Miao, Manchurian, Mongolian, Puyi and Korean. Those numbering less than a million and more than fifty thousand include the Hani, Thai, Li, Lisu, Kawa, She, Tunghsiang, Nasi, Laku, Shus and Jinghpaw. Many members of these tribal or minority groups reside interspersed among other groups. The Hui, for example, are found in over a thousand provinces, Manchurians in over eight hundred.

The major languages spoken in China are Mongolian, Tibetan, Manchurian and Korean, but there are many others who also have their written languages and their own printed books and newspapers. More neatly, the non-Han languages may be divided regionally into major groups: Sino-Tibetan in the south-west; Turkic in the north-west; Mongol in the north; and Tungus in the north-east. The Mon-Khmer is the only linguistic group in south-west China that does not belong to the Sino-Tibetan family. The Sino-Tibetan languages are spoken by a larger population than any other minority language. Presumably, they originated in the Pamirs and then branched out over the eastern half of the Asian continent from the Tibetan plateau eastward to the coastal regions of China, and from the Indochina peninsula northward to Sinkiang, Mongolia and Manchuria. The Sino-Tibetan family includes, besides Chinese, three groups: Kam-Thai, Miao-Yao and Tibeto-Burman.

The Thai language is used by approximately nine million people: by different ethnic groups in Kwangsi, Yunnan and Kweichow. Northern Thai includes some of the Chuang dialects spoken in Kwangsi, and southern Thai is spoken mostly in South-east Asia. Closely related to Thai and often classified together is a group of dialects known as Sui-Kam-Mak.

The different ethnic groups of China display a remarkable heterogeneity. There are a variety of physiques, cultures and languages. There are herders and farmers and traders. There are Christians, Buddhists, Lamaists and Moslems. Socially, the minority groups show considerable variation: small-scale tribal groups, feudal societies or groups almost completely assimilated to the wider Han society. Contemporary political and economic changes have made great inroads—in fact, much of the information known about Chinese minorities is pre-Communist and may already be historical.

Many of China's tribal groups are indigenous groups who have been settled in their homes since ancient times. Others have moved to their present homeland only in recent centuries. Migratory routes have been different and there has been a general southward movement from the deserts and plateaux of the north to the Yellow River plains, and from the central south and south-west regions towards the tropics. Northern groups, such as the Mongols, Manchus and Tungus have repeatedly pressed southward and been repeatedly pushed back by the Han Chinese. Southern groups on the other hand, have penetrated beyond the Chinese national boundary into Burma, Indochina and Thailand. Examination of these fringe peoples—and we will look at some of them now in more detail—will show the capacity of many ethnic communities even in such a monolithic state as Communist China to preserve intact much of their cultural heritage, despite all the forces which tend to persuade people to conform to the stereotype of the modern working man.

Mongolians include the Oirat and Buryat of Inner Mongolia and the Mongolian Republic, who are related to the Khalka. Small numbers of people of Mongolian origin are found in Sinkiang, Manchuria and Kansu. They are mostly nomadic pastoralists, raising horses, cattle and sheep, like the Kazaks of Central Asia, but there are also sedentary and semi-sedentary Mongols. The settled Mongols live in Chinese-style mud houses and are grouped into villages or settlements composed of clay, yurt-like structures. They are, or were, mostly followers of Tibetan-Lamaism and prior to Communist rule, the lamas were a powerful and privileged clan in Mongolian society. The Mongolians celebrate a number of annual festivals, especially an elaborate Spring New Year festival.

OPPOSITE:
Living on a barge which carries rice down to Canton, China.

OVERLEAF:
Lama outside a temple in Peking. Lamaism incorporates ritual based on mysticism and is a form of Buddhism.

The ger, or nomadic tent, of this Mongolian woman is made from wool beaten into felt.

Sinkiang, enclosed on the north, south and west by great mountain masses, and on the east by a barren plateau, is largely desert, and is the home of the Uigurs. In parts of the dry desert, oases make agriculture possible. The Uigurs (or New Uigurs or Turks), generally call themselves after the names of their adopted cities. They share a number of values adopted from Islam—polygamy is permitted and they practice tenets of the Sunni with much of their old religion still playing a role. Other groups in north-west China include the Hui, Kazak, Kirghiz, Monguor, Tajik, Tartar and Uzbek, most of whom are connected with larger groups in the U.S.S.R.

Tibetan-speakers are principally distributed in Tibet and in the Chamdo regions of Szechwan; some are found in Tsinghai and Kansu, where their neighbours include the Monguor, Salar and Turki. Tibetans are both nomadic and sedentary, the former occupying the northern plateau where they pasture sheep and yak for the greater part of the year, descending into the Brahmaputra valley for only the coldest months. The majority are farmers, once tenants on monastery lands or serfs of large land-holders and nobles. They grow barley, turnips, potatoes and wheat. The peasants traditionally lived in villages under headmen, while the nobles lived in cities and were descendants of the families of former Dalai Lamas. The nomads live a life similar to other nomads of Central Asia. Lamaism was the formal religion—it is an adaptation of Buddhism. Today, the basis of Lamaism— the Tibetan monastery system—has everywhere been abandoned.

The Miao and Yao are not closely related, but they are usually classified together and constitute one of the most important groups in south and south-west China. The Miao are distributed widely over the mountainous areas of Kweichow and Yunnan in the west to Hunnan, Kwangtung and Kwangsi in the central south. The Kwangtung group, located on Hainan Island, is descended from Miao soldiers brought there centuries ago by the Chinese government to quell the rebellious Li. The Miao are divided into the Red, Black, Blue, White and Flowery Miao. The Yao inhabit the mountainous regions of Kwangtung and Kwangsi. The Miao and Yao are

farmers who have been influenced for centuries by the Han Chinese. Among the two peoples, while there are traces of clan organization, the elementary family is the basic unit. Settlements are built on mountain slopes beside streams and the villages are surrounded by mud or stone walls. Both native and Chinese religions, each with its own priesthood and ritual, have been practiced.

The Chuang number over six million and constitute the largest ethnic minority in China. This is a Thai-speaking group located mainly on the plains and in the valleys of western Kwangsi.

The Yi are principally found in the Liang Shan area on the borders of Szechwan and Yunnan. They are marked by clan divisions and are divided into the Black Lolo, who own all the land and control the villages, and the lower classes, divided into White Lolo and Han Chinese slaves. The Yi or Lolo were animists, the chief religious specialist being the Pimu priest, a sorcerer who inherited his role patrilineally.

The Puyi or Chungchia, originally Thai-speakers, are distributed in low, marshy areas around Kuei-Yang and in south-western Kweichow province. They are a homogeneous group assimilated into the Chinese communities. They are not at all despised by the Han as the Miao were. The Puyi believe in a plurality of gods and spirits common to Chinese folk religion.

Smaller tribal groups include the Lahu and Akha of Yunnan. The Lahu are believed to have come from somewhere near Tibet. There are 250,000 of them in China, Burma, Thailand and Laos. They rely on slash-and-burn agriculture, although their preferred occupation is hunting. Villages are found above 4000 feet and usually number no more than a couple of hundred people. The Akha number 50,000 in Yunnan. Like the Lahu, they build their villages on steep hills, usually just below the crest of a ridge. Village gates often have carved wooden figures on top and at the sides, representing male and female fertility deities. The Akha women are very distinctive in their elaborate head-dresses—covered in coins, beads, buttons and feathers—which fall down either side of the head and are intertwined with their hair. Faced with problems of exhausted soils and population growth, the Akha are welcoming Chinese help and technology.

Central Asia

Central Asia is an arid area of grasslands, deserts and plains in the heart of the Eurasian continent, habitable only to those who know where to find water and exploit it. These open plains have never been an obstacle to the movement of ideas or peoples between east and west, north and south. Waves of migrants have entered the area; many have passed on to Europe or southern Asia, some have remained and adapted to the harsh way of life. With the immigration of sedentary farmers, cultivation based on irrigation increased, the farmers building villages along the rivers flowing out into the plains as well as beside high streams in the valleys where the waters have their source. In time, a chain of oasis-towns, set amid gardens, orchards and fields of grain, extended in a strip across Central Asia from the delta of the Amu-Darya (the ancient Oxus), south of the Aral Sea, to Lop Nor on the borders of China. North of these oases are grassy steppes suitable for pasturage and a life of nomadism, centred on horses—the people living by and for their animals, independent of the sedentary cultivators of the river valleys. And, between the farmers and the nomads, there have always been marginal groups of semi-nomads or semi-sedentary peoples, whose way of life is transitional between the steppe and the farm.

It is difficult to separate out the history of the peoples, races and ethnic groups of Central Asia, as so many different people flowed through. Many of those who stayed blended with those who were already there, and so identities became blurred. In the sixth century, Herodotus described the pastoral nomads: north of the Black Sea were the Scythians, and far east of these, astride the Syr-Darya, were the Sacae. South of these tribal territories were the fortified towns and villages of the oasis-dwellers. Along the middle course of the Amu-Darya was the Persian satrapy of Bactria with its capital at Balkh in what is now northern Afghanistan.

Throughout history, nomads have often threatened the oases: in Alexander's time, they were known collectively as the 'Scythians' and seem to have been of Indo-European speech. Then came the Huns and Turkic tribes, and the Mongols under their most famous leader Genghis Khan. In the fourteenth century, Timur, a Turko-Mongol descendant of Genghis Khan, conquered an empire extending from

China to the Mediterranean. Of the Iranian, Turkic and Mongol tribes who wandered through western Central Asia over the centuries, some remained in the area and became assimilated into existing populations. Eventually, nearly all the tribal peoples became Turkic-speaking, sorting themselves into groups, with their cultural identities in the main deriving from their adaptation to the ecological niche they moved into. Thus, by the nineteenth century we have six relatively independent ethnic groups—the Tajiks, Uzbeks, Turkomans, Kazaks, Kirghiz and Karakalpaks.

During the nineteenth century and along with the Russian conquest, there began a flow of Slavic peoples into the area. Later, under the Soviet regime, other ethnic groups, many of them non-Russian exiles from other parts of the Soviet Union, were settled in Central Asia.

Racially, the people of Central Asia have been classified as Turkic, although the pastoralists and agriculturists are mixed with Caucasoid strains. Body-build may generally be said to be robust, with a very broad face and prominent cheek bones, a round head and frequently abundant beard. On the whole, the eyes are not Mongoloid, but often have the external fold. Linguistically, the area contains three branches of Altaic-speakers: an eastern branch in East Turkestan; a central branch, consisting of the Kirghiz of the mountains of Tien Shan and the Pamirs, as well as the Tartars of the Volga and the Caucasus; and a western branch comprising the Turkomans of Iran and Russian Turkestan and the Azerbaijani (Turkicised Iranians).

In Russian Central Asia we thus still have language and cultural groups who remain passionately attached to their old traditions despite years of aggressive propaganda on the part of Soviet authorities to persuade them to conform to the socialist norm. Uzbeks, Tajiks and Kirghiz have undergone a spectacular change over the past three generations; they have been organized into collective farms; nomads have been partly brought to a sedentary way of life and made to cultivate crops. Almost all the Central Asian tribes represent a mixture of elements which, largely through a common history, culture and residence, came to have enough feeling of ethnic identity to accept these classifications. Yet, there is no national solidarity between Turkoman tribes and they often show as much hostility towards each other as towards non-Turkomans. Oasis people have generally identified themselves as belonging to a certain locality, rather than as Uzbeks or Tajiks. Nevertheless, many peoples of Central Asia still hold on to many of their

Turkomans are famous for rugs made with red and indigo wools, and for colourful embroidery, such as that in the cap of this girl on a collective farm.

ancient traditions tenaciously. For this reason alone they deserve a special place in this book; and after first taking a brief look at the great diversity of peoples in Central Asia even today, we will consider the Kazaks in greater detail.

The Karakalpaks, or 'Black Caps', are a people of mixed origin living in the delta of the Amu-Darya, along the southern shores of the Aral Sea. There are groups of Jews and Gypsies, who have for centuries managed to retain their own way of life and ethnic identity and avoided absorption into the more populous peoples around them. The Jews are all settled in Samarkand, Tashkent, Bukhara, Kokand and Khatyrchi and all speak a dialect of Tajik Persian, at least in the home. The Gypsies—known as Luli or Chugi—live in Tajikstan and Uzbekistan. Some provide music and singing at weddings and other family celebrations in small villages and among the mountain-Tajiks. In the 1950s, there were 7,600 of them in Tajikstan and Uzbekistan. Jews and Gypsies are both described more fully in the section on Europe. There are Arabs in Uzbekistan living in small compact enclaves in the eastern oases; they believe themselves to be descendants from the Arab armies which conquered Turkestan in the seventh and eighth centuries. Persians, in Central Asia, trace their origin to the Persian inhabitants of Merv, who were led into captivity when the Emir of Bukhara captured the oasis in 1785. They have maintained their identity through a strict adherence to the Shi'a faith. Uighurs constitute the basic population of the oases of Chinese Turkestan and are closely akin to the Uzbeks (see p. 126). Dungans are Chinese Moslems who sought refuge on Russian territory at the end of the nineteenth century, after an unsuccessful revolt against the Manchu government.

The Kazak Tartars are mainly Moslem teachers and merchants who obtained their eminence in Central Asia not only because of the strategic position of Kazan on the trade routes between Russia and Central Asia in the eighteenth century, but

The active Khodja-Akhrar mosque in Samarkand. Islam has prevailed in this area since 750 AD when the Arabs invaded Central Asia.

because of their origin as descendants of the Golden Horde. Further minorities include communities of Indian traders in the larger towns, western Mongols in the easternmost region of Kazakhstan and, in the south, some Kurd and Baluchi tribesmen in Turkmenia, and Koreans—descendants of former Kulaks—live in Uzbekistan. Under the Soviet regime, Azerbaijani Turks and Armenians have been encouraged—or obliged—to settle in Central Asia. During the World War II, when several autonomous republics of southern Russia were liquidated, many of their inhabitants were themselves exiled to Central Asia—the most numerous of these are the Volga Germans and the Crimean Tartars.

The Tajiks of Central Asia were originally speakers of Indo-European languages as well as being primarily Caucasian in physical type, with a culture similar to that extant on the Iranian plateau. Most of them spoke dialects of eastern Persian akin to those spoken in Afghanistan and the Persian province of Khorasan. In isolated villages of Central Asia, Iranian languages are still spoken. The mountain Tajiks are thus an important example of a people who have stayed outside the main cultural stream over the years and retained not only their old speech, but also many elements of the Zoroastrian fire cult, which flourished in the plains before the introduction of Islam. They eventually became Moslems, but, since they are remote from the main oasis-centres of Moslem learning, they adopted the Moslem Ismaili faith, led by the Agha Khan, introduced into the mountains from India in the nineteenth century.

The peoples of Iranian speech have been subject to influences both from the Iranian plateau and from the Turkic steppe-nomads who settled among them over the centuries. The Turks have increased in number and the Tajiks living on the oases have adopted the Turkic speech, though retaining their old oasis way of life. Because of this language change, the number of Tajiks clearly identifiable as such has steadily decreased. Their culture has become very little different from that of the oasis-Uzbeks, although their conservatism is still demonstrated by the retention of Persian speech in isolated cases and a general resistance to changes in their way of life.

A Tajik farmer on the best form of transport for this mountainous region.

The Uzbeks, Turks who settled in the oases, adopted the oasis-culture of the Tajiks but retained their own Turkic speech and indeed transferred it to many Iranian-speakers. In the early sixteenth century, the oasis cities were conquered by Turko-Mongol dynasties, tracing descent from an ancestor named Uzbek. From this time the name Uzbek came to be applied to the dynasties and some of their tribal followers, but the Turkic town and village dwellers became known as Sart—an Indian word meaning merchant. In current Soviet usage, the name Uzbek has come to include all the tribes who lead a partly pastoral life on the fringes of the desert, including the Kipchaks and Kuramas as well as the Turks. The Uzbeks consequently represent a mixed group with a physical appearance varying between Caucasoid and Mongoloid, although on the whole they are much less Mongoloid than the Kazaks or Kirghiz. The Uzbeks today are the most numerous indigenous peoples of Central Asia and comprise a majority of the inhabitants of the oases. Over six million of them live in the Uzbek S.S.R., and in Tajikstan.

Turkomans, or Turks, occupy the arid south-western part of Central Asia, a territory extending from the Amu-Darya into northern Iran and north-western Afghanistan. They are descendants of the Oghuz Turks who remained in Central Asia, when most of their number moved on into south-west Asia in the eleventh century. Physically, most are Caucasoid, which distinguishes them from the Tajiks and most other Turks. Their language is related to that of the Azerbaijani Turks of Turkey and Russia. Over a million Turkomans live in the Republic of Turkmenia.

LEFT: Tourist interests have, in many parts of the world, revitalized attempts to preserve national distinctions in art. Here, a Tajik man is painting chess pieces in the traditional local style in Dushanbe, Tajikstan. RIGHT: An old Uzbek man. His cloth turban is a hallmark of his Moslem faith.

The Kirghiz, proper, originally dwelt round the headwaters of the Yenisei river in southern Siberia. Some of them migrated south-westward to their home in the western Tien Shan in the tenth century AD. Those who remained in the north came under the rule of Genghis Khan in the early thirteenth century, and under the Jungars in the seventeenth. Like the Kazaks, they are Mongoloid in appearance and the two peoples speak related languages. Cultural differences are chiefly a reflection of the difference in habitat: in the high mountains, for example, the yak replaces the horse.

There are about a million Kirghiz in Kirghizia, although this large number must not suggest that they were once an organized nation with an overall political structure. Some primitive peoples may amount to a few hundred, even a few dozen individuals—this is true of hunting and gathering groups in South America, say, the whole 'nation' comprising only a few families. In other cases, and Africa provides many examples, tribes may number several million. They are a tribe, usually, because they speak the same language and practise similar customs. Nevertheless, like the Ibo, they will not even have the same name for themselves or be organized into political communities larger than a village or a group of neighbouring villages. Social and political life is carried out on a face-to-face, local level.

The Kazaks

The Kazaks constitute one of the largest indigenous groups of Central Asia. They came into being in the fifteenth century, when the White Horde occupied their territory in the days of Ghengis Khan; they are also descendants of Turko-Mongol tribes from the grasslands of north Central Asia and southern Siberia. The Kazaks are classic, Central Asian horse-breeding nomads and they retained their purely pastoral way of life longer than most of the tribes of Central Asia. However, when the Russians began to expand beyond the Urals, the Kazaks were the first to feel the restrictions of encircling Cossack fortresses. Then, Russian farmers moved into their fertile lands, while mineral resources were found in the less fertile areas.

The Kazaks are Mongoloid in physical type and most strongly so in the north. They speak a Turkic language distinct from both Uzbek and Turkoman. About three million of them now live in the Soviet Republic of Kazakhstan, with others in Uzbekistan, Turkmenia and Kirghizia.

Kazak pastoral nomadism is centred round the horse—the small, shaggy horse, fast and endowed with great endurance; the possession of large numbers gave prestige to their owners, a prestige related to quantity rather than their economic value. Horses gave the Kazaks mobility in times of war and during blood-feuds and were the object of cult attention. Children learned to ride at an early age—between two and four, and every real Kazak would disdain to walk even a hundred yards on foot. To the nomadic Kazak the horse is what the automobile is to a community devoted to the internal combustion engine. A Kazak is happiest grooming his horse, riding his horse, communing with his horse. To a Central Asian nomad the idea of a man devoting his sabbath morning to the cleaning of his Ford, starting up the engine in order to go fifty yards to the newsagent's, or merely sitting in it to get away from the wife, would be perfectly understandable. The Kazak man has his horse; the Englishman or the American has his car. Often, groups of Kazaks rode great distances for entertainments (tamasha), whether for an exchange of news or gossip, to greet a notable visitor, or to attend weddings or funerals.

Although the horse was the ritual focus, sheep were, and are, of greater economic importance; only the richest chiefs had enough horses to permit the eating of horseflesh or the drinking of mare's milk in any quantity. Small families had from twenty to thirty horses, while some chiefs had over three thousand. Some camels, two-humped Bactrians, were also kept for the transportation of belongings. Cattle were rare until the end of the eighteenth century.

The Kazak family migrated continually. In winter, their portable dwellings were set up in sheltered spots in the foothills under the bluff of a river or among bushy thickets of reeds, following the fresh growth of grass northward—or, for eastern groups, upwards—into the mountains. Some groups which wintered in the south-west travelled as much as a thousand miles to summer pastures in Siberia, while those wintering at the base of the Ala Tau ranges often ascended no more

OPPOSITE:
Eskimo in Kotzebue, Alaska,
wrapped in a fur hood.

A local game called Kyz-Kumai,
'Catch the Girl', played at many
village celebrations in the Kirghiz S.S.R.

than twenty-five miles to the high pastures of mid-summer. Migration followed traditional routes and was never haphazard. Usually, families returned to the same location each year for winter-quarters, where many clusters of tribally-related families camped near each other. In spring, this large group set out on its seasonal migration with smaller groups fanning out into the summer residential unit, the *aul* or camp, which consisted of from three to as many as fifteen tents.

Kazak nomads stored no fodder; in the summer and the autumn, the animals grew fat, grazing in their rich pastures; but the rigours of the winter reduced them to bags of bones by the spring. When snow lay on the ground, horses were turned into the pasture to break through the snow with their sharp hooves and eat the tops of the grass. Then the camels were turned into the fields followed by, finally, the sheep which nibbled the remaining grass down to the soil. In a bad winter many animals died of cold and starvation and if thawing snow froze into ice, too hard to be broken by the horses' hooves, entire herds and flocks sometimes perished. If the winter was not too severe, the spring migration was a time of rejoicing, when people dressed in their finery and sang as they rode towards summer pastures. Summer and autumn, when food was plentiful for man and his animals, were the best times of the year for the Kazaks.

In the summer, the Kazaks lived mainly on milk products. For the chiefs, who owned many horses, the chief nourishment was *kumiss* or mare's milk, fermented in a skin bag with frequent stirring. Those less fortunate made a similar drink from sheep's milk or added a little water to curds made of boiled milk. Cream and buttermilk were drunk. Various cheeses were also made and stored, including hard cakes made from cooking down curds to a rock-like consistency, which were used for travelling and as food in the winter, when it was pounded and softened in milk or water.

The Kazak dwelling, known as the yurt, is still used by some nomads. It is admirably adapted to both the nomadic life and the severe climate. Its walls are made of flexible, latticed wooden sections which can be contracted for carrying and expanded, once the yurt is set up. From five to nine of these sections are set up in a circle with an opening for the doorway; curved rods are tied at intervals and

Sheep are essential to the Kazaks and are a main source of income.

the upper ends are set in holes in a circular wooden rim which crowns the dome-shaped dwelling. The wooden framework of the yurt is covered with several pieces of heavy felt, held firmly in place with ropes. In winter, a felt lining is added for greater snugness, while in summer, the walls of the yurt are replaced with openwork reed matting. Inside, the ground is covered with covered rugs and decorative felts. On the woman's side, at the right of the door, are domestic utensils, sacks and bottles for storing milk and wooden bowls and ladles. In summer, kumiss bags hang there. In the centre is the hearth over which a large, iron cauldron is suspended from a tripod. The men's side contains saddles, harness, weapons and other male belongings.

Kazak family life was patrilineal, but when sons married they received a yurt to set up within the father's group. Only the youngest son remained in the paternal yurt to help the parents in old age. The extended family was limited by the number of animals that could be pastured within range of one camp site. When the number of conjugal families became too large and the animals too dense for the pasture-lands available, a son asked for his share of the family livestock and moved off to form his own extended family.

Kazaks all believed that they were descended, in the male line, from one primogenitor, and the Kazak nation and all its subdivisions were regarded as the ramifications of an extended family group, although genealogies were always highly idealised. They provided a fictional framework for tribal life, the largest subdivision being territorial units, traditional territories within which the smaller member groups were free to migrate.

Political organization followed tribal, genealogical lines. Being nomads they could move to new territories if they resented the imposition of authority. Leaders, or chiefs of larger and smaller subdivisions in the tribal genealogy, settled disputes. Strong leaders of the larger subdivisions really only functioned in times of war. Usually, leadership was paternalistic and informal, however. Unlike many egalitarian nomadic groups, such as the Fulani in Africa, there was an hereditary class principle at work among the Kazaks. An aristocratic class called 'White Bones' traced their descent from illustrious ancestors and maintained their elite status by endogamy—marrying only amongst themselves. Commoners were called 'Black Bones'. There were also slaves of sorts among the Kazaks—war captives, or children who had been sold by their parents in times of famine, and a group known as the Telengut, who, according to tradition, were descended from slave retainers of earlier sultans.

Kazak religion centred on cults, which were a mixture of an ancient, steppe-spirit cult, supernatural practices emanating from Iran by way of the oasis peoples, and beliefs associated with Islam. In the eighteenth century, they became nominal Moslems, but avoided some of the recommended practices, like circumcision, the shaving of the head and the wearing of embroidered skull-caps. Mullahs, Moslems learned in theology and sacred law, attended weddings and funerals, but traditional rituals always accompanied the Moslem practices. Among some tribal groups, rich men who died in winter were wrapped in felt and were left to hang from a tree until spring. Their bodies were then taken for burial to the town of Turkestan, where there was a famous saint's tomb venerated by all Kazaks. Rites centring on the horse were basic to Kazak religion; the birth of the first foal in spring was marked by feasting and rites as was the drinking of the first kumiss of the season. In some groups these rites lasted until the twentieth century. Shamanism, a religious phenomenon characteristic of all Central Asia, Siberia and the Far East, persisted into this century as well. The shaman—believed to be possessed by a spirit control—went into a trance state in order to cure patients, foretell the future or find lost property. In his incantations, the shaman invoked Allah and such Judaeo-Moslem saints as Noah, Abraham and David as well as indigenous Central Asian spirits. The shamans were much respected by the Kazaks; they wandered from camp to camp, evoking ancient heroes in their chants, keeping alive the old legends and religious traditions among the nomads. The Kazaks also sought protection by wearing amulets consisting of passages from the Koran. In addition, there was a cult of saints (holy men) and a tree cult, when trees were draped with votive offerings in the form of pieces of cloth, skin or horse hair.

Entertainments and feasts and ceremonies for marriage and death involved contests such as long-distance races between men and others between young men and girls, the girl trying to elude the young man, who sought to cut across her path. Archery contests tested skill in shooting both from a standing position and while riding at full speed. The chief entertainments were wrestling and eating contests and singing ritual or improvised songs.

The Kazaks have felt the Russian influence since the sixteenth century. In fact, it was Russian expansion that had caused the dislocation of earlier tribes (the Golden and White Hordes), thereby contributing to the very formation of the Kazaks. By 1725, a line of Cossack fortresses extended along the Irtysh River in the north, from Omsk to Semipalatinsk, and in the west through Kazak territory to the Caspian Sea. By 1865, when Tashkent was captured, most of the Kazaks had long since been brought under Russian administrative control.

Russian immigration meant that Kazaks suffered pressure on their pasture-lands. And with the appearance of trading-posts and seasonal fairs along their borders, manufactured novelties were introduced and exchanged for animals and furs. Russian policy, moreover, as a result of the unsettled conditions of the steppe, tended to favour wealthy Kazaks, who were sometimes more concerned with augmenting their own power than with assuming the kind of paternalistic responsibility normally expected of their leaders by pastoral nomads.

In the 1870s, Russian colonists began to arrive in large numbers: the worst was an unauthorized movement of Russian peasants into the most fertile part of the northern steppe; by 1914, almost half of the total population of these regions was Russian. Moreover, Russian pacification of the Kazak steppe encouraged land-hungry Uzbek peasants to extend their cultivated fields along the southern edge of the steppe.

Under the influence of the settlers, the Kazaks began to change their way of life. They stored fodder, settled down for winter and changed their house styles. Russian clothes were accepted with enthusiasm and a sleeveless, velvet redingote jacket, fashionable among Russian ladies in the nineteenth century, became fashionable among Kazak women (compare them with Navaho velveteen jackets). Craft works were developed by some, and in the early twentieth century, craft centres were organized, making felt, stone and bone objects. Many Kazaks were forced to give up pastoralism, taking up fishing if they lived near the lakes, or farming—planting a little millet or other grain at their winter quarters and leaving a poor family or two to care for the fields, while the rest of the group went on its summer migration. Others hired themselves out as mine-workers or farm-labourers; some were tempted towards the towns.

CENTRAL ASIA
some names mentioned in the text

MONGOLIAN REPUBLIC

Mongol

Lop Nor

C H I N A

Kazak   S.S.R.

Kirghiz S.S.R.

Dungan

KOKAND

TASHKENT

Uighur

Tajik S.S.R.

Syr-Darya

SAMARKAND

BUKHARA

Amu-Darya

Tartar

Aral Sea

AFGHANISTAN

Karakalpak

Uzbek S.S.R.

Turkmen S.S.R.

Kurd

Baluchi

Caspian Sea

I R A N

Black Sea

T U R K E Y

All this followed a pattern of change typical of a colonial situation. The Russian administration certainly disrupted Kazak culture: the money tax meant that the Kazaks could no longer be self-sufficient, depending on barter. Now, they had to enter alien markets, where money could be obtained by selling goods or services. Russian officials were corrupt, did not speak their language and gave local interpreters and clerks enormous power. The weakening of tribal structure was sudden and swift and soon there were even law suits among near kin and an ever-widening gap between rich and poor. The poor were no longer helped by richer relatives and were forced out of the pastoral way of life into settlements. Kazaks, influenced by the Russians, introduced the private ownership of land, which before had been held communally. In some areas, rich Kazaks became landlords reducing their less prosperous fellow-tribesmen to the status of tenant-farmers. Schools were introduced, but education in Russian schools was designed chiefly to train clerks and interpreters for the Russian administration. Most Kazaks remained illiterate, more concerned with their pastoral affairs or the struggle to survive on the fringes of settled life.

The First World War brought an initial decline in the number of Russian colonists, but there were many disadvantages: higher prices for commodities which the Kazaks had become accustomed to; higher taxes and the drafting of young men for war work. Alarmed, the Kazaks and Kirghiz rose against the Russians, some 300,000 fleeing to China, and there was much bloody fighting, starvation and the wholesale loss of animals. After the revolution and fighting against the Bolsheviks, the Soviets finally set up a government for the Kazaks with a capital at Orenbur, a Cossack settlement at the edge of Kazak territory. In 1924, it was moved on to the steppe. The Kazaks and their neighbours, the Kirghiz, were the last of the Central Asian peoples to be accorded full status as Soviet Socialist Republics in 1936.

Soviet administration was much less cautious than that of the Tsarist government; the new men pressed for change on the firm belief that agriculture was a higher and more desirable way of life than pastoralism. In 1921-2, government land was distributed among poor Kazaks and later more land re-distributed from wealthy Kazaks. The state also confiscated animals and redistributed their stock, a move which marked the beginning of a collectivization programme, which under the direction of Russian officials was rushed through too fast, far ahead of plan and more rapidly even than in Russia itself. Thousands of nomadic families were forced into collective encampments, where their animals often starved for lack of grazing. Many more Kazaks fled to the Chinese side of the border and others to Afghanistan—between 1926 and 1939 the Kazak population in the U.S.S.R. decreased by 900,000.

Collectivization was accompanied by the exile, liquidation or impoverishment of their leaders. Throughout the land, mining and industry was introduced. During the Second World War, many thousands of dissident Koreans, Ukrainians, Volga Germans, Crimean Tartars and others were transplanted to Kazakhstan and there was an influx too of Russians. In the fifties the plan was to convert the remaining grasslands of northern Kazakhstan into a granary for the whole of Russia.

So how do most Kazaks live today? Despite revolutionary changes, nomadism has survived to the present day in a modified form and has even been accepted by the administration as the most efficient way of exploiting grassland and desert. Today, nomads are 'rovers', herders are 'specialists' skilled in the care of livestock, and the nomadic family is a 'brigade' with each member holding an official title. They are, nevertheless, still pastoral nomads moving in family groups according to season in search of pastureland. Livestock numbers have risen and of the 2,800,000 Kazaks (1959), two and a half million were attached to collective farms and state farms. Perhaps half a million Kazaks migrate from pasture to pasture throughout the year, while as many as two million raise some livestock but also plant grain, engage in dairying and live in yurts during a part of the year. All Kazak kolkhozes, or collective farms, have herds of horses and sheep and continue to make kumiss.

By the 1960s, the great drive of the twenties and thirties to turn the pastoral nomads into settled, cultivators had passed. The Soviet economy needed the meat hides, wool, karakul fur and dairy products all traditionally produced in the steppes and deserts of Central Asia. It is recognised that many parts of Central Asia are best suited to stock-breeding and that livestock are best cared for by a nomadic way of life. Even the private ownership of a few animals is allowed—one cow, one milk-mare and five sheep.

In a Kazak kolkhoz, the number of workers ranges from 120 to 400. Usually, each kolkhoz has a social centre, but in some cases several small kolkhozes share a centre where there is a miller, a blacksmith and a carpenter as well as a cultural club and an elementary school. Most services are provided by regional centres, where there is a store, a clinic, hospital, school-library and a post-office. These regional ventures serve as links with the outside world. There are greater changes in such things as clothing, yet the old crafts continue, particularly in the making of felts and weaving on the traditional horizontal looms. Perhaps the greatest change has

The horse is still of great importance to the Kazaks and despite gradual movements away from pastoral nomadism, they cling to their traditional ways of life with vehemence. This is a sheep-breeder on a collective farm in Kazakhstan.

been the introduction of bread and meal (the Kazaks receiving grain as part of their pay), and potatoes in the winter, in addition to the dried cheese. The traditional diet, however, persists and in spring and summer, Kazak kolkhozniks live largely on milk products and probably the average Kazak consumes more kumiss than his ancestors. Meat is not served, except on ceremonial occasions. Even miners still eat on the floor with old people and guests seated in the traditional place of honour; solid food is served on a platter from which people dip with their hands.

Some nomads seldom go to the kolkhoz centre and in recognition of this, Red Yurts—mobile centres for adult education—are sent out to visit the wandering families. Many do have dwellings at the centre, where older members of the family and school-children reside during the winter months. In summer, school-children and elders join their families at summer pastures and often the centre is completely deserted for months at a time.

Kolkhozniks are formed into brigades with each assigned to tending either a flock of sheep or a herd of horses, camels or cattle, or else to take care of and cultivate the fields. In practice, the brigade is not very different from the old extended family. It consists of a family group, animals, riding-horses and pack camels. The yurts are still constructed in the traditional way, though utensils are modernised and there are kerosene lamps and iron stoves.

Co-operation between men and women is still necessary among horse and sheep-breeders. The kolkhoz itself is made up of closely related families of a tribal kin segment. When collectivization took place, families were migrating in the traditional territory of the tribal subdivision to which they belonged and the smaller kolkhozes of this period consisted of related families which normally moved out together in spring. Larger kolkhozes, when formed, usually brought together larger kin groups by virtue of their traditional sharing of a common territory. The formation of kolkhozes in traditional territory has even led to the strengthening of kinship ties. The sense of kinship is so strong that non-kin (book-keepers and truck drivers, etc.) remain very much outsiders. Tribal chiefs have disappeared as such but have often reappeared as district administrators in some places—all key positions are held by members of a single aristocratic lineage. The kolkhoz head is normally also chief of his tribal kin group and the head of the extended family is still a person of importance.

Even such primitive customs as the levirate (by which a dead man's brother or next of kin has to marry his widow) and polygamy have not disappeared, despite the latter being a 'crime based on tradition' in Russian law. Kolkhoz presidents are the worst offenders; they are the very men who, because of their prosperity in the past, would have been obligated to marry a relative's widow under the levirate. Bridewealth payment continues, though in a disguised form. Modern weddings conform to the traditional patterns, lasting several days at the home of the bride after which a feast takes place at the home of the groom. Shamans are still called in and Islam has not declined—circumcision is universal, the shrines of saints are visited, and so on.

The Kazaks of twentieth century Kazakhstan are very different from the primitive nomads of the fifteenth century and there is no possibility of returning to old ways. But there has been no loss of the sense of ethnic identity. Along with a strong tendency to cling to traditional occupations, most Kazaks are still primarily conscious of sub-tribal or regional identity, while there is a new sense of 'narodnost' identity—nationality—based on pride in being Kazaks.

Circumpolar Peoples of Eurasia and North America

The peoples of the circumpolar region include Eskimoes, Lapps, sub-Arctic Indians of the New World, and Siberian reindeer-herders and fishermen. They inhabit the inhospitable circumpolar regions of northern America (including Alaska), Greenland and Siberia. They all belong to the same broad racial category— Mongoloid, and in fact represent a classical section of that race. They include such peoples as the Tungus, the Buryats and the Samoyeds.

The environment has had a great influence on the make-up of these peoples. The extremities of their bodies—the limbs, ears and nose—are short, for example. The Eskimoes have very short legs, toes, fingers and noses. The Tungus, who live in the coldest part of the earth, are of the most extreme Mongoloid type, and have short, thick-set bodies, flat faces, fat-lidded eyes, coarse black hair, and scanty beard and body hair. Such a physique has been moulded by climatic engineering, protruberances being flattened to reduce surface area to a minimum, and the face padded with fat to prevent the loss of heat. Beardlessness is convenient as well, since breath freezes on a beard and then freezes the face underneath.

The peoples of this area also need enormous quantities of fatty food because the fat they eat is quickly expended as heat loss. The effect of chewing tough food is also seen in the size and form of muscles and teeth, and the bony structure of the race, particularly in Eskimoes.

Perhaps more than any other 'primitive' peoples, the Eskimo, Samoyed, Tungus and Chukchi have suffered from a confrontation with expanding capitalist and communist societies. Eskimoes and North American sub-arctic Indians soon came into contact with fur-trappers and gave up traditional pursuits for quick ways of earning money or Western consumer goods—often of little more value than cheap alcoholic liquor. In Siberia they have become outnumbered by immigrants from the central Slav regions of Russia and forced to become members of collective farms. In Alaska, the discovery of oil, the pressure from government and religious agents have contributed to an almost complete loss of traditional culture. In

Greenland the Danish administration has succeeded in fostering a sense of pride in Eskimo culture, combined with the adaptation of beneficial European ways. The Tungus and Chukchi of Siberia are also encouraged by the administration to retain certain culture elements. In particular their children are educated in elementary schools where their indigenous languages are taught. As in other parts of the world where minority groups are nervous of losing their identity, the insistence on retaining the language is an important step in standing apart from the majority culture.

The Eskimo

The Eskimoes are the best known of all the peoples of the far north, with their unique and exotic way of life; they extend over 5000 miles of Arctic and sub-Arctic coast-lands embracing the U.S.S.R., Alaska, Canada and Greenland. Their total population, less than 100,000, is very thinly distributed, being concentrated at ecologically favoured places along the complex coastlines. No other primitive people shows an equal uniformity in physical type, language and culture over such a wide area. Eskimoes are readily identifiable by their stocky build, their long heads and short faces, and the narrow slanting eyelids and Mongoloid fold. Even their different languages are mostly mutually intelligible. All Eskimoes base their economy on hunting; everywhere they refer to themselves as 'inuit' or 'the men', in this respect emphasizing their own identity in contrast to people around them of different physical type, language and culture. The homogeneity of the Eskimoes derives from their having spread from their homeland around the Bering Straits in waves of migrations over two or three thousand years without any competition from other peoples until the present century. Moreover Eskimoes have not developed frontiers between isolated groups which might have allowed a degree of physical and cultural differentiation; they interact frequently over long distances for trade and social intercourse.

On the whole, the features that distinguish the culture of the Eskimo from that of all other native peoples of the circumpolar zone are their well-nigh-exclusive residence in the Arctic and their dependence on the sea, although there are some riverine Eskimoes and 'land' (or 'Caribou') Eskimoes. Their adaptation to the northern climate has become almost proverbial—the igloo, or snow house, is the best possible structure that can be built with the materials available. They use the dog sled and the kayak, and tailor their clothes so that the seams are waterproof. Slit goggles are made from ivory to protect against the blinding sun reflected from the snow. They invented the smokeless stone lamp that burns sea oil. Their tools are beautifully made and remarkably efficient for the struggle to survive in small isolated groups. The Eskimo feeds on migrant animals which he hunts over great distances; this nomadic life means contacts between family groups are rare, but by no means non-existent. Larger groups are connected by blood and marriage, each individual having rights and obligations towards others—caring for the sick and the aged, protecting widows and orphans.

Despite widely-publicized tales of wife-swapping and wife-lending, marriage is an important institution among the Eskimoes, a man marrying as soon as he can hunt with sufficient skill to feed a wife and family. As in most primitive groups a single man is in a hopelessly disadvantageous position—marriage must be a practical affair, the husband and wife forming an economic and social unit which is basic to Eskimo life. Wife-lending should also be seen from a practical point of view—the exchange of women is the best way to formalize economic partnerships or social alliances. When two men agree to become partners in some activity, they exchange wives for a while and in effect become 'relatives by marriage'. In northern Alaska, wives were exchanged as a sort of guarantee of the friendly relationship between two men. The partnership arrangement also extended to the child, a child calling his father's partner by a name which meant 'the man who has had intercourse with my mother'.

Copper Eskimos travelling in winter by dog team. Despite external influences, Eskimos may still travel by sleigh.

Contact with Europeans has inevitably brought changes in weaponry and hunting methods. This Copper Eskimo is returning to camp after hunting.

In Eskimoland there are long 'hungry' periods, the people alternating between feasting and famine. For this reason, co-operation, exchange and friendship are essential. In primitive society close-knit communities recognise the importance not only of kinship and close family ties but of friendship between unrelated people. Often brothers-in-law are considered 'best friends'. Small children may be converted into ritual friends by a special ceremony which sets up an unbreakable bond between the two. As a result they help each other in time of trouble or illness, share their wealth, sometimes even exchanging their daughters as wives. Blood brotherhood—the custom of exhanging blood between two unrelated men in order to establish a ceremonial friendship—is a common means of sanctifying an emotional relationship between comrades. In the case of the Eskimo, exchanges between allies and kin are not gifts; an Eskimo praises another for the way he harpooned a sea-mammal—he does not thank him for sharing it. Sharing is inevitable: an Eskimo who is successful in spearing seals automatically shares his bonus meat with unluckier hunters, in this way insuring himself against want during his own unlucky periods. The Eskimo is not necessarily more altruistic and generous than other peoples, but he knows that the best way to store his surplus is by giving it away, because sooner or later he will want his gift repaid.

Conflict, often violent, occurs between Eskimo males, usually over women. Adultery is usually the cause—that is, when a woman has sexual intercourse with another without the express approval and prior knowledge of her husband. Wife-swapping, wife-lending or organized sexual games (known as 'putting out the lamp'), when sexual partners are chosen at random, do not constitute adultery, since these variations are condoned by the husband. In case of adultery, there is usually a history of prior antagonism between the two men, and the sexual delict is an excuse for a violent quarrel which often ends in murder.

The winter home of these Copper Eskimos is a caribou-skin tent, surrounded by a windbreak of snow blocks.

Once a murder occurs, it must be revenged by the kin of the murdered man and this usually results in further retaliation. Feuding is very much feared however, being disruptive of the close-knit family life of Eskimo communities and every attempt is made to prevent a quarrel leading to homicide. Outlets for ending disputes include buffeting, butting, wrestling and song duels. Opponents fell each other with forceful blows or butt each other with their foreheads, while wrestling may end in a death. In Alaska and Greenland, disputes are settled by 'singing' insults and obscenities at opponents to the delight of the spectators. The songs aim to deride, humiliate and shame and the greatest applause decides the victor.

Today the life of all Eskimoes has changed, for the whites have introduced new techniques that have completely revolutionized the relationship of the sealer and whaler to his environment and to other Eskimoes. Commercial fishing has encouraged the small bands to move into large, settled villages and live in wooden western-style houses. The Eskimo buys tinned, preserved foods from Western nations to help him through the hungry periods of winter. Instead of fishing and harpooning he earns money by working in fish-canning factories or by carving soapstone for tourists. This is a common situation for primitive communities once they come into contact with modern industrial society, usually through the medium of a colonial administration. To buy the new consumer goods he has acquired a taste for—clothes, utensils, alcohol—and also to pay government taxes, the primitive must join the system and either sell the goods he produces outside the community or sell his labour. In many cases primitive peoples have been converted from self-sufficiency to a dependence on external markets by being forced to spend most of their energy on cultivating cash crops such as coffee, cocoa and cotton. With the cash they earn they buy subsistence food; but in times of depression this income may disappear overnight and misery result. Yet, despite these overwhelming changes the Eskimo in America has managed to salvage more of his culture than the Indian groups who inhabited the temperate and tropical zones to the south.

A classification of Eskimo groups presents several problems, mainly due to the lack of clear distinctions in language and culture between the various cultural

Copper Eskimos fishing for polar
cod at a lead in the ice.

groups. The unit which might be regarded, and has been regarded, as a tribe, is
purely geographical and does not correspond to any degree of cultural or
political differentiation. (The following summary of Eskimo tribal groups is
derived primarily from Birket-Smith).

In the Aleutian Island chain with its fourteen large islands and over eighty
smaller ones live the Aleuts where 20,000 lived over two hundred years ago. They
are one group which should be distinguished from the Eskimo proper, mainly
through linguistic divergences. They include the Atka on Andreanov, Rat and
Near Islands, the Unalaska on the Alaska Peninsula up to Cape Stroganov on the
north side and Pavlov Bay on the south side, as well as Fox and Shumagin Islands.
The Aleuts hunt birds, fish, shellfish and sea-mammals. Like so many other peoples
their history of contact with both Russians and Americans has been disastrous,
involving slaughter, enslavement and exploitation for fur-trading. During
World War II the Aleuts were removed to the mainland and after three years in a
camp in south-east Alaska, those who wanted to go were returned to the islands,
but by then the total number of known Aleuts had dropped to less than a thousand.
A number were also carried by the Russians to the north-east point of Kodiak and
the opposite coast of the mainland.

The Pacific Eskimoes, including the Palûgvirmiut, Tatitlarmiut and Shuqlur-
miut all at Prince William Sound, are collectively known as 'Chugach'. Asiatic
Eskimoes include the Nookalit, the Aiwanat and Siorarmiut. The Bering Sea
Eskimoes live or lived on Bristol Bay (the Aglemiut and Nushagagmiut), on
Nunivak Island and the opposite mainland coast, and in the delta of the
Kuskokwim and Yukon. The North Alaskan Inland Eskimoes are known as the
Kûvagmiut, the Nunatâgmiut and Kangianermiut; and the North Alaskan Coast
Eskimoes as the Ungalardlermiut, Malemiut, Nuvungmiut, etc. Various groups
come under the general names of Mackenzie Eskimoes, Copper Eskimoes, Netsilik
Eskimoes and Caribou Eskimoes. The Iglulik inhabit Repulse Bay and Roe's
Welcome and are now in Southampton Island as well. The original Southampton
Eskimoes (the Sadlermiut) became extinct in 1903. In South Baffinland live the

OPPOSITE:
A Lapp with his reindeer and dog. Reindeer are used as a source of income, providing food, pelts for trading and clothing.

Preservation of fish of the rivers along which the Eskimos live is a seriously important aspect of survival. Fish supplements their diet during the winter months.

Akudnirmiut, the Oqomiut and Nugumiut. On the Atlantic coast of America are the Labrador Eskimoes. Greenland Eskimoes are divided into Polar Eskimoes, West Greenlanders (inhabiting the coast between Melville Bay and Cape Farewell) and the East Greenland Angmagssalingmiut.

Indians of the Sub-Arctic

South of the tundra domain of the Eskimo of northern America, from Newfoundland westward nearly to the Bering Strait, lies the thick green carpet of the sub-Arctic forest where game of all sorts abounds—deer, elk, moose, bears and herds of caribou along the tundra/forest border. The American Indians who still live in this zone belong to two large language families, the Algonkian and the Athabaskan. Those living south and east of Hudson Bay speak Algonkian and include such bands as the Montagnais and Naskapi of Labrador, the Micmac of New Brunswick, the Penobscot of Maine, the Chippewa or Ojibway of Ontario. The Indians to the west of these speak Athabaskan and include the Yellowknife, Chipewya, Kaska, Slave, Beaver, and Kutchin.

Despite the differences between the two language families, the Indian cultures over this immense area have many things in common. Originally they hunted mammals, fish and birds, but with the establishment of French and British trading posts, they soon switched to trapping. Although their climate is as rigorous as that of the Eskimo, the sub-arctic Indians differ from them in important ways. They build conical skin tents (wigwams) rather than igloos; they use toboggans instead of dog sleds; their feet are covered with moccasins rather than sealskin boots; and they use the birchbark canoe instead of the kayak.

But there are differences between the Indians, too. Many Athabascan-speakers are caribou hunters scattered through a remote and inhospitable land. Those living along the streams of the Pacific drainage basin take advantage of the several varieties of salmon that ascend the rivers to spawn. Meat is smoked and fish dried. They have a simple, undifferentiated social organization, with few group ceremonies and rituals, most of their religious life involving individual dreams and guarding spirits. A common division is therefore made between Athabascans inhabiting different river valleys or sections of a river valley. Perhaps the most well

146

known of the northern bands are the Kutchin, a matrilineal people who were once organized in ranked clans. Today the Kutchin live in a number of settlements with populations ranging from about a hundred to six hundred.

The Algonkian-speakers, on the other hand, have beliefs which centre on totemism. Totemism is another institution found across the world, but not of course in all primitive societies. This special relationship between a clan and some animal or object may be of overriding importance in tribal culture as it is in Australia and North America. In other cases clan totemism amounts to no more than the animal name by which a clan is known. The totem becomes a family label just as members of a Scottish clan wear their own tartan. In tribes where the totem plays an important part in the religious system totemic animals are revered because they symbolize the unity of their social groups. In regarding their totems as sacred they regard the social groupings as sacred and in respecting the totemic animals they are expressing the relationship of individual members of society to the society itself, as a source of their moral traditions and their very sustenance. What may seem a strange primitive custom on a closer view becomes a system of merging the individual in his society and providing him with a book of rules for behaviour. Each family has a particular animal as its emblem and personal names derived from these animals. Descent is claimed either directly from the animal or from a legendary animal associated with it. The very word 'totem' is derived from the Algonkian language of the Ojibway. These peoples also have strong beliefs in reincarnation; clear 'proof' that a person has been reincarnated comes when he has a dream about events in an earlier life.

The traditions of the Algonkian-speaking Penobscot, that live near the Maine coast, demonstrate the elaborate beliefs connected with totemism. Groups of families claimed association with certain aquatic creatures divided into two categories: salt-water totems (whale, sculpin, crab, sturgeon, perch and lobster) and fresh-water totems (frog and eel). One single myth explains the origin of each totem—a giant frog swallowed the world's water, causing a universal drought, but a mythical hero slew it and released the water. Thirst-crazed people rushed into the water where they were changed into various animals and those who were saved assumed their animal names and became the founders of the various Penobscot families. Thereafter the different Penobscot groups believed that the particular animal whose name they bore was especially abundant in their territory and when this animal was killed particular rituals had to be performed: permission had to be asked of the animal to kill it and afterwards apologies were made to it. But the interest of this kind of totemism is not because the Penobscot and other totemic

LEFT: The Kutchin tribe live in the Yukon River area. The dress and moccasins of this woman reflect her Indian origin. RIGHT: Chilkat Indians carving totems. Totemism is an integral part of their life, even today.

peoples were concerned about filling their stomachs, but because totemic organization reflects a general symbolic notion of duality, associated with marriage. The Penobscot divide aquatic animals into fresh-water and salt-water types. The Ojibway divided their bird totems into opposites of aerial and aquatic birds (such as the eagle and the loon). Totems help determine marriage relations — if an Ojibway man and woman both belong to an Eagle totem, they may never marry. But if one is Eagle and the other Loon, then the duality of the totems guarantees that they are of different blood and therefore permitted to marry. Among the Australian aborigines, described elsewhere, the totemic affiliations are much more complex but serve the same social functions.

The Lapps or Samek

The only European peoples who traditionally inhabited the circumpolar zone are the Lapps. Today, the Lapps live in the marginal lands of northernmost Scandinavia, number 35,000 or less and pursue a number of different life-styles of which reindeer-herding is only one. Their language is of the Finno-Ugric branch of the Ural-Altaic stock, found in Hungary and in North and Central Russia, and is most closely related to Finnish. Their lands stretch approximately 1000 miles east to west, from the tip of the Kola Peninsula in Russia, through the top of Finland, Sweden and more than half-way down the Atlantic coast of Norway. They are normally considered in four groups — the Coastal ('Sea Lapp'), Forest, Mountain and Eastern Samek. For two millennia the Samek or Lapp has had relations with powerful outsiders and has maintained his identity in spite of an increasing number of cultural changes and a history of colonial status. Some still live as

CIRCUMPOLAR PEOPLES
OF EURASIA AND NORTH AMERICA
some names mentioned in the text

Tuvan
Khakasy
Altay

Manchu   Buryat   U.S.S.R.

Tungus   Samoyed
          R. Lena

          Yakut

          Dolgan

                                        FINLAND
                                    Lapp
Chukchi   SWEDEN
                                        NORWAY

                                            ICELAND

NUNIVAK I.   Kuvagmiut
                   N. Alaskan
                   Coast Esk.
          Kangianarmiut   Polar Eskimo
Nushagagmiut   Nunatagmiut   GREENLAND
          R. Yukon   Mackenzie   W. Greenland
glemiut   Alaska   Eskimoes   Eskimo   Angmagssalingmiut
          Kutchin
Chugach   Akudnirmiut
Prince William Sound
                   Copper
                   Eskimo   Netsilik Eskimo   Nugumiut
          Kaska   Yellowknife
                        Iglulik
                   Caribou Eskimo
                Slave   Labrador Eskimo
          Beaver   Hudson Bay
                   Chipewya   Naskapi
     C A N A D A   Montagnais
                                        Micmac
                   Ojibway
                              Penobscot
                   Great Lakes

ARCTIC CIRCLE

Lapp clothing may vary in style according to region. Certain elements of traditional dress survive, such as the jacket and turned up moccasins worn by this Lapp in Norway. Others are affected by alien trends. Note the women's footwear.

reindeer herders; and most feel the need to stress their differences from Norwegians, even though they live side by side. In 1939, most Lapps lived in Lapp-style huts and wore Lapp clothes. Today the language remains the only obvious Lapp trait, although Norwegian is increasingly taking over.

Siberia

Despite the fact that the overwhelming majority of the inhabitants of Siberia are Slavs today (Russians who began to colonize the region in the sixteenth century), almost a million non-Russian indigenous peoples still inhabit their traditional lands, and these persistent minorities are what concern us here. They include quite large groups—Yakut, Buryat, Altay, Khakasy and Tuvan, and many so-called 'small nationalities'. Some of them number less than a thousand. These non-Russian native groups belong to various linguistic stocks. Most of them speak Turkic languages (the Siberian Tartars, Altays, Shors, Khakasy, Tuvans, Tofalars, Yakuts and Dolgans). The Buryat speak a Mongoloid language. Speakers of Tunguso-Manchurian languages include the Evenks or Tungus, described in more detail below, the Evens and Negidals, the Nanays, Ul'chi, Orochi and Udegeys. Not many more than 5% of Siberian people speak Tungus-Manchu languages, but they are territorially widespread from the Yenisey to the shores of the Okhotsk Sea and Bering Strait. The peoples of north-west Siberia speak Samoyedic and Ugric languages (related to that of the Lapps). The Yurak, Tavgin, Entsy and Sel'kup speak Samoyedic languages, while Ugric languages are spoken by the Ostyaks and Voguls. The Ugric languages include Hungarian and are part of a larger Finno-Ugric group.

Other languages, particularly those of a number of people in the north-east and far east cannot be placed in these linguistic groupings. Examples are the languages of the Chukchi, Koryak, Itel'men, Yukagir and Gilyak. These languages have been called 'Paleo-Asiatic', a term which stresses the antiquity of the languages and their vestigial nature. A separate place among Siberian languages is occupied by the Eskimo and Aleut, already mentioned earlier in this chapter. Finally, there is the language of the Ket, a people living along the middle course of the Yenisey River in Turukhanskiy, which seems to be an isolated language.

The Yakut, who number over a quarter of a million, are the most numerous of all the peoples of the circumpolar region. They are, in fact, intruders to the north, as their Turkic language shows. They migrated centuries ago from the southern regions of Asia to their new homeland centred on the Lena River, bringing with them a pastoral economy based on horse and cattle breeding. They traditionally lived in chiefdoms, a form of organization unique in the North. In total contrast to the Yakut, the Yukagir are a small group of inland arctic hunters in the north-east, now extinct or near extinction. In modern times, the Yukagir have already suffered a drastic decline and exist as small scattered groups surrounded by alien peoples, newcomers to Yukagir country like the Yakut, the Tungus, the Chukchi and the Russians.

The Tungus of Siberia and Manchuria numbered about 75,000 at the end of the last century, of which about half were reindeer herdsmen, keeping small herds which they used mainly for transportation, but also for food when no other sources were available. As in all circumpolar societies the shaman plays a central role, the word 'shaman' coming from the Tungus language. Today the peoples of Tungusic speech are the most numerous and widespread linguistic group in north-east Asia. They fall into two broad divisions, the southern and northern Tungus: the southern Tungus of Manchuria and Outer Mongolia are mainly farming peoples today who also raise livestock; the northern Tungus practise only a little agriculture today and only as a result of Russianization. The Northern Tungus are nomadic herdsmen on the whole, combining reindeer herding with a hunting and fishing economy. The Tungus of the Amur River basin and the Pacific Coast are fishing peoples who use dog sledges for transport. The Tungus domestic reindeer

Yakut women working on the ornamentation of fur boots. Reindeer provide a large source of income.

is larger than the wild animal and there are white, black and brown varieties which contrast with the uniform grey-brown of the wild reindeer. The milk is highly valued, and is sweet and rich like cream.

The Chukchi, relatives of the Koryak and the Eskimo, numbered 12,000 at the end of the century, inhabiting the tundra section of Siberia that juts out towards Alaska. They are divided into reindeer groups of the hinterland and the maritime groups of the coast. The reindeer herders, unlike the Tungus, have not completely domesticated the reindeer, who resemble the wild animals in appearance. Since these reindeer are half wild, they cannot be milked, nor so easily ridden or broken-in to draw sledges. Nevertheless, the reindeer means meat, clothing, shelter and leather to the Chukchi, whose diet of meat is supplemented by fish and tea and the fly-agaric mushroom.

In this century, of course, the Chukchi have become Russianized and outnumbered by Russian immigrants. Reindeer herding has become a profitable form of husbandry, producing more than 100,000 tons of meat a year. The poor, nomadic Chukchi has become well-off. Yet acculturation to Western ways was not easy for the Chukchi. The tsars had a theoretically humane policy to all the Siberian peoples—Yakut, Yukagir, Chukchi and Tungus, but the actual policy was of general neglect. The Chukchi were the last of the minority tribes to submit to Russian rule. Clad in Japanese armour they fell upon the Cossack bands and Russian colonists with spears and lances and stolen flintlocks. Toward the end of the eighteenth century they began to pay an annual tribute to the tsar, for which they were rewarded by bouts of smallpox and syphilis, and the vodka trade. Whole camps were carried off by disease and their precious fish and fur stores were sold off for alcohol. Until the revolution, therefore, the Chukchi remained illiterate, and generally lacking the benefits of western medicine, while a host of unscrupulous traders exploited the people and demanded tribute in furs, labour and services.

With the revolution changes came fast. Their official name became Luoravetlan—their own name for themselves, meaning 'the people'. During the period 1917–35, the Chukchi, along with other Siberian peoples were protected

Chukchi hunters in Siberia. These are part of the maritime group of the Chukchi, the other group being the reindeer herders. Economic development is based on reindeer meat and fishing.

from harmful outside influences and prepared for collectivization by the formation of local political organizations. From the thirties to the World War II, the great majority of households and camps were collectivised and their territorial divisions incorporated into the U.S.S.R. The Chukchi National District became a national homeland and steps were taken to protect the national language and culture of these minority peoples. The Chukchi and other Siberians, within Soviet Russia, have their own states, collective farms and co-operatives. Importantly the major part of Chukchi economic development has been based on traditional occupations—hunting, trapping, sea-mammal hunting, fishing, reindeer breeding. In addition to agriculture, fur-farming, mining and lumbering have assumed a new importance. Modern mechanized techniques, such as motor-powered whaling boats, have revolutionized the way of life of the Maritime Chukchi. The Reindeer Chukchi provide necessities such as furs and meat to thousands of Russians.

In their own territory today the Chukchi are outnumbered by Russians, and with the growth of towns and the movement of peoples from the southern areas to the north, they are nervous of losing their identity. Tchersky, a former camp site, is now a white man's town of 10,000 Russians living in apartment blocks in an administrative centre for a gold-bearing region the size of Holland and Denmark put together, where workers claim the highest wages in Russia. At the same time, universities are encouraging Chukchi studies and written scripts have been established in the Chukchi language. At schools the first stage of learning is conducted in the Chukchi language. The political and cultural development of these Siberian lands is not only a wholesale adoption of the culture and ways of the west, but in large measure represents a merging of Western and Siberian cultures.

Europe

Primitive peoples in Europe? Perhaps there are no naked head-hunters, or nomadic hunters and gatherers; nevertheless there are groups which may be considered sufficiently small-scale and isolated from the main culture of a nation to be considered 'primitive'. We have already mentioned the Lapps, former reindeer-hunters, who now speak an archaic Finnish language, but are distinct historically and physically from their neighbours, the Samoyeds, east of the Urals. The Lapps display such features as short arms and legs, small hands and feet, broad faces, small teeth, flaring cheekbones and almond-shaped eyes. Their territory stretches across the northern extremities of Norway, Sweden and Finland and north of the Russian Kola peninsula.

Apart from the Lapps, it would be difficult to distinguish other ethnic groups racially; Jews have mostly taken on the physical characteristics of the larger groups among whom they live, even if they retain specific cultural patterns. Gypsies, although still attached to nomadic ways of life, have tended to stay within traditional areas, adopting the language and some of the customs of their surroundings. The Basques are one of the few groups which have a specifically characteristic physical type. However, race is no determinant of the primitive. Throughout Europe, there are local folk cultures, and though industrial capitalism has engendered a monolithic conformity in cities, towns and suburbs, based ironically on a theory of individualism, village life is still largely swayed by collective aceptance of codes of behaviour and morals based on tradition. In an Italian or Welsh village everyone knows everyone else and everything to do with them; collective knowledge penetrates all social relations and every technical field. Villagers know the family history, social connexions, religious beliefs and working habits of all their neighbours—even sexual behaviour is not unobserved. A Greek peasant is acquainted with all the technical know-how of the village specialists, such as the blacksmith and the cartmaker, even if only one person actually does the work.

According to the criteria for 'primitiveness' established for this book—that is, smallness of scale, isolation from the main cultural streams (the 'high culture'), interdependence of members and quasi-self-sufficiency, whole cultural blocks of peasant people can be classified as equally 'primitive' as an African or Polynesian tribe. This is particularly so in the 1970s, when almost no part of the world is not dependent in some way on Western capitalist techniques and consumer goods. Moreover, in Europe, there are groups which are very distinctive culturally from their neighbours: the Welsh from the English, the Breton from the Norman, the Swabian from the Prussian. Sarakatsani, Koutsovlachs and Karagouni in Greece are noticeably different in dress, language and livelihood from other Greek peasants. In southern Italy, there are peoples of Albanian descent and Greek-speaking communities who maintain life styles distinct from the Italians around them. Part and parcel of being a minority is to stress cultural differences such as language and dress. In Communist Europe, between the large regions inhabited by homogeneous German-, Italian- and Russian-speaking populations, there are a number of people whose lands have alternately been enriched and laid waste by the ebb and flow of empires, but who have insistently maintained their cultural integrity—Ukrainians, Mordvins, Letts, Lithuanians, Slovaks, Serbs, Croats, Slovenes, Magyars, Romanians, Bosnians and Montenegrans. Even a country seemingly as homogeneous as Denmark has a variety of different indigenous groups—such as Greenland Eskimoes, Faroe Islanders, as well as minority immigrant communities.

In some ways, immigrant or minority religious and national groups within larger cultures can be said to have 'primitive' characteristics—this is particularly so when the minority is anxious to retain its distinctive quality in the face of pressure from outside. These groups may develop double lives, one to deal with the world around them, one to mark relationships with their own people. There may be emphasis on dress, such as in 'Pakistani' communities in England, but more often it is culturally orientated, with newspapers, schools, and social meeting places. The Jewish and Moslem communities in England, Germans in Denmark, and Americans in Paris, are active defenders of their heritage against complete integration into their surroundings.

The cultures of Europe may be as heterogeneous as those of New Guinea, nevertheless there are common factors which make for unity: the great majority of Europeans are 'Caucasians' and speak a variety of Indo-European language. The non-Indo-European languages represented in Europe are Finno-Ugrian (Finnish, Estonian, Karelian, Lapp and Magyar), Turkic (spoken by Turkish and some European groups in European Soviet Union), Semitic (spoken by the Maltese), and the mysterious Basque.

There is also a good degree of racial uniformity. While Europe can be divided clearly on the basis of nationality, language, religion, political ideology, no clear-cut racial groups can be claimed. Moreover, scientific research has thrown little

Asian immigrant women shopping in London's Southall High Street demonstrate their need to preserve cultural characteristics by wearing saris.

light on the race or races from which Europeans are derived—the only general trends being paler-to-darker and taller-to-shorter as you go further south. Nevertheless while it is difficult to talk of European 'races', there are general characteristics distinguishing 'peoples'.

Of course, people who are racially 'European' (or Caucasians as they have long been known) are not confined to Europe, for the native inhabitants of large parts of Africa and Asia belong to this race. In India, the dark-skinned populations of the south-east (and of north Ceylon, who speak Dravidian languages) have been classified as Caucasoid, while the Australian Aborigines and the Hairy Ainu of Japan are said to have 'Europoid' characteristics. Northern Indians or 'Mediterranean' Indians include many Hindu groups who speak Indo-European languages. In north and north-eastern Africa, the Hamitic-speaking Berbers and the eastern group of Egyptians, Ethiopians and Somalians have European characteristics.

Within the European classification, we have Mediterraneans: they include Basques, Portuguese, Spaniards, Dinarics (a term now out of use, but once applied to the dark, long-faced people among the Bosnians), Montenegrans, northern Albanians, Serbs, Croats, Slovenes and Tyrolese; Nordics—another term rarely used scientifically—are taller than southern peoples with longer, higher and narrower noses, more pronounced chins and, on the whole, fairer complexions; Alpines—mixed with Nordics and Mediterraneans—have been postulated as a physical group concentrated along a line extending from France eastward through the Alps and the Balkans into Asia Minor towards Russia, and are supposed to have a large degree of brachycephaly (broad-headedness). On the whole this categorization is shaky, to say the least, and most French Alpines can hardly be differentiated from their Spanish Mediterranean neighbours. Finally the blond, round-headed inhabitants of north-eastern and eastern Europe have been broadly grouped as East Baltics. These people carried Finno-Ugrian languages of the Uralic linguistic stock to Europe.

Race and language theory give no very clear-cut guideline to European cultural divisions. Nor does religion, since Christianity has imposed a relative homogeneity

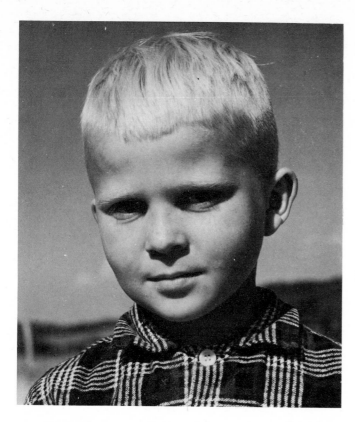

Clearly from the north—a young Danish boy.

on all peoples, apart from a few Moslems and Jews. Historically, Europe has been subject to innumerable invasions, both peaceful and aggressive, which have left their confused mark on the cultural and racial map.

For example, there were the irruptions into eastern Europe in historical times by the Huns—Asiatic in aspect, short, squat, round-headed, broad-faced, snub-nosed with slanting eyes, ochre skins and lank, black hair. After them came successive waves of Turkic-speaking warriors, robustly built with massive round skulls, profuse body-hair and beards. These are, in fact, types still familiar in Russian Turkestan and Azerbaijan today. In the sixth century, Turks settled around the Caspian and sent raiding parties across the south steppes into eastern Europe and became collectively known as the Tartars or Tatars. While out-and-out Asiatic types are rare in Europe, where they occur (apart from the Lapps and Samoyeds), they appear as a recombination of traits introduced by these waves of invaders.

Over 250,000,000 people speak Slav languages, and include the Russians, Poles, Czechs, Slovaks, Yugoslavs and Bulgarians. They constitute the largest linguistic group in Europe. Over 1500 years ago, their linguistic progenitors were an obscure, little-known people scattered thinly through the extensive woods and marshlands of east Central Europe, between the Vistula, the Dnieper and the northern slopes of the Carpathians. Then the Slavs began to spill in all directions—into Germany (where the Sorbs still speak Slav), Holstein and westward to beome the ancestors of the Polish, Czech and Slovak peoples. Southwards, the Slavs crossed the Hungarian plain to the eastern Adriatic, and thence through the Balkan valleys as far south as Greece. To the east, the Slavs moved across the Ukrainian steppe into White Russia, mingling with a variety of autochthonous peoples, most of them Baltic, Finno-Ugrian speakers.

The area to which the Baltic languages (Lithuanian and Latvian or Lettish) are now confined, represents a meagre portion of the territory in which they were formerly spoken. Before the encroachments of Teutons, Slavs, Finns and north Germans, the Baltic culture-province embraced a sizeable section of western Russia. Balts, from the first century AD, were engulfed by expanding Slavs, who either absorbed or displaced them. Following the Soviet occupation of the Baltic states in 1940, over 90,000 Lithuanians and Letts, together with 6,000 Estonians, were deported to Russia. These national groups may be permitted to preserve cultural traditions but any element of political nationalism has been ruthlessly crushed.

Russia still has the most complex mosaic of ethnic groups in Europe—Russians, Ukrainians, Poles, Bulgarians, Lithuanians, Moldavians, Greeks, Gypsies, Armenians and Jews speaking Indo-European languages, while the special Caucasic groups include Georgians, Kabardines, Circassions, Lesghians, Laktsians and Agulians. Finno-Ugric languages are spoken by Karelians, Lapps, Voguls, Samoyeds and Ostyaks. Turkic or Altaic speakers include the Chuvash, Tartars, Bashkirs, Kazakhs, Azerbaijani, etc.

Cossacks do not constitute an ethnic group, but are Slav families who lived on the Russian frontiers and gave military service to the Russian empire. Each man fought from the age of eighteen to thirty-eight. There are now eleven scattered Cossack groups from the Amur on the Chinese border to Kuban and Jerek in the northern Caucasus.

People who have been variously called Teutons or Nordics, or even 'Gothones', were originally migrants from Scandinavia and the Vistula region. They formed such nomadic nations as the Goths, Vandals, Langobards and Burgundians, who became absorbed by local populations in France, Germany, Spain and North Africa. The Franks and Thuringians even carried their Teutonic languages into the former Celtic parts of central and southern Germany. Their former neighbours, the Anglo-Saxons of Schleswig-Holstein, implanted their very similar, western Gothonic dialects into England.

The profound influence of Norse speech on both English and Gaelic languages in Britain also indicates the substantial numbers of Scandinavians who invaded and settled in Britain. In remote areas, such as Caithness and the Orkneys and Shetlands, the Norse vernacular persisted until the eighteenth century. In Scandinavia today, apart from the Finns and the Lapps, the Nordics or Gothonic-speaking peoples there are culturally and ethnically homogeneous.

Don Cossacks in the Rostov Region of the Soviet Union. The woman in the centre is extending the traditional welcome of salt and bread to her guests.

Let us look now more closely at a number of European groups some of which are racially distinctive, some of which are set apart just by their language, and some of which exist as entities only because of a persistent sense of cultural identity and separateness from the peoples they are in contact with, even if this feeling has often little practical foundation.

The Celts

'Celtic', like 'Hun', is rather an emotive term, which has given rise to many fanciful, historical and cultural lines of thought. Originally, the Celts were an iron-age people who made a spectacular expansion throughout Europe in about 500 BC, crossing the Alps into Italy, sacking Rome in 390 BC, and settling large traces of later, 'Slavic' country in eastern Europe. They passed through the Balkans into Greece and into Asia Minor. They spilled west into France mingling with the natives to become Gauls and passed through Belgium to Britain, the only place in Europe, apart from Brittany, where their languages are still spoken. It is believed that even before the iron-age invasion, Celtic dialects had arrived in Britain. Afterwards, however, further waves arrived, bringing the remnants of continental tribes defeated by Caesar, such as the Veneti, who settled among the Dumnonii in Cornwall, the Cantii, the Atrebates and the Catuvellauni. Before the Anglo-Saxon invasions, the Celts covered the whole of the British Isles. Now, their languages are confined to the westernmost fringes of Britain (western Ireland, western Scotland and north Wales) and Brittany. Irish, Scots and extinct Manx Gaelic represents 'Q' type Celt, while Welsh is the sole representative of the so-called 'P' type.

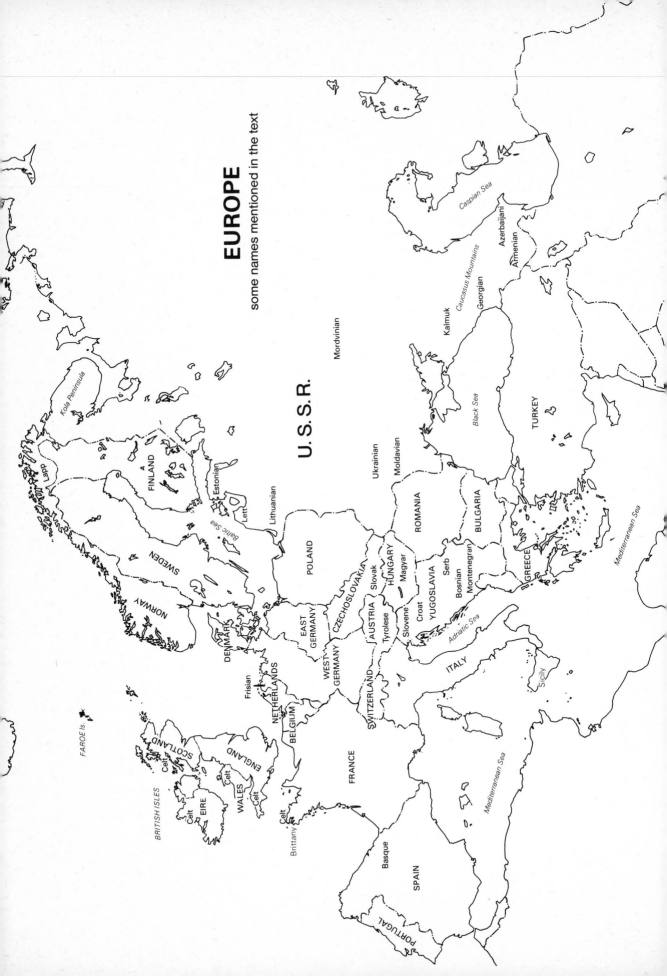

EUROPE
some names mentioned in the text

This Welshman is carrying his coracle from the river. Coracles are made from animal skins stretched over wicker frames and used for river fishing.

Today a Celtic identity is important for certain minority groups from Scotland, through Wales to Brittany. The Celts of Great Britain in particular have a long history of being treated as outcasts and primitives. James I justified his oppression of the Scots and later the Irish on the grounds that they were primitive. The wild Celts of the mountains were held to be on a par with the American Indians: the English decided they should be pacified, moved into reservations or even exterminated, and their lands put to a civilized use by civilized peoples. Of course the Celts were as primitive as American Indians in their social organization, methods of farming and political system based on the clan. The Scottish clans and Irish tuaths (petty chiefdoms) were tribes in the same sense as we call African groups 'tribes'. However racial prejudice does not always stem from colour; the Celts were as white if not whiter than their Anglo-Saxon neighbours. Moreover, despite their Celtic speech the Irish and Scots were of Nordic, that is Viking blood.

This is ancient history but it is remembered by the descendants of the Celtic minorities who assert their cultural and political independence from the English crown today. In the seventeenth century Celtic lands were distributed to Anglo-Saxons, their customs undermined and their chiefs removed from power. In Ulster plantation schemes were introduced and the 'natives' were ordered to leave the country or enter special reserves. Eighty thousand natives of Ireland were shipped to the West Indies as chattel slaves. In Scotland and Wales local languages were suppressed and the wearing of native costume banned. The cleverest move of all, perhaps, was to send the 'primitive' Celts to English schools. These are some aspects of the historical relations between the Anglo-Saxon overlords and the primitive Celts which are remembered by the minority groups of Great Britain, adding fire to their intense desire to maintain a separate identity. The Welsh, for example, like the Basques, have been able to perpetuate a separate identity as an ethnic enclave, and for 2000 years, Wales has been a refuge for recalcitrant groups. Their cultural distinctiveness is reinforced by strong anti-English feeling and makes the northern Welsh, in particular, partisans and fighters for ethnic identity. In Wales, there is a distinct dual division of cultures—some people would say between 'High' (that is, 'international') and 'Low' (that is 'folk'). In very broad

A Breton woman in St Cast, Brittany. Lacemaking is an important and long-standing tradition in Breton life. Tall, lace headdresses, distinctive in every community, are often worn on Sundays and holidays.

terms, the countrymen are Welsh in culture, while townsmen are English. The 'real Welsh' speak their native tongue and are deeply religious; they have a powerful sense of identity and a famous musical tradition.

Brittany is an isolated zone, or at least was until World War II, and its inhabitants are still proud of belonging to the Celtic fringe, maintaining the ancient Celtic tradition of oral literature and annual festivals. During recent years, Bretons have begun to organize pressure groups rather as the Welsh have, to keep the last remnants of their culture from being over-run by France.

Frisians

In Tacitus's day, Frisians occupied the whole of coastal Holland from the Rhine delta to the Ems and inland around the margins of Lake Fleva. The interest of Frisian as a language is that it is the closest living continental relative of English, although it is restricted to certain country districts in the province of Friesland and the West Frisian Islands.

Finno-Ugrians

While most of the important languages of Europe belong to the Indo-European group, nine representatives of the Finno-Ugrian family still survive in isolated enclaves. Of these, only two—Finnish and Hungarian—are spoken by more than three million people. Finno-Ugrians there never represented a cultural, let alone a political, unity. With the Estonians, before their arrival in their present Baltic homeland, the Finns probably had a dispersal centre somewhere in Central Russia, between the Oka and the Urals. The presence, in Finnish and Estonian, of early Teutonic and Baltic loanwords indicates that the ancestral Finns and Ests were in long and intimate contact with some east Teutonic peoples and with the forerunners of the modern Latvians and Lithuanians. The Baltic Finns are thought to have reached their present home in Finland, Estonia and Russian Karelia early in the Christian era.

Magyars are also Finno-Ugric speakers and constitute another influx from Asia. Their language is still the dominant speech of the Hungarian plains and adjacent parts of Romania, with the nearest living relative of this language—Vogul— spoken 1500 miles to the north-east of Hungary. Akin to the Magyars are the Bulgars, who invaded the lower Balkans in the sixth century. They lost their Ugrian speech, which has left barely a trace on the Slavic language of modern Bulgarians.

Mediterraneans

As a racial term, 'Mediterranean' has been used to cover Basques, Arabs and Spaniards, Italians, Irano-Afghans of Persia, Afghanistan and Baluchistan and North-West India, and Armenoids. Spaniards are the 'classical' Mediterranean type combining narrow skulls and slender fine-boned features with dark hair and eyes. From the beginning of neolithic times, the Mediterranean culture was the most important in the history of the Western world. Probably having their original homeland in the Middle East, the Mediterraneans spread out after 5000 BC, along the north and south coasts of the Mediterranean, eventually reaching France, Switzerland and the British Isles.

The Basques are unique in being considered as the survivors of these early Mediterranean peoples. Descended from Neolithic cattle-herders, they have remained isolated until recent times and have always inbred. Their speech, known as Euskarian, is a non-Indo-European language and may be linked with that of the Ligurians, the first historically recorded inhabitants of Switzerland. About three quarters of a million Basques live in northern Spain and south-western France (there are also a great many in South America). The blood-group frequencies of the Basques show wide deviations from the normal European pattern and emphasize their uniqueness and isolation; they have the lowest incidence of group B in Europe and the highest rhesus-negative frequency.

Basque isolation and distinctiveness, both racial and cultural, has often been exaggerated. In the eighteenth century, the Basque Abbé Lahetjuzan, with typical ethnic pride, 'proved' that Adam and Eve were the Basques. They are not, in fact, as different from their neighbours as many other European minorities. Except when they put on folklore displays, men, women and children dress in modern Spanish clothing. Housing is somewhat distinctive. Apart from the language which has no proven contemporary relatives, the Basque characteristics are primarily those of temperament and personality. What differenes do exist, however, serve as symbols of ethnic diversity—having failed to *become* a nation, they cling to what remains of a distinctive heritage. Their desire for separate identity is today reinforced by active revolt.

Caucasian peoples

The Caucasus mountains between the Black Sea and the Caspian contain an astonishing number of languages and human types. Valleys, effectively *culs-de-sac,* hide vestiges of all the peoples who have passed this way during the last two thousand years. Many of these groups have migrated or been resettled in recent years as far away as Central Asia.

The ancestors of Armenians who ocupy the southern reaches of the Caucasus may have been linguistically akin to such Balkan peoples as the Thracians and Phrygians. The Ossetes language is a member of the Iranian group which includes Persian and Pashtu, and folklorists have drawn attention to the striking parallels between certain Ossetic legends and some of those related in the Norse Edda. The Kalmuk shepherds of the northern Caucasus, of whom some are Buddhists, are the most 'Mongoloid' people of eastern Europe. They also speak an eastern-Asiatic language, spoken by their ancestors (the followers of Genghis Khan), who settled in the region in the thirteenth century. The bulk of the nation was deported to eastern Siberia after World War II.

The Caucasus therefore presents a remarkable ethnic mosaic, with dialects and looks as varied as a similar region in Africa or India. There are descendants of silk merchants from China, furriers from Russia, Greeks, Romans, Arabs, Moslems, who often violently conflicted and sometimes existed peacefully side by side.

The most well-known of the Caucasian people are the Georgians, a people who represent a fusion of peoples and speak a language which has Indo-European, Turkic and Semitic elements. They are wine growers and proud horsemen (they play polo); some of them are fishermen living in the swampy areas near the Black Sea in wooden houses built on stilts. Georgians were never organised into a unitary

Harvesters in the Svan area of the Georgian Republic in the U.S.S.R.

group until the Soviet era, when the mountain tribes were included in the nation of Georgia. Today, many still cling to their separate languages and cultures. Two remarkable features of the modern Georgians—their love of music and their longevity—are celebrated at Sukhum on the Black Sea, where a full orchestra composed entirely of men aged over 100 strikes up twice a year. Many Georgians are vegetarians and some of them strong drinkers.

Physical types in the Caucasus also vary, the Ossetes being tall and blond, while the people around Tbilisi are stocky and dark. Many ancient traditions and customs are kept up in the Georgian valleys: the Khevsurs and Svans are strictly endogamous and marry preferably their first cousins. They depend to a large degree of hunting.

Other Caucasian groups include the Abkhas, the Armenians (who live on both sides of the Turkish and Russian border), and the Chechens of the central mountains. The Circassians were dispersed by Stalin; the Daghestanis of Daghestan are Moslems.

The Jews

Jews are an ethnic group living dispersed in every country of Europe. Like the Gypsies, they come from a wandering tribe, although in most cases, their wanderings have been forced upon them, rather than being a voluntary way of life. Some Jews, no matter where they live, maintain a cultural distinctiveness in close association with local industrial and urban populations. Their history and biblical tradition is nomadic; devotion to traditional ways and, for some, their aversion to intermarriage with the majority population makes many of them, in a sense, as tribal or even more tribal than the Fulani of western Africa.

Jews have been in Europe since the early Iron Age. Coming from the Middle East, they first entered Italy during the consulship of Marius, in the last century BC. As traders and merchants, they followed the victorious armies of Julius Caesar into Gaul. During the eleventh century, the western European or Ashkanazi Jews suffered persecution at the hands of the Crusaders and settled in Poland and Russia to become dealers in jewels and precious metals. They were forbidden to own land and forced to live in ghettos. Their descendants still speak yiddish—a form of mediaeval German enriched by Hebrew and Slav words. Finally, violent anti-semitism forced many Jewish families out of Eastern Europe; some settled in Germany, some came to England, and many crossed the Atlantic to the US.

The Sephardic Jews, those who were expelled from Spain during the Inquisition, fled north to Holland and England, whilst others went to the Balkans. Their descendants still speak Ladino—a form of Spanish permeated with Hebrew terms.

In fact there is a whole range of 'Jewishness' in Europe from separateness to integration. Before World War II and the Nazi programme of genocide, the Jews of eastern and central Europe lived in ghettos, where they maintained a culture which was highly distinctive, speaking their own language, wearing clothes and grooming their hair in a typically Jewish fashion. Their whole way of life was aimed at symbolising their differences from non-Jews. Nowadays, of course, Jews are predominantly city people, not living in ghettos, and they remain only marginally distinctive. Like the Moors, the Jews originally spoke a Semitic language—Hebrew. But over the years, they began to lose their language at the same time as they began to lose their genetic distinctiveness, becoming thoroughly assimilated to the European types among whom they lived. The Jews are physically 'composite', and the large-headed, full-lipped, hook-nosed, abundantly bearded 'caricature' Jew is not Jewish at all. This type is commoner in Anatolia and Armenia, rather than Palestine itself. Jews everywhere generally conform to the prevailing norm in whichever locality they are found.

Early Jewish communities were forced into distinctive dress and custom partly by surrounding prejudice, but also by their own highly complex religious traditions. Family life and education was carefully laid down almost hour by hour in the Torah, the book of tradition and custom for religious Jews everywhere.

In England there are about half a million Jews although they have never been counted as a group—they are merely people who go to a different church. Nevertheless there are in fact special laws for Jews and they receive special treatment in some circumstances. The court of law even supports the Jewish

An Orthodox Jew displaying symbols of faith: the black hat, the 'tefillin' on his forehead, and uncut hair tied in a knot below the temples.

religious authorities in the performance of their duties in relations to the Jewish public (as they do with other religious groups). However on the whole the Jew is a simple citizen without special status.

As a distinct ethnic group they are noticeable because in London they often created their own communities with synagogues, voluntary associations, kosher butcher shops and groceries. Nevertheless, such neighbourhoods are not concentrated enclaves and cannot be thought of as ghettos like the Jewish centres in Eastern Europe. The East End of London (like the Lower East Side on New York) was once a flourishing Jewish centre, especially for new immigrants from Russia and Poland. As they grew prosperous, Jewish families flowed further north, not because they were fleeing their brethren but because they wanted better housing, gardens, and better schools. Golders Green, Hendon and Edgware are the end-points of this movement.

To be an orthodox Jew can be a full-time job. One may belong to countless clubs and societies of interest to women, students, refugees, ex-servicemen; there are countless friendly societies, and associated with each synagogue are a multitude of social, charitable and education activities. An observing Jew must obey a number of prescriptions and proscriptions governing relations between himself and other men, between himself and his environment, and almost every aspect of his daily life is covered in the total system of belief. Laws governing kinds and classes of food are only the better known of these rules, or taboos, and are still observed although the large majority of such rules originated for reasons of basic cleanliness and dietary health at a time when public sanitation and food control was unknown.

A good Jew observes the Saturday Sabbath, requires special methods of processing his food and organises his life in a particular way. This religious conformity is a means of setting off the Jew from his neighbour, be he Arab or English. In recent years, outside pressure has abated. Nonetheless, many customs particularly in terms of family life, have remained very strong, although their roots in the Torah have been forgotten. This is especially true of the Ashkenazi, since the majority of European Jews stem from that group.

A new development has come with the establishment of Israel in 1948. Some Jews chose to return to their traditional homelands but many, although proud of progress and development in Israel, have recognised that they have become, almost without realising it, part of their adopted land, in England and America in particular. Perhaps more interesting is the change in Israel itself. A religious and racial ideal has become a nation, and the growing quite unique cultural distinctiveness in Israel has set the new generation of native born Israelis apart from other Jews, in ways occasionally upsetting to traditional European communities and visitors.

Like the rest of the western world, religious belief in terms of regalia has declined in recent years. In England only roughly a third of the Jewish population are active members of synagogues; moreover, Anglo-Jewry today has lost that intensity it once had. The comparative openness and freedom of British society, at least today, by taking the pressure off Jews, allows the majority to remain Jewish without following all the ancient rules. Petticoat Lane in London with its jellied eels, nylons, countless clothes stalls, the constant spiel and salt beef, is a relic of an old Jewish culture of the East End which is fast disappearing. The delicatessens are still full of smoked salmon, sauerkraut and chopped liver, however. Here the orthodox took their baths on Fridays at Scevzik's Russian Vapour and went to

The Sabbath: Jewish men, with their heads covered in accordance with religious custom, read prayers in a synagogue.

Jewish theatres in the Commercial Road. Our language has been enriched by yiddish words, such as schmalz, clobber and spiel. Much of Jewish culture is now British culture.

The synagogues have split roughly into three groups: the orthodox, who adhere completely to the old way of life as well as to services in Hebrew; the Liberals, who believe that Judaism is a way of separate worship, but who feel that obsolete dietary laws and use of a language most people do not understand is counterproductive for modern life; and the middle group, who compromise.

Nevertheless, there are many traditions still alive. The European Jews perpetuate traditions based largely today on family celebrations and rituals in order to achieve the same thing. Bar Mitzvahs, to celebrate a boy's coming of age, and weddings are usually an occasion for a huge family splurge with food, music, and as many relatives as one can afford to entertain. The comparison between this and the American Indian potlatch ceremony, with its feasting and present-giving which sets a seal on a specific tribal site, is not so far-fetched.

What has often remained most strongly is the emphasis on family life and community care and family celebrations such as the sabbath, and Jewish New Year. Like the Celts, the Jews are attempting to preserve elements of a culture which symbolises and stresses a valued ethnic identity.

The Gypsies

Compared with Jews, the European Gypsies are recent arivals in Europe, the Roms first appearing in the Balkans during the fourteenth century as wandering tinkers, fortune-tellers and clothes-peg manufacturers. Over the next 200 years, they appeared in every country of the European continent. Both in their outward appearance and even in their bloodgroup frequencies, the Gypsies stand out from the local peoples among whom they roam, and these differences are accentuated by

Gypsy children in their encampment in the Forêt de Sénart in France. Modern vehicles have generally taken over from the traditional wooden caravan.

underlying differences in economy. In parts of southern Europe, whole neighbourhoods of settled Gypsies are found in the poorer parts of towns and cities and even in larger villages. Many of these 'gitanos' or 'zingari' are not true gypsies, but pimps, prostitutes, entertainers and beggars. Nevertheless, along with the true Gypsy, they are all looked down upon as dirty, thievish and uncivilised. On the other hand, nomadic Gypsies may often be romantically admired. The wandering Rom often maintain their own language—one or other dialect of Romany—and they wander almost at random, following traditional trades: in southern and eastern Europe, they function as horse traders, peddlers, tin-smiths and professional beggars. We find gypsies (there are over five million of them) by the sides of roads, on the edges of woods and near towns, where their invisible presence is attested by the sign 'No nomads' or 'No Gypsies'.

The Gypsies are an exceptional case—only paralleled by the Jews—of an ethnic group which, through space and time for more than five hundred years, has achieved a great migration without any alteration as regards the originality and singleness of their race. This has occurred even despite the active hostility of their hosts—the fact that 400,000 Gypsies were hanged, shot or gassed in the Nazi concentration camps, in precisely the same way as the Jews, is a fact, if not a greatly publicised one.

It is generally accepted today that the Gypsies are of Indian origin—not Egyptians, biblical tribes or Bohemians. One thousand years after the appearance of Aryans in northern India, the people suffered from successive penetrations of Greeks, Persians, Scythians and Kusheans, and in the fifth century of our era, other nomads from the Huns invaded the north, followed by the Moslems. The ancestors of Gypsies felt less at ease during the attempts of the invaders to settle them in one place; occupying powers all over the world are damaging to the interests of conquest. It is not certain at what date the Gypsies left the Indian territories, nevertheless it is a fact that they were suddenly found scattered all over the East and the year 1000 AD may be posited as the beginning of an exodus which is still

Gypsies are a distinct ethnic group despite being scattered throughout Europe. This woman is in Paris.

continuing. Another theory has it that the name by which certain Gypsies are known in Europe—'zingari', or 'gitanos', is derived from that of the Athinganes or Untouchables, a half-Christian, half-Pagan sect of the Byzantine empire, who shared with the Roms a reputation for sorcery and other practices. Linguists, however, have clearly shown that the Gypsies and their language are ultimately of North Indian provenance.

There are three principal Gypsy groups—the Kalderash Gypsies, the Gitanos and the Manush. The Kalderash are the only authentic Gypsies, according to themselves; they are tinsmiths and coppersmiths, as their name indicates ('caldera' being Romanian for copper pot, or cauldron) and came fairly recently from the Balkans, then from Central Europe. They may be divided into five groups: the Lovari, called 'Hungarians' in France; the Boyhas from Transylvania, well-known as animal-tamers; the Luri, who still have the name of an Indian tribe; the Tschurari; and the Turco-Americans who emigrated from Turkey to the United States before returning to Europe.

The Gitanos are found in Spain, Portugal, North Africa and southern France and differ from the Kalderash in physique, dialects and customs. The Manush are traditional 'Bohemians', their name meaning 'true men' in Sanscrit. They are divided into three sub-groups: the Valsikanes, who are travelling showmen and circus people; the Gaygikanes or German gypsies; and the Piemontesi, or Italian gypsies, of whom the most famous are the Bouglione family.

Outside these three groups are the English, Irish and Scottish gypsies, who resemble all of these groups in one way or another. The Irish 'Tinkers' are often horse-dealers, but their ethnic connexion with true Gypsy stock is uncertain. There remain the 'Nomads', who are not gypsies: basket-makers, chair-menders, mountebanks, jugglers or tumblers, watermen and various 'travelling' people.

Mostly the Gypsies are workers in metals, musicians and mountebanks, horse-cops and dealers, fortune-tellers and exhibitors of animals. One of the strangest facts about them is that they have at all times resisted attempts to encourage them to take on different occupations, possibly because these necessitated a sedentary life. In India, the system of castes and its strict occupational divisions condemns the pariahs and outcastes to keep to occupations which are distasteful for some reason to the upper classes. Looking at the list of curses and occupational prohibitions contained in the Laws of Mamu, it is clear that the Gypsies have followed precisely those occupations that were considered accursed. And it was in India that the Gypsies learnt how to work in metals.

As horse-dealers, the Gypsies follow a cult of the horse, like many peoples of central and western Asia. The importance of this animal in mythology and the role it played in the historical and economic development of Europe and Asia are well known, since the great migrations and conquests were equestrian. There are striking parallels between the beliefs of the Gypsies and those of other Asiatic peoples. A Gypsy salutation is not 'Live long!', but 'May your horse live long!' Like the reindeer, in Nordic cultures, the horse is also a funeral and ceremonial animal. But the Gypsy is a poor horseman. For him the horse is a pack animal. The true business of the Gypsies is in concealing the animal's defects; they are not content just to buy and re-sell animals, but are justly proud of their art and their reputation of 'putting right' dilapidated beasts, which they show at fairs. In Central Europe, the sale of horses takes place at special horse fairs, which end in more or less prolonged gatherings in taverns, where they sing and dance.

After the horse, the bear is the animal most closely associated with Gypsies; it is a familiar figure in their folklore and magic. In the Balkans, they use bears for show purposes and up till World War II Gypsies and their bears could be found in the Pyrenees in France. The Balkan Gypsy 'bear-leaders' are all nomads, but this is a nomadism of a particular form. It was long the custom for the women and children to remain in camp, from which the men left, in little groups of from two to five, to show their animals throughout the country. During the off-season, or when bears were lacking, they returned to the camp and devoted themselves to their forges and horse-shoeing.

The Gypsies are also famous musicians, particularly in Hungary. Gypsy musicians in the past led the way in great processions and other celebrations, and were even invited to lead armies in battle, their violins in front. Besides violins, they also use lutes, drums and tambourines. The *flamenco* was probably of Gypsy origin and throughout Europe, Gypsy women are well-known as dancers. They are also great fortune-tellers, specialising particularly in palmistry. They not only practise chiromancy (the art of predicting the future by the hand), but also chirology, the aim of which is to discover from the hand natural predispositions and

Community feeling is strong among the Gypsies. Children are of particular importance to the group as a whole.

psychological tendencies. Palmistry is an 'occupation'; gypsies never have recourse to fortune-telling among themselves, and it plays no part in their fundamental beliefs.

Gypsies may be Christians or Moslems or Greek Orthodox Church, but at the same time what is obvious is an intense religious faith outside of any specific religious dogma or persuasion—they give proof of a special enthusiasm in matters of faith which is astonishing. An important part is played by the Gypsy Tradition, with its tales and legends and mythology, its solar and lunar cult and its annual cults, such as that of Sara, the Black Virgin.

Sara is a genuine Gypsy saint. She was of noble birth and was chief of her tribe on the banks of the Rhone where the Gypsies worked metals and traded and practised a pagan religion involving the worship of the Babylon god Ishtar. One day Sara had visions that the Christian saints were arriving by boat across a rough sea, and the boat was sinking. Sara threw her dress on the waves and, using it as a raft, she floated towards the saints and helped them reach land. Nowadays on 24th and 25th May each year the Gypsies have grown accustomed to follow the Catholic pilgrimage of Saintes-Maries-de-la-Mer, a Catholic ritual, and they identify this Catholic Saint as Sara, the Black Gypsy Virgin. Up to 1912 only Gypsies were allowed into the Church crypt where they spend a whole night among themselves. In this crypt there is an old pagan altar, a Christian altar and the statue of Sara, painted black. The Gypsies keep watch there, usually with bare feet and the head uncovered. The women stroke the statue and kiss the hems of her many dresses and then hook up clothes beside her or torn pieces of cloth. Then they touch the saint with miscellaneous objects such as medals or photographs they have brought along with them. This rite of hanging up garments is known in Iran and also in India where certain groups believe that the linen and clothes of a sick person become impregnated with his illness and that he will be cured if the clothes are purified by contact with a sacred tree. After this the Gypsies proceed to the sea and the symbolic immersion common to many fertility cults.

Like the Eskimoes and many other peoples, the Gypsies are a homogeneous ethnic group, who are known as the 'Men' (Gypsy *Rom*) and regard themselves as one people. In most primitive societies there is no need for the community to give itself a name—the members of the group are simply 'we, the Men' or 'the human beings', outsiders being considered in some way unhuman or somewhat less than human. The collective of Gypsies is made up of so many diverse groups that the only social link is the general 'Gypsy Law'. There is not and there has never been a Gypsy King and the 'dukes' and 'counts' of old texts refer to tribal chiefs. In fact each Gypsy tribe, the importance of which may vary from ten to several hundred tents or caravans (the equivalent of households), recognises the authority of a chief elected for life, usually a man of middle age, known for his intelligence and sense of justice. He presides over the Council of Elders and decides about migrations.

Within the tribe, the essential nucleus of the Gypsy people is the family, where authority is wielded by the father. The mother and other women have a certain power, which is often unofficial and occult, but undeniably real. Within the extended family and local groups, disputes are settled by the elders according to a Gypsy tradition or collective whole of customs. Sterility is the greatest misfortune that can strike a Gypsy woman and it is often attributed to a magical cause, stemming from beliefs in witchcraft and sorcery. Fertility spells are therefore many and varied, and the pilgrimage to Sara, the Black Virgin, often involves an invocation to the saint to help a sterile woman conceive. After birth, babies are soon baptised, usually by immersion in running water and by the conferring of a secret name. Gypsies have, in fact, three names: one is secret, the second is reserved for use among the kith and kin and their third is used in the outside world. Other rites of a simple nature occur during betrothal and marriage; there are apparently no initiation rites at puberty. Their death and funeral rites are distinctive. Like many peoples, a Gypsy does not die in his tent or caravan, but is carried outside to render up his soul, thereby preventing the pollution of the home. The funeral wake begins before death, the witnesses waiting for the death after which the corpse is washed and dressed in new clothes. On the announcement of death, the whole tribe begins to weep and cry out, men, women and children showing much, often exaggerated, sorrow. Burial usually follows the local Christian or Moslem practice. After burial, the clothes and personal belongings of the dead person are burned or perhaps sold; in any case, no member of the tribe can inherit any of them. Among the Gypsy funeral chants are some of their most beautiful poems.

The Middle East

To many geographers and political writers 'The Middle East' is an expression for the whole area from Afghanistan through the Arab world to North Africa and the Atlantic coast of Morocco and Mauritania. It has been made to include the Sahara and the Mediterranean coast of Africa as well as the Arabian Peninsula, Iraq, Turkey, and Iran. This broad cultural unit covers the land of Islam, and includes the Sudan, Egypt, and Algeria. However, as in most other world regions, there is a diversity of peoples in an area of general homogeneity, and certainly not all of them are Moslem or speak Semitic languages (the languages of the Arab majority and Hebrew).

For my purposes, it will be convenient to treat North Africa separately, but to include Egypt in the classic Middle East zone. If Islam were the sole criterion for including or excluding nationalities from the Middle East, there would be a strong case for including countries such as Pakistan, Niger and Mali, where the majority of the population is, or will soon be, Moslem; it would exclude whole Semitic-speaking nations, such as Israel, which are not Islamic, but are certainly of the Middle East.

The Middle East is not inhabited by an ethnically pure race, any more than Europe is. Human accretion has diluted and modified any stock which may have been original or pure, and race has in no way conformed to, or created, any present-day boundaries. Consequently, populations throughout Iran, Iraq, Turkey, the Arabian Peninsula, Egypt and, particularly, Israel are composed of a score of ingredients which are very mixed. Throughout history, vast numbers of people dispersed from Arabia to other regions of the Middle East. Examples of this process are the early wanderings of the Jews; the settlement of north-eastern Africa by colonists from the Hadhramautä; the occupation of parts of Somalia and Ethiopia by Sabaens from the Yemen; the expansion of the Arabs after the death of Mohamet.

Only in a small number of cases will there be found a visible survival of some feature held to be characteristic of a 'racial group'—the small-boned fineness of a Najdi Arab, the flat back-of-the-head of an Anatolian Armenian, the Mongoloid eyes of a Turk, the recognisable Arab-Berber-Negro mixture in some Egyptians.

Country women in the Yemen. The woman in the centre draws her veil over her mouth as is demanded by the Moslem faith.

The purest nucleus of Mediterranean Arabs is in fact found in the Yemen. The Yemenis of the fertile plateau are slender and relatively long-limbed, with a long head, very long upper face, high forehead and a narrow nose. The Jews may have originally been of a small, Mediterranean type similar to the present Yemeni Arabs; today they are intricately mixed. An 'Irano-Afghan' strain is common in Iran as well as Afghanistan and Baluchistan. The Persians of Iran have facial dimensions similar to Europeans. The Kurdish nomads of Iraq, Iran and Turkey include a blond minority and may have an admixture of ancient Nordic. A strong Irano-Afghan element, mixed with Mediterranean, is also said to be present in the inhabitants of Iraq; the post-Islamic infiltration of Arab blood does not seem to have affected the population which is still much the same as it was in Sumerian and Babylonian times. Iraquis are taller than Arabs, with a larger face, longer and broader nose and a heavier jaw. Beard and body-hair are very heavy, a trait which is characteristic of Irano-Afghans as a whole.

These remarks are culled from the statistics of physical anthropologists. However, none but the expert can tell Turks from Kurds or Arabs from Persians, unless they are confronted with an ideal type. Everywhere, apart from small isolated pockets, we have people with dark-to-white skin, brown-to-black and grey eyes, and general Caucasian or Mediterranean features. Moreover, nationality and race are often determined more by cultural factors: a man's passport, his religion (Jew or Moslem), his language (Semite, Indo-European or Ural-Altaic). There are Greeks speaking Greek and practising the Greek Orthodox religion in Egypt. There are Persians in Iraq and Circassians from the Caucasus in Jordan. There are cultural groups living among majority people of quite a different history and language—Turkomans in northwest Iran, Iranian and Iraqui Kurds, the Arab tribes of the Iranian Karun. Thus, while language and religion often determines a person's culture and nationality as well as where he lives, apart from the communities of the Arabian peninsula, nowhere is a country's population limited to a single race. Turkey, Iran, the non-peninsular Arab states and Israel all have minorities, and it is within these smaller groups that tribal customs and primitive

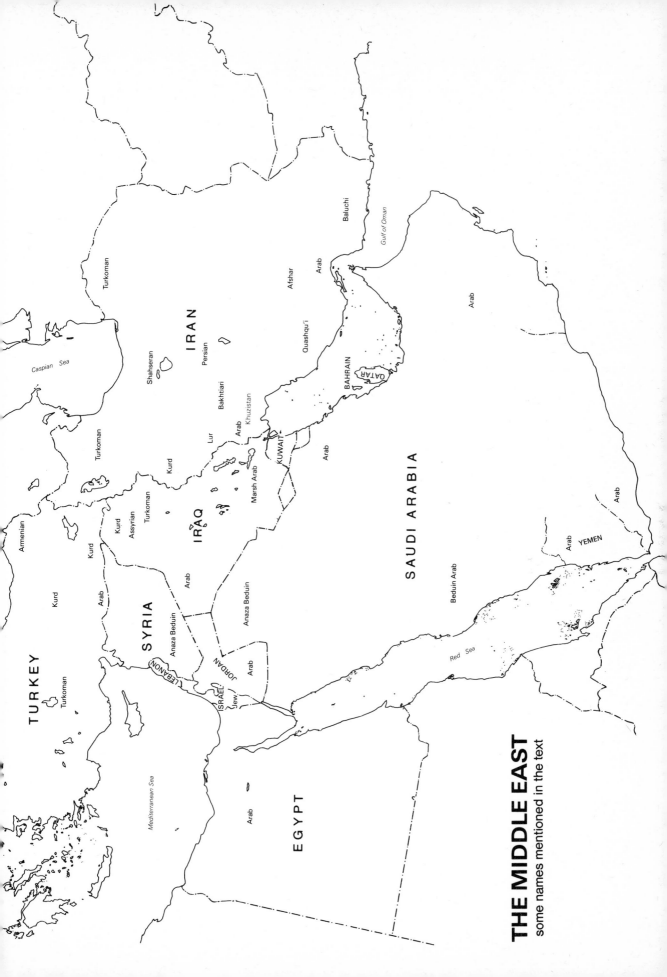

THE MIDDLE EAST
some names mentioned in the text

OPPOSITE:
A nomad with his camel in the desert of Saudi Arabia. Camels are still very important, but wealthier sheiks have bought cars to boost their prestige in the desert.

Islam is one of the strongest bonds between Arabic peoples of the Middle East. This is the entrance to the mosque in Meshed, Iran.

traditions are encouraged by communities intent on preserving their own way of life in the face of the unitarian and monolithic culture of Arab Islam.

The Middle East, therefore, despite its apparent homogeneity based on a near-universal religion and language, is at once a patchwork of dispersed peoples and languages and a fragmented area of enclaved ethnic groups, locally dominant over others scattered among them. Of the languages spoken, apart from Arabic, the most important are Turkish, Persian, Hebrew, Armenian, Kurdish and Syriac or Aramaic (the latter surviving as a spoken language among certain Christian communities in the northern edge of the Fertile Crescent and a few villages near Damascus). Caucasian dialects are spoken by immigrants who came out into the Arab world from the Caucasus in the nineteenth century. The most important are the Circassians and the Chechen, who were settled by the Turks on the edge of the Syrian desert. Armenians speak an Indo-European language and still continue their highly developed literature and traditions in many parts.

In the Middle East, religion is a good guide to membership of cultural groups. All Arabs follow Islam, the religion par excellence of Western Asia, and all the national states, apart from Cyprus and Israel, claim some form of belonging to the House of Islam. The majority are Sunnites, of whom most belong to the Wahabi Sunnites, followers of the purist doctrine of Mohammed Ibn Abd al-Wahab. A small minority are Shi'ites, particularly in Iran, while other groups include the Alawus, Isma'ilis and Druzes. Other religious communities include the Shabak, the Baha'is (mostly in Iran), the Jews, the Karaites and Samaritans. In many cases ancient religious rites have been preserved within smaller communities in order to

A Jewish elder in Istanbul.

OPPOSITE:
Marsh Arab children in a boat in the reeds, Iraq. The marsh Arabs make their homes on reed platforms.

stress the distinctive nature of their culture or their way of life. Traditions have often been castigated as primitive, idolotrous or even pagan by majority groups jealous of attempts by ethnic communities to preserve their special identities.

There are also half-isolated topographical enclaves of Arab-Christian communities, which successive waves of conquest and penetration have not wiped out. Christian communities include: Greek Orthodox found in Turkey and Alexandria; the Nestorians of Syria and Iraq, known as Assyrians; the Copts and Monophysites of Egypt, Syria and Armenia; the Roman Catholics. They also include the Kurdish Yazidis and Maronites. In the Lebanon, Christians in their various communities form a majority. Lebanese Maronites amount to 30% of the population and are prominent politically, economically and culturally. Various other Catholic groups include the Chaldaeans, and the Latin-rite Catholics of Jerusalem. Groups of Arabic and Turkish-speaking Greek Orthodox communities are found in the Middle East and are subject to one of the eastern Patriarchs of Antioch, Alexandria or Istanbul. They are strongest in Turkey, Syria, Lebanon and Egypt. Nestorians or Assyrians are a poor remnant of the once powerful and widespread Chuch of mediaeval times. They number about 75,000 in Iraq and Persia. Copts are confined to Egypt and number more than one and a half million. The 'Riverside' Sabaean are a Mandaean community of Lower Iraq. There are 150,000 of them and they are famous as 'Christian' silversmiths.

The Arabs

The Arabic-speaking people form the great majority of the population of the Middle East, numbering approximately 55 million and divided into sovereign states: Iraq, Syria, Lebanon, Jordan, Sa'udi Arabia, the Yemens, Egypt and several minor independent units which are of ambivalent status—including the United Arab Emirates, with Qatar, Bahrain and Kuwait. Arabs also live in Iran (Khuzistan, formerly Arabistan), the southern fringe of Turkey and Israel. Throughout the Middle East, the Arab language is spoken, the sole considerable enclaves of non-Arab speaking peoples being those of the Kurds, the Turkomans and the recently intruded Jews of Israel. Arabian speech and consciousness, along with Islam, provide the strongest bonds—the language, plus a shared way of life and traditions, is that of all Arabs everywhere, whether the speaker is a tribesman, a nomad, a village-dweller or a townsman.

Arabs throughout the Middle East look upon Arabia as their ancestral home. And it is not the language of the capitals, but the Arabic of the peninsula, of the Beduin tribes, which is the popular ideal. Only the Beduin are considered 'pure' in race and language. And the customs of the Arabian Beduin are looked upon as symbolising the highest and truest qualities of Arabness: simplicity, bravery, generosity and independence. Beduins are also the models for the general traditional stereotype of the Arabs held by Westerners, and in the sense that we have used the word in much of this book, they can be considered primitive, their lives centred round small face-to-face groups, rather than the monolithic bureaucracies we know so well in the West.

The Arabs of Arabia distinguish among themselves not on the basis of racial differents which are never clear as we have seen, but along lines of tribal affiliation and social status. The largest component of the population are the Beduin tribes, nomads whose pastoral life is based on the herding of camels, sheep and goats, and who follow regular migration routes. Sedentary Arabs, on the other hand, are farmers or they follow trade or non-pastoral pursuits; many are employed in the oil industry. They greatly outnumber the nomads who constitute only one fifth of the population. Curiously, there is very little difference in dress between the Beduin nomads and the sedentary town-dwellers.

The Beduin occupy tracts of coarse grassland, which afford permanent vegetation and water-holes, penetrating the sandy desert only for short-season pastures. For nine to ten months of the year, they live in the interior arid pastures. Of the tribes, the northern 'Anaza' control the steppe-lands between Aleppo, Damascus and the Hauran plateau on the west, the middle Euphrates on the east, and the Shammar mountains in the south. The largest and most important faction are the Ruwala. A single tribe may contain 20,000 tents—that is, 20,000 households—and over half a million camels. While forming a homogeneous unit, they are by no means a close-knit group; rivalry and enmity are almost as common as alliances.

A Beduin in Jordan. For centuries, the Beduin have roamed the desert with flocks of camels, goats and sheep. They consider themselves the only true Arabs.

The life of a Beduin camp is not, therefore, one of peaceful migration from pasture to pasture. It is punctuated, more or less frequently, by raiding expeditions against enemy tribal segments and their herds. Raids are not undertaken merely for the lust for possession, although the size of a camel herd *is* the mark of wealth and power; still less for the sheer satisfaction of any innate bloodthirstiness. More important is the thrill of succeeding, and the consequent prestige of a victory. Mostly these raids are minor affairs, but large expeditions may involve half the fighting strength of the camp under a commander who leads the individual kin groups. Most tribes have a number of traditional enemies, and preparation for raids and precautions against attack are a part of life.

One of the initial causes of raids is the need to expiate a blood feud. For the Beduin, murder must be avenged by the victim's kin, by the killing of the murderer or one of his near kin. The murderer may sometimes take sanctuary with a chief and the feud be settled by the paying of 'blood money'. As among the Yanomamö Indians of South America and the New Guinea head-hunters, both of which are described elsewhere in this book, aggression is not permitted to continue unchecked. A number of practices enable the tribes to afford themselves some protection from perpetual attack and enable them to travel across tribal territories. These include the universal institutions of friendship between individuals or alliances between tribal segments. And throughout the Beduin world, there is a genuine respect for strangers and travellers, which allows for a degree of mobility on the part of small groups and individuals.

In southern Arabia, there are more than a hundred Beduin tribes with a membership of over a thousand. The Anaza is the largest and, along with the Harb, belongs to the Nejd group. In the eastern province, the Ba-harniah is a grouping of settled Shi'ites numbering 100,000. The tribes of Al-Hijaz include the Buqum, Fahm, Munijihah, Shanabirah, Surur and Utaybah. In Asir, the camel-breeding Shubah tribe is partly of Sudanese stock and is ruled by Arab sheiks. The Bal-Aryanals are also of African origin. The Naju and Sanhan are nomadic tribes, while the Malik and Raysh are now completely settled. Asmar, Abs, Air, Bahr, Durayb, Hilal, Qarn, Shahran, Shihr, Thawab and Zayd are tribes containing mixed, nomadic and settled, Arabs.

Beduin goatskin tent on the road to the Dead Sea in Jordan. To the Beduin, hospitality is a sacred duty.

Throughout the Middle East, nomads wander through a vast region, where land is plentiful and water is in short supply. It is interesting to look at one group of Arabs who inhabit the great marshes of southern Iraq, where conditions are exactly the opposite—almost all water and no land. The waters of the Tigris and the Euphrates overflow and spread over 6000 square miles before gathering in the Shatt al-Arar and emptying out into the Gulf. Since before the times of recorded history, people have lived in these marshes, building houses on piles of reeds and developing a technology particularly suited to 'living with water'. The marsh-dwellers are as specialised as their neighbours, the desert nomads.

About 400,000 marsh-dwellers live in small self-contained communities exploiting open lakes and channels, small islands and permanent, seasonal or temporary marshlands. The lakes and channels are used for fishing and transportation; the islands provide limited land where reed-framed houses may be built and some crops planted; while seasonal and permanent marshes offer the best environment, for here land can be diked, drained and cultivated or left to the natural growth of reeds.

Throughout this zone, there are three major groups of marsh-dwellers. One group raises cattle and sheep and produces summer crops of rice and millet. These tribal farmers are proud of tracing their descent from tribes of the Arabian peninsula and look down on the buffalo breeders—the Ma'dan—whom they regard as inferior by birth and occupation. This fact has reserved for the latter a monopoly over buffalo-breeding and a unique position as aquatic nomads on the marshes. Among the settled marsh-dwellers live holy, respected men who provide religious and magical services in exchange for gifts in kind.

The Ma'dan, the second group, live in scattered settlements, making their homes on man-made islands of reed matting which rise and fall with the floods. Their buffaloes' main diet is reeds. Ma'dan are organised into clans and lineages. Each member is bound to share in the compensation payments levied against their tribal division for killing or injuring another. They are Shi'ites.

A third major occupation-group are the reed-mat-makers and there are thousands of them who weave mats of all shapes and sizes for the commercial markets throughout Iraq. As far as the farmers are concerned, mat-weaving is considered an even more lowly occupation than buffalo-herding.

186

A marsh Arab boy in Iraq. The lives of the marsh Arabs and their social organization are quite different from those of the Beduin.

The marsh-dwellers have their own idiosyncratic social system (very different from that of Beduins and other tribal groups), which is organised according to occupations and the division of labour at work in the marshes. Each community has its sheik who settles disputes with other respected elders. It is the sheik who is responsible for the building of the tribal house, which is the centre of men's lives and of the political and judicial lives of the tribes. Prayer meetings and ceremonies are held here, where there is an elaborate and formal etiquettee for greeting and seating among tribesmen, demonstrating the different social, religious and occupational status of both groups and individuals.

Israel and the Jews

Formerly, Jews lived in various Arab countries, Syria, Yemen and Turkey—where Istanbul Jews had their own rabbi—but, with the arrival of militant Zionists, they have been persecuted and most have migrated to Israel. In Palestine-Israel, the composition of the peoples has undergone a radical change. In 1919, there were 90% Arabs—in 1940, 65%. Since then the great majority of Arabs have departed from the main part of Palestine and the numbers of Jews rapidly increased. Now there are nearly three million Jews and less than 200,000 Arabs.

The Jewish colonisation movement began in the 1880s and is still continuing. The majority came from eastern and western Europe, and their confrontation with immigrants from Arab countries led to a division into Oriental and Occidental Jews, a division which was deepended by social and ritual differences. A third

Qashqu'i children outside their school, a tent made from felt. Their elaborate dress is worn every day.

schism within Israel arose between Orthodox and non-Orthodox Jews, the result of a paradox that Israel is a 'religious' state, where—unlike the Arab countries—the majority of the population is not religious.

Minority groups

Many different dialects of the Turkish language group (a member of the Altaic family) are spoken throughout much of the Middle East, where it constitutes one of the four most important language groups (the Jews, Arabs and Iranians forming the other three). Not all the inhabitants of Turkey speak Turkish, since there are important communities of Arabs, Kurds, Lazer (a Moslem people of Caucasian origin) and Christian groups. Turks are more or less uniform in physique. Their racial history involves mixtures of aboriginal Anatolian peoples with Phrygian, Hittite, Lydian, Kimmerian, Thracian, Persian and Greek groups, with mediaeval additions from Russia and Central Asia, from Arabia and the Levant, and the Balkans.

In modern Iran, the Turkish speakers are loosely called Turkomans and they comprise diverse and important groups. They are found in the Azerbaijan province, in the provinces of Gurgan and eastern Mazandaran and also in the north-eastern provinces of Khurasan. These are migratory tribes who claim descent from early Turkic colonists left by Genghis Khan. Turkomans are found in a fairly solid block in Anatolia, and small adjacent areas in European Turkey. Other Turkish nomads include the Qashqu'i of the Fars province (who show more traces of Mongoloid physique) and a part, but not all, of the five tribes of the same province. The Afshan of Kirman speak Turkish as do the Shahseran in Qum and Saveh. Turkomans also live in Iraq, strung out in townships along the old Baghdad trunkroad from Qara Tepe to Arbil.

The Aryan, or Indo-European, language group includes the Iranian languages—Zend, old and new Iranian (Persian) as well as Sanskrit. The modern languages of western Asia include modern Persian with its dialects and Kurdish and, perhaps, the Baluchi language. The Persian-speaking citizen, however, is not the pure 'Aryan' type but a mixed bag of aboriginal Iranians, Indo-European migrants and Central Asians, Mongols and Arabs. Iranians today are mainly farmers, the pastoral tribes being largely minorities, such as Kurds or Turks. The Persians, as distinct from other Iranian and non-Iranian elements (Kurds, Lurs, Baluchis, Turks and Arabs) are concentrated in the north, west-centre, north-east and east of Iran. Baluchis are Sunni clansmen and peasants with a typical tribal organisation, part pastoral and part sedentary; they inhabit the coastal area of Makran province. The Lurs are tribesmen of the middle stretch of western and south-western Iran; they are villagers and grazers. The Bakhtiari live farther south and east and form a distinguishable part of the Lurish complex. The majority of these groups are still seasonably nomadic, moving northwards and eastwards from the confines of the Khuzistan flatlands to the vicinity of Isfahan.

The Kurds speak a number of dialects akin to Persian. The tribes are Moslem, but they are scarcely united enough to be called a nation. Their main centre has always been the mountainous region of Eastern Anatolia, usually called Kurdistan. They are divided between Turkey, Persia, Iraq, Syria and the U.S.S.R. Kurdish nationalism today is a persistent and well-nigh hopeless affair without a realistic programme or valid leadership. The Yazidis are a puzzling fragment of Kurdish peoples who practise a separate religion; they live in Iraq and eastern Syria.

Other minorities include the Somali in Aden, Pakistani traders in coastal districts of Oman, the Persian Gulf and the Red Sea. In the Persian provinces of Kirman, Yazd and Teheran there are long-enduring communities of Zoroastrians, who are close kinsmen of groups of Parsees of western India.

Armenians lived formerly to the south of the Caucasus in what is now both Turkey and the U.S.S.R. They have a continuous story as a national group since ancient times. In the course of time they have spread as peasants and merchants throughout Asia Minor. Their settlements were largely destroyed by the great massacres of the last two generations, but they still have communities in the Balkans, and the Americas as well as several Arab countries. The largest community is in the Caucasus and is now a Soviet socialist republic, self-governing in political affairs and the centre of a flourishing Armenian culture.

Northern Africa

In describing African societies in a book on 'primitives' we are up against a certain difficulty. African societies, seen from a technological point of view, vary enormously, from small communities of hunters and gatherers which are found throughout the continent, to large farming, peasant groups and developed state systems. Descriptions of African societies, in both the northern and tropical regions, reveal a level of political and cultural sophistication which rival much of our own European culture. At the same time within these large groups, these elegant kingdoms, small communities have survived for centuries and maintain a way of life which has provided a wealth of material for anthropologists which is usually considered by the debased term 'primitive'. African cultures are exotic and worthy of description for that reason alone. They have their own method of agriculture, their own systems of belief, their own way of dealing with calamities and misfortune. By attempting a survey of African cultures I am not implying that this vastly heterogeneous continent is on the same level of 'primitiveness'; instead I am trying to assert the richness and variety of their cultures. The primitive label became stuck to the whole continent during the nineteenth century when cultures so obviously different from that of the European middle classes automatically were labelled 'primitive'.

Throughout northern Africa on both sides of the Sahara we have groups who live in towns and villages, practise agriculture, commerce, and hunting and gathering, and pastoral nomadism. There are Negro farmers and Mediterranean farmers; Negro cattle-herders and Mediterranean nomads. For convenience I have divided Africa into cultural and geographical zones as far as the farmers are concerned, but treated the migrating nomad in a special category. The Fulani cattle-herders are an example of a people who demonstrate the many problems of a book of this kind—they speak a Negro language, but have the physical characteristics of Mediterraneans for the most part; they wander from state to state across the lands of many different tribal groups of settled farmers; and although they number several million their political and social communities may consist of only a few families or lineages.

Much of North Africa belongs to the Mediterranean, Islamic civilization—the Middle East culture zone—rather than to the Negro world of tropical Africa. For nearly 1500 years, from the foundation of the first Phoenician colonies in North Africa in about the eighth century BC, until the Arab conquest of the seventh century AD, nearly all the Africans living to the north of the Sahara belonged in some sense to this Mediterranean civilization. The people, of course, were not Negroes, but fair-skinned Caucasians whom the ancient Greeks called Libyans and whom they clearly distinguished from the Ethiopians—the men with the 'burnt faces', as they called the Negroes. The Libyans spoke languages of the Afroasiatic family (or Hamito-Semitic) and their purest descendants today are some of the more isolated Berber groups in the mountain regions of North Africa.

Nevertheless, relations between 'white' North Africans and 'black' Africans—the worlds of the Mediterranean and the Western Sudan—were close even from Roman times. Caravans, armies, embassies crossed the desert in both directions trading cloth, salt and especially gold. Today, however, the unifying cultural theme in the northern African region, in which I have included the Mediterranean farmlands, the desert and the sahel, is Islam. Of the block of peoples extending from the Mediterranean to these sahel and savannah lands, the great majority are Moslems and they include many isolated Negro groups who, until this century were pagans.

What are the racial characteristics of the area? In skeletal and skull measurements, the mountain Berbers of Tunisia and Algeria (the Shawia and Kabyles, for example) are almost identical with northern Europeans, though blond colouring is rare. Among the people of the Riff of Morocco, blondness is a striking feature: the skin is often pinkish-white, freckles are not uncommon and the eyes are commonly mixed in colour or light greenish-brown. The hair is wavy to curly, sometimes black, sometimes reddish, generally some shade of brown.

The Moroccan Berbers, a southern group, includes the Berbers of the Middle Atlas, a group of Senhaja tribes which are part-pastoralists, part-agriculturalists; they are very tall, with long faces and a convex nose. Tuareg cattle-nomads, while classified as Berbers, have developed a specific physique. They—or at least the aristocratic class—are tall, lean with long limbs, narrow shoulders and hips, very long and narrow hands and feet. While skin colour may be fair, there is frequently a good deal of admixture with the Negroids of the western Sudan.

Eastern Mediterraneans include the Egyptians, the Beja from the Red Sea area, most Ethiopians—such as the Amahra, Galla, Somali and the Bu Nubians. All these people are racially Mediterranean with Negroid admixture, particularly in the ratio of limbs and trunk. The Somali, for example, have a very narrow face and

Nomadic woman in the market at Nabeul, Tunisia. Many nomadic tribes now tend to bring agricultural produce and traditional crafts to town in order to subsist.

jaw, a long skull, straight nose, brown skin, narrow hips and fine hands and feet. More Negroid than the Somali, but with Mediterranean characteristics, are the cattle herders of eastern Africa—the Hima, the Tutsi, the Masai and Turkana.

The problem of racial classification presents itself here. Throughout the area which I have rather arbitrarily called northern Africa, and which covers not only the northern littoral but also the desert and the sahel and northern savannah zones which have long been in contact with the Mediterranean world, we have groups which have been variously called Mediterranean (implying Caucasian, White, Nordic elements) and Negro (Bantu, Black). Although there are ideal anthropological types which might be classified as Mediterranean (the Berber with the fine features, the pale skin and light-coloured eyes) and Negro (the West African with his black skin, stocky build, prognathous jaw and everted lips) it is very difficult to divide up *cultural* groups in this way. Thus the Tuareg of the savannah and desert are considered Mediterranean, but many I have seen have very European features associated with black skin and frizzy hair. There are also black Berbers. Whatever the facts are about genetic races for this whole region the only truth we may state is that if one stands on the north African coast and looks southwards people tend to get darker the further one goes. Egyptians and Berbers are more or less Mediterranean Caucasoids and as you go south the inhabitants of the Sudan and West Africa have a dominant Negroid stereotype. There are, however, no lines to be drawn racially nor racial distinctions to be made between tribes. Even the most obviously Negroid tribes have individuals with light skins and pale eyes and fine features. On the other hand we must not deny that some

Nubian woman and child. Her Arab features and covered head suggest links with the world of Islam.

groups, especially those who have lived for long periods in specific environments have developed special physical traits. The slender, tall, handsome black Nilotics are one example.

Negro Farmers of northern Africa

Under the rubric northern Africa, I have also included the peoples of the sahel and northern savannah, of regions known as Eastern, Central and Western Sudan and speaking Sudanic languages. The 'Sudan' is not here to be confused with the political state, which corresponds roughly with the Eastern Sudan. Most of them have been Islamicised for centuries. In the Eastern Sudan, the Nubians were swamped by Beduin invaders and some of them (the Gaallin peoples, for example) have become Arabicised in language and culture. The mixed population between the first and fourth cataracts of the Nile, the Barabra nation, is Arabicised, but still speaks a Nubian language. Other Nubian speakers include the Anag, Birked, the Dilling of the Nuba Hills of Kordofan, the Midobi and the Nyima. The Nuba, it must be stressed, are a distinct Negro people south of Nubia and west of the White Nile; protected by their mountain environment, they have remained relatively untouched by the movements of peoples and cultures. There are a quarter of a million Nuba—very negroid in appearance—who have lived until recently their traditional lives and speak a language independent from the general Sudanic stock. Another independent people are the Sidamo of the south-western Ethiopian plateau. Their total population may be as many as two million.

All the tribes of the Central Sudan zone are fully negroid in physical characteristics and all speak Central Sudanese languages. They include the Sara, Madi and Mangbetu groups. The Mangbetu in the south-east live in former Pygmy territory into which they infiltrated roughly 1000 years ago. The Mangbetu farmers entered into a close relationship with the Pygmies and for years fought off other Negro farmers, who began to penetrate the area from the north-west and south-west. In the late nineteenth century they were conquered by the aggressive Azanee.

In the vast Western Sudan, there has been a striking confrontation between small-scale pagan groups, often living in refuge zones in mountains and valleys, and the Moslem inhabitants of large states which have risen and fallen in the savannah-sahel zone between Lake Chad and the Atlantic. Linguistically very uniform, cultures vary significantly: matrilineal states, patrilineal pastoralists, pagans and Moslems, warlike predators and peaceful tillers.

A block of Negro people, known as Voltaic, largely inhabit the watershed of the Volta River. Their population is probably something like six million and they mostly inhabit small independent village groups, in contrast to the larger, aggressive, conquest states found to the east. They include the Senufo, the Bobo, as well as the Lobi, the Gurunsi, Tallensi, Mamprusi and Mossi. Their Mande neighbours have been foremost in cultural and political movements in the western Sudan, trading with the Berbers across the desert, some of them maintaining complex state systems. The Mande include the Bambara farmers, Bozo fishermen, Dialonke, Soninke, and Malinke. Perhaps the best known of these Voltaic and Mande peoples are the Dogon.

The Dogon, for some centuries, have entrenched themselves in a harsh, semi-desert environment on the bend of the River Niger, on the fringe of an immense stone plateau where they have built their villages, strange huddles of terraced houses and granaries, all with thatched, pointed roofs, and constructed from the rocks fallen from the overhanging cliffs. Looked at from these cliffs, the Dogon appear to be living in a lunar landscape: there is no colour and the contours of the villages are blurred by a permanent heat haze. Stretching into the horizon, there is nothing visible but a plain of sand dotted sparsely with villages. The people cultivate millet; their fields sometimes form tiny valleys which divide the plateau into furrows, or cling to the cliff slopes. Some farm-gardens on the slopes are only a few yards long, supported by walls of sun-bleached stones, and can only be reached from the plain by means of a rope-ladder.

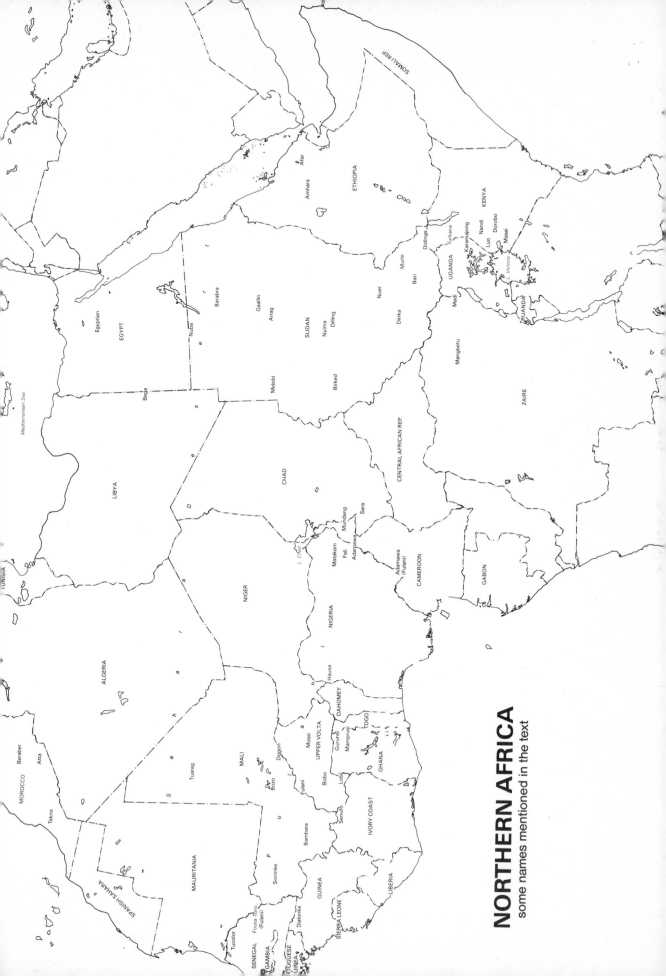

NORTHERN AFRICA
some names mentioned in the text

Dogon villages, such as this one in Sangha, North Nigeria, are built in clusters of terraced houses and granaries from rocks fallen from overhanging cliffs.

Perhaps because they have lived somewhat sheltered from major culture movements, the Dogon have preserved a civilization rich in detailed myths and symbolism, and with a splendid cultural heritage, inspired by their religion. The Dogon view of the world is as intricate as its technology is simple and might also be compared to medieval cosmology: medieval, European thinkers saw the world like a ball, the shell of an egg, the sky a place of spiritual air which angels crossed to bring messages to mortals, and with the four elements—fire, air, water and earth—disposed concentrically in this globular space.

Such a fantastic, if inspired, vision of the universe is equalled by the Dogon version of their cosmos. The stars came from pellets of earth flung into space by the god Amma; the sun is a pot raised to white heat and surrounded by a spiral of red copper; with another lump of clay the god created the earth extending east and west, north and south, the separate members like the foetus of a womb and the body of the earth facing upwards resembling a woman—its sexual organ an ant-hill and its clitoris a termite hill . . . and so on.

Here, I shall only touch on one aspect of Dogon cosmology—their attitude to twins, a common enough theme in African ethnography. Throughout the continent twins are treated with the greatest respect or the greatest disrespect—worshipped or put to death. To the Dogon, twins are perfect births, echoes of a primordial world when twin births were the rule.

Twinship has been the rule among the Dogon since the beginning of time. Twinship symbolises the complementarity between all kinds of bonded pairs: friends, traders, husbands and wives, a man and his shadow, a man and his placenta. Even the rich and the poor, children of aristocrats and descendants of slaves, become twins once they have gone through circumcision and the ordeals of initiation together, thereby experiencing a new social state. People who form alliances of any kind are seen as a single entity—albeit divided into two parts—like twins. The two parts are not identical, but complementary and equal.

The Dogon universe, as a whole, issued from an infinity of smallness, created as we have seen by the Word of a single God, called Amma; this is symbolised today on earth by both the fonio seed (a Sudanese staple grain crop) and the egg of the mudfish; it is symbolised in space by a satellite of Sirius, the star Digitaria. This infinite smallness developed and formed a vast womb, called the Egg of the World, which was divided into two parts and contained two placentas, which eventually gave birth to twin couples, pairs of mixed twins, living and animated beings, prototypes of men, who possessed the creative Word. These beings had the form of the mudfish and, by the Dogon, are likened to human foetuses in the water of the womb. From one half of this egg, one of the male twins, the fox, was born prematurely, and in order to gain possession of the nascent universe for himself, he rebelled against his creator. Tearing off a piece of his placenta, which had formed a kind of arch, he climbed down into empty space on it. The torn-off piece of placenta became our planet. He went inside it in order to look for his twin sister, since without her he was powerless to realize any of his ambitions for domination. Walking in every direction he made five rows of twelve holes in the still wet and bloody soil. In this way he set out the first field of the future, with its sixty plots. When his searches on earth came to nought, he went back up into the sky. But Amma had given his twin to the pair in the other half of the egg, so that he should not get hold of her; and Amma had put the rest of the placenta out of his reach by turning it into a sun—that is, burning fire.

The Fox, archetypal rebel and trickster, then stole eight seeds of cereal created by Amma and sowed them in the earth; the humidity of the placenta, which had not yet entirely dried out, caused one of the fonio seeds to germinate and become red and impure. The premature intervention on the part of this audacious creature, the incest he had committed by penetrating his own placenta, that is the womb of his 'mother', and above all his theft and planting of the fonio seed, the 'sperm' of his father Amma, permanently disturbed the order of creation and made it incomplete and impure. Amma, in order to remedy this situation, had one of the twins in the other half of the egg castrated and offered in sacrifice to heaven. This twin shed his blood to purify the universe; he was given the name of Nommo and his body was cut into sixty pieces, and one by one they were thrown into space at the four cardinal points of the compass; some of them fell to earth and were transformed into plants, symbols of the purification wrought by this sacrifice.

Nommo, however, was brought back to life as a human couple—a man and a woman, made from the stuff of his own placenta. With the same material, he created four pairs of mixed twins, who were the real ancestors of mankind, the sons of Nommo. In another version of the creation myth, Nommo, male and female himself, drew two outlines on the ground, one on top of the other, one male and one female. Nommo stretched himself out on these two shadows of himself and took

A Dogon man in Mali. The Dogon live in a semi-desert environment on the River Niger. Sheltered from major cultural movements, they still preserve their unique traditions.

OPPOSITE:
A Moroccan Berber feast celebrated with displays of horse skill.

both of them for his own. The same thing was done to create women. Thus it came about that each human being, from the first, was endowed with two souls of different sex, or rather with two different principles corresponding to two distinct persons. In the man, the female soul was located in the foreskin and in the woman, the male soul was the clitoris. Each person then had to merge himself in the sex for which he appeared best fitted and circumcision and cliterodechtomy are seen as the removal of the external feminity and the internal masculinity. An incestuous act in creation, therefore, had destroyed order based on the principle of twin or androgynous births; and order was only restored by the creation of human beings; twin births are replaced by dual souls. Dual souls were implanted in each new-born child by Nommo, who held them by the thighs over the etched outlines in the ground.

From the union of the original Dogon ancestors, mankind grew apace, and life became organised on Earth. Meanwhile, the rebel, the Fox, a single being without his twin sister, was incapable of achieving his wished-for domination. He was fated to pass his time vainly pursuing his lost twin who was at the same time his female soul. Nommo's role as a complete being, a pair of twins, was to limit the disorderly activities of the Fox and to do this he divided up all the constituent elements of the universe and placed them in categories, keeping them under his constant control.

Twins express exchange, complementarity and equality as well as duality and order and, as such, they symbolise friendship and alliance. Twinship even expresses the violent friendships between the Dogon and the Bozo—a fisherfolk on the banks of the Niger; the two peoples exchange wild jokes and insults in token of an ancient friendship. The Bozo are 'fish' and in mythical times the mudfish and man (i.e. the Dogon) were twins. The Bozo are of the water and the Dogon traditionally refer to them as walking fish; while the Dogon are of the land. The pact between the two peoples, who are by no means near neighbours, has always been expressed by insults and joking, the Dogon believing that once upon a time a part of the vital force of each group was deposited in the other. Thus each Bozo possesses in himself part of a Dogon and vice versa. When the relationship is

198

In Mali, a Dogon man in the compound of his living quarters. The thatched buildings in the background are used to store grain.

The Ginna (as the house of a Dogon priest is known), inhabited by the oldest man of the village. To explain the origins of man the Dogon have evolved a complex cosmology.

activated, each party then acts on that part of himself which is in the other—his twin and his friend—and which forms a sort of foundation in that person on which he can work.

What about actual Dogon twins? They are delicate creatures who must not be grumbled at or they die. They are visionaries with second sight and can see the forest spirits and the recently-dead, who fly around the village. They lose their second sight and fragility once they become adolescents. Dogon twins are also given special names and a year after birth there is a ceremony on exactly the same lines as the installation of the Dogon priest-chief, the Hogon. Both the twin ceremony and the installation of the priest are beneficial to soil fertility and human prosperity in general. The twins are given special necklaces of eight cowries and a special pointed hat like the priest's bonnet, with cowries sewn on it.

For the Dogon, the ideal and perfect birth is twin birth. Single children upset the social and cosmological order of things. At every childbirth, the intermediary spirit, Nommo, prays to God for the birth of twins, but Nommo's prayers are not always answered, of course, and that is why he has given two souls to every child. A child's body is one, but his spiritual being is two. And until his initiation rites, he remains spiritually, symbolically and physically 'androgynous'—until puberty dual children retain their foreskins and clitorises; their 'masculinity' and their 'femininity' thereby remain equally potent. For a girl, the clitoris is a symbolic twin, a male makeshift with which she cannot reproduce herself and which also prevents her mating with a man. She has it removed, since anyone trying to mate with an unexcised woman would be frustrated by opposition from an organ claiming to be his equal. Similarly, when a boy is circumcised and his foreskin is transformed into a lizard, he loses both his feminity and his twin.

The duality and complementarity of male and female is associated with the duality and unity of twinship. Twins correspond to the number 2. Duality between male and female corresponds to the opposition between the masculine symbol 3 and the feminine 4, which added together gives seven, which is the Dogon symbol of the complete being. Twinship here is a useful concept for understanding the relationship between two people who are symbolically one, and

Dogon woman and children in a market. The woman on the left is buying a spindle.

the androgyny of the male and female parts of a single person, made up of two. In this complex and original way, twins have been converted by the Dogon into a mode of thought.

Twins, as an ideal unit, also express the alliance and duality of friends, traders, joking-partners and husbands and wives. Each member of these dyads has in a sense found his other half. Most people are nevertheless born alone, and to compensate the Dogon for this misfortune, each child is linked to an animal who represents his unknown other half—his unborn twin. This animal twin himself has a twin, another tabooed animal and so on and so on; thus the aggregate of Dogon families is connected with the whole animal kingdom through the essential notion of twinness.

Let us move from the Western Sudan to the Atlantic coast. The people of Senegal and Gambia are Negroes with a strong Islamic element. At one time, they extended farther north into coastal Mauritania, but when the Arabs began pressing the Berbers, the main people—the Wolof—were pushed southward to near the mouth of the Senegal River where the Serer lived. The Tucolor of the middle Senegal were politically dominant at the time and accepted Islam and proselitysed the Wolof. Islamic influence among these people is seen by an elaborate multiplication of stratified statuses—royalty, aristocrats, free commoners, soldiers, peasants, servants, slaves and despised endogamous castes.

The trans-Saharan trade between the Sudan and the Mediterranean was felt first and strongest by the Negro people inhabiting the northern fringe of the Sudan. They enjoyed economic prosperity for centuries and adopted cultural elements from those with whom they traded. They have long constituted the African frontier with the Moslem world and the great Middle-Eastern culture area. Elements of Arab culture are very noticeable. Today, this frontier has been extended further south, as far as the equatorial forest. At the termini of the four major caravan routes, strong African states developed in Darfur, Wadai, Bagirmi and Bornu. The Gadames trail from ancient Carthage and modern Tunisia ends at the major cities of the Hausa states and provinces. Timbuktu, inhabited by the Songhai and the cities of ancient Ghana, were also great mercantile centres. The Hausa people, probably as a result of their long experience of the northern trading routes, achieved a degree of cultural unity comparable to that of a great European nation. They adopted the Arabic alphabet for writing their own language and have produced an extensive literature.

Nomadic Peoples of Negro and Mediterranean Africa

Nomadic peoples of many different languages and cultures tend cattle, sheep, goats and donkeys across the savannah lands of Africa north and south of the Sahara. They are considered here for convenience, but really transcend the division between the northern zone and the tropical and southerly areas of the next chapter. Some of them are organised into large-scale tribes and as in Somali form the majority and governing class. Others are small groups which rarely make contact with neighbours or larger sections of their community. At the present day, particularly in West Africa, attempts are being made to settle many of these nomadic groups which may migrate with their cattle over vast zones. Recently dreadful droughts have encouraged this sedentarisation throughout Africa.

Nomadic peoples, almost as a universal rule, display a degree of xenophobia and racial pride which is much stronger than that of settled peoples. Like the Gypsies, the cattle-herders of western Africa and north-east Africa have had to stress their differences from surrounding farming peoples in order to survive. They insist on endogamy—that is marriage within the local group. They spurn the customs of other people and praise their own way of life as the only activity of real men. Usually they are forced to live in very restricted groups, communities larger than a few families only coming together during seasons of plenty when grass is available for larger herds. During these periods community ceremonies such as circumcisions occur. For the greater part of the year the extended families of a herding group are on their own.

The Bega of north-east Africa, who first appeared in European history about 2,700 BC, at which time they already seem to have been nomadic pastoralists, belong to the Mediterranean race, resembling the Beduin of the Arabian peninsula. Three other pastoralist nations—the Afar, Somali and Galla—inhabit the arid desert and swamp country of the desert horn. The Nilotes are Negro pastoralists who occupy a large territory extending from the border of Kordofan in the north-west, through southern Sudan, northern Uganda and western Kenya, to northern

Hausa fishermen trying their luck in the Argungu Fishing Festival in north-west Nigeria. The river is not fished for eleven months of the year and then competitors from all over Nigeria are given half an hour to catch as many Nile perch as they can with bare hands, a net and a calabash in which to put small fish.

Tanganyika and from the edge of Ethiopia to Zaire. They include the Didinga, Murle, Dinka, Luo, Bari, Karamajong, Nandi, Masai, Beir and Nuer. Nilotes also expanded southward where they encountered the farming Bantu tribes of Uganda. The descendants of these migrants are the Hima. In the Ruanda region, the Tutsi brought local Bantu farmers, the Hutu, into subjection.

When the Phœnicians and Greeks, and later the Romans, colonised the North African coast, they found the region occupied by a people of homogeneous culture known collectively as the Berbers. Although they occupied a few marginal oases, they had not penetrated into the Saharan desert. In the seventh century, the Berber nations were shattered by Arab conquests and even more disastrously by the mass Beduin immigration beginning in the eleventh century. Some fled to the desert, others submitted and became Arabicised; today they have become part of the Middle Eastern culture area, although Berber speech survives in some mountain fastnesses. Some tribes have also retained their original language and preserved their ancient customs. The main Berber-speaking groups include the Atta, the Beraber, the Gadames, Guanche, Tasymsa, Tekna and Tuareg. When the Berber groups were dispersed by the Arabs, the Tuareg sought refuge in the Sahara and adopted a nomadic and predatory mode of life modelled on that of the Beduin invaders. Though long since completely Islamicised, the Tuareg still bear witness to their Christian past in the retention of the cross as their favourite decorative motif. While Tuareg are part Berber and part Arab, their culture is unique. They are camel nomads, despising agriculture, leaving it exclusively in the hands of their Negro serfs. They live in migratory bands and live in tents, covered with tanned sheep or goat hides dyed red.

The Beduin invasion began about 1045 and continued at a decreasing rate for several centuries. Pouring first into Egypt, they spread through the former Berber regions of North Africa. Nomads, they took over former agricultural land, converting fertile fields to pasture, their flocks destroying the natural vegetation cover. There exist still hundreds of tribes and factions and religious groups, which include Algerians, Cyrenaicans, Egyptians, people of the Fezzan, Moroccans, the Sanusi, Tripolitanians and Tunisians.

Tuaregs in Tessoum, north Nigeria. Nomadic Tuaregs depend on camel, goat and sheep herds for subsistence. Reduction of herds due to drought has caused some tribes to settle in the cities.

Scattered throughout the Western Sudan, from Senegal in the west to Cameroon in the east, live the Fulani (or Peul, or Fulbe), cattle-herders living among settled farming groups, such as the Bambara, Dogon, and Hausa, as important minorities. They are a vast group, linguistically and racially distinctive. The main patterns of their cultural and social life appear to be essentially the same whether they are the Adamawa Fulani of Cameroon or the Fouta Toro group of Senegal, except where some have become politically dominant through conquest. The initial migration of the Fulani was not one of conquest, but a dispersal of an unobtrusive people living symbiotically with farming peoples and economically linked to them by exchanging cattle for farm products.

Where did the pale-skinned Fulani come from? They have been variously explained as a lost tribe of Israel, Syrians, Gypsies, Beduins, even a Hindu caste. They are probably of Berber stock and moved down the west coast of Senegal about a thousand years ago, where they acquired their present language. From their small beginnings, the Fulani managed to expand from a small community of migrants to a population of six million people. Within this vast world, independent Fulani communities are very small. Their very presence is not at all obvious to the traveller as he drives for miles past the farms and villages of the Islamic Hausa, the circular huts of the pagans and the flat-roofed market towns with their busy stalls and mosques. The Fulani keep away from other people, but across the fields you may catch sight of a tall, copper-skinned boy playing his flute as he watches a milling herd of cattle or another like him leaning against one of the cows for

Sedentary Fulani village women grinding sorghum with large wooden pestles.

support, caressing its lyre-shaped horns and chanting to it in a soft voice. Even their camps blend in with the bush; their household equipment is meagre and their temporary shelters are made from branches torn from a nearby tree. Within hours they may strike camp and disappear like the wind which blows through the bush; and when they have gone, all that remains is a few stripped branches and a patch of bare earth.

This temporary, camouflaged homestead is the real world of the Fulani, the formal centre of life which shifts with them as they lead their cattle from the dangers of the tse-tse fly or to a distant water hole. When they arrive at their destination a patch of earth is cleared, a calf-rope is set up and the women erect their frame beds and store away their bundles of ceremonial clothes, jewellery and decorated calabashes. The herd mills around the fire in the men's section at night and their formation, too, oddly reflects the formality of the Fulani family; the bull lies nearest the fire, the stronger cows next to him but a little apart, while the young bulls and the heifers remain on the edges and the calves are tethered to the rope which divides the Fulani homestead.

A man's life is spent pasturing his cattle, seeing to their needs, curing their illnesses and drawing water for them from deep wells every morning and evening. Cows are beloved members of the family, known by name and treated with an

Nomadic Fulani herdsmen in southern Nigeria. Their sleeveless caftans, worn over loose trousers, and their covered heads are marks of Islamic influence.

affection amounting to devotion. If a man loses his cattle through disease, his world comes to an end; in such cases a Fulani has been known to go mad, tearing off his clothes and wandering naked through the bush calling the names of the dead beasts. Looking after cattle is their only fully rewarding occupation and they never complain of the hardships it brings. In the wet season particularly, when the cattle are herded together in restricted pastures away from the tse-tse fly, they have to be watched night and day. Herds stampede at the sight of strange cattle moving in the bush, or through sheer excitement when they feel the pouring rain after months of drought. Hyenas abound and annoy them. For the men at those times there is the extra work that must be done—de-ticking, felling trees for fences and seeing to the seasonally increased amount of animal sickness.

Fulani boys learn their masculine roles early. From childhood a boy is immersed in the world of cattle; even his games are conceived with a life-time of cattle-herding in mind. Little boys dig tiny dry-season wells and model cows, calves, bulls and pack oxen in mud. After circumcision a boy moves out of the women's half of the patch of ground which is a family home, crossing the calf-rope to sleep on the men's side. He receives his first leather wrap and his first calf, and begins to imitate the older men in their handling of the cattle, caressing them, singing to them, removing their ticks. As he grows up he becomes betrothed and watches his own section of the herd grow.

Today the Fulani are becoming semi-sedentary, particularly with the changing, and often disastrous, climatic conditions of recent years. Islam is now almost everywhere the predominant religion.

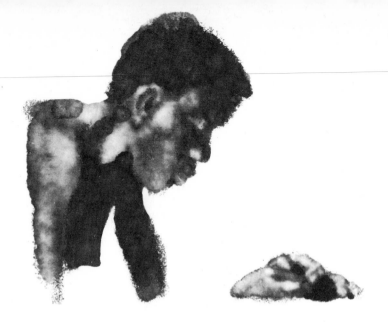

Tropical and Southern Africa

To many of us equatorial Africa conjures up dripping jungles, small thatched villages in vast expanses of black forest, hunters with spears or bows, farmers felling huge trees to clear a space for their manioc or yams. Africa, of course, now has its cities, its towns, its networks of railways and roads, its plantations of coffee, cocoa and cotton. And much of it is rolling plains, savannah lands where grains such as millet and corn are grown; and people have always lived in large villages under chiefs or even kings. But there is a great difference between the impersonal, bureaucratic government of the modern industrial state and the traditional rule of, say, the Bamileke chiefs who are described later in this section.

The Bamileke are related to a heterogeneous group of people who live in the uplands of Cameroon and speak Bantu or Bantoid languages. The Cameroon Highlanders constitute a large variety of tribes of all sizes, from the Bamileke who number over almost a million, to the Bafia, the Bafut, the Kom, the Bali, the Bamum, Nsaw and Tikar. These peoples are not quite Negroid and not quite Bantu, not quite a savannah people and not quite equatorial. And here we have in a nutshell the problem of classifying and ordering peoples and tribes according to race (Negroid), language (Bantu), or environment. However, in this section we must try and look, in broad lines, at the racial, linguistic and cultural zones of Black or Tropical Africa, excluding the predominantly Moslem peoples of the northern sahel and desert fringe.

In 'Black' Africa, all the main races of the world are represented: Caucasoid in East and Central and South Africa; Negroid throughout the continent; Bushmanoid in the South and East; and Mongoloid in South Africa and Madagascar. Scientifically, however, there is little more than this we can say. As far as West Africa is concerned, for example, we can only avoid racialist fantasies by saying that starting in the north and working down, the people tend to get blacker and their hair frizzier; but there is nowhere any sharp differentiation. Negro, as a word, has been traditionally used for Africans of West Africa, sometimes to distinguish them from so-called Bantu peoples of the centre and southern regions. However, it is a term with physical implications, while Bantu is a linguistic term, in the same way as Hamitic and Semitic are purely linguistic concepts.

In the north of our zone there is a group of tribes speaking non-Bantu languages, which includes the peoples of Adamawa (Mbum, Mundang, Fali), and an equatorial group partly in the zone of tropical rain forests (Azande, Banda, Baya, Wute). The inhabitants of the central plateau region of Nigeria and Cameroon are typically Negroid. They include so-called Bantoid peoples: the Bassa, Birom, Jarawa, Jukun, Katab, Mada, Mambila and Tiv; and the Chadic peoples: the Angas, Gerawa, Kapsiki, Margui, Matakam and Gbara. Among all these peoples Islam is making inroads.

Bantu is by far the most important of the African linguistic groups, a large family of languages spoken by Negroes over most of Africa south of the equator. As little as two thousand years ago, Bantu may have been a single language spoken in an area much smaller than that occupied by its modern descendants. The 'birth' of Bantu probably took place in the south-east Nigerian Cameroon regions, where the Bamileke speak a Bantoid or semi-Bantu language. The expansion of the Bantu-speakers was the expansion of farmers armed with iron tools who invaded the equatorial forests towards the beginning of the Christian era. In the course of this dispersal, groups of hunters and gatherers, presumably of Pygmy and Bushman type, were destroyed or hunted into the inhospitable deserts of the south-west or the deepest corners of the Zaire forests. Right down the highlands of east Africa, the descendants of Hamitic-speaking cattle-herders (as we saw earlier) held out against the expanding Bantu farmers, some of them becoming farmers themselves, others specialising as pastoralists on the dry, savannah lands of the plateaux.

Modern linguists have now decided that the vast Bantu family of languages is really a sub-family of an even larger group known as the Niger-Congo family which is divided into seven sub-families. Bantu languages cover most of central and southern Africa. (The second large family is Sudanic, spoken by the Dogon and related peoples of the western Sudan, the area of the middle Niger River and the eastern Sudan.)

Afro-Asiatic languages, generally further north, are related to the Semitic group, a sub-family of Afro-Asian. This group includes Ancient Egyptian, Cushitic as well as Berber, Tuareg, the various languages spoken around Lake Chad, and Hausa.

'Click languages' is the term given to remnant languages still spoken by the Bushmen and Hottentots and by a few remnant peoples in Tanzania.

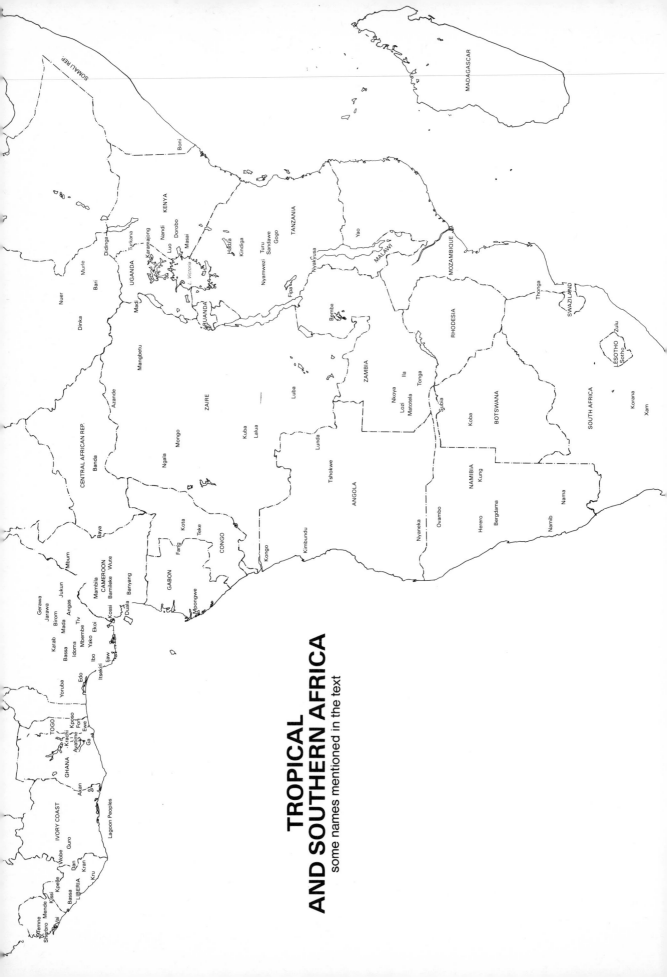

TROPICAL
AND SOUTHERN AFRICA
some names mentioned in the text

SOMALI REP.

MADAGASCAR

Boni

KENYA

Nandi
Luo Dorobo
Masai

TANZANIA

Didinga
Turkana
Karamojong
Hadza
Kindiga

Yao

MOZAMBIQUE

Murle

Bari

UGANDA

Madi

Turu
Sandawe
Gogo

Nyamwezi

Nyakyusa

Thonga

SWAZILAND

Nuer

Dinka

L. Victoria

Fipa

Bemba

MALAWI

RHODESIA

LESOTHO
Zulu
Sotho

RUANDA

Mangbetu

ZAMBIA

Ila
Tonga

Korana

Xam

Azande

ZAIRE

Luba

Nkoya
Lozi
Matotela

Subia

Koba

BOTSWANA

SOUTH AFRICA

CENTRAL AFRICAN REP.

Banda

Kuba
Lalua

Lunda

Tshokwe

ANGOLA

NAMIBIA
Kung

Baya

Ngala
Mongo

Kimbundu

Kongo

Nyaneka

Ovambo

Herero

Bergdama

Namib

Nama

Farig
Kota
Teke

CONGO

Mbum

Mambila
CAMEROON
Bamileke Wute

Banyang

GABON

Mpongwe

Gerawa
Jarawa
Jukun
Mada Angas
Birom
Tiv

Karab
Idoma Mbembe
Bassa Yako

Ibo
Edo

Ekoi
Kossi
Duala

Yoruba

Itsekri

Ijaw

TOGO
Kposo
Krachi Fon
Avatime Ewe
Ga

GHANA

Akan

Lagoon Peoples

IVORY COAST

Guro

Wobe

Dan
Kran

Kru

Kpelle

Bassa
LIBERIA

Kissi
Mende

Sherbro

Vai

Kissi

Toma

Dialects of English are spoken as the mother languages of populations in Liberia and Sierra Leone on the west coast and as well as English, a dialect of Dutch (the new language called Afrikaans) has developed in South Africa. There are also *linguae francae* in Africa apart from English, Portuguese and French—the colonial languages. There are large areas centring on Tanganyika, Zanzibar and Kenya and overlapping into Uganda and Zaire where Swahili is used. Hausa is used throughout northern Nigeria and neighbouring countries. Lingal and Kikongo are important in Zaire.

Caucasoid peoples speaking Indo-European languages are found in some numbers primarily in the central and southern parts of Africa. In South Africa 68% of the population is African, 10% Coloured and 3% Asian. The European people—the remainder—who call themselves 'Whites' are the descendants of people of many nationalities, but principally of the Dutch and English. There are also groups of French Huguenots and Jews. The Asians—many of them also Caucasoid and Indo-European speakers—are called 'Asians' and are of East Indian or Pakistani origin. 'Coloured' is a residual category including all people not classified in the other three groups. Cape Malays are a Moslem minority of Indonesian origin. Thus, in South Africa, we have four racial castes with 'Whites' at the top of the hierarchy. The socio-economic gap is wide and unbreachable; the groups are endogamous (marriage between castes is forbidden by law and tabooed socially); membership in castes is ascribed by birth; and being a 'White' entails full humanity and citizenship plus special privileges for the master race.

Nevertheless being a master race and economically predominant, does not mean that the immigrant white tribes are more civilised or less primitive than the Africans. Many small communities live 'Amish-like' (see p. 266) in the farm valleys of the Transvaal and Natal. These endogamous, isolated groups maintain their traditional English or Afrikaans worlds, using symbols and sharing values to maintain their ethnic separateness and sense of community. In these communities they intermarry not only into White groups, but into residential groups. Terms such as Afrikaans-, or English-speaking South African are in this sense not only linguistic, but racial and religious, and exclude the majority of the population, even if many black Africans are, literally, 'English-speaking South Africans'.

The population of Madagascar is over five million, and this country too is a composite of racial and cultural strains, with African Negroid predominating in the west coast. Mongoloid (Indonesian) strains are found in the interior plateau with a scattering of Arab (Caucasian). The languages are, however, basically similar and of undoubtedly Malayo-Polynesian (or Austronesian) type.

Ngamiland Bushmen in Botswana carrying long hunting-bows and poisoned arrows rest in front of a rock painting.

Let us now look in more detail at the peoples of the area in turn.

Bushmen

While it is difficult to separate out groups which we conveniently call Caucasoid, Mediterranean, Negro, or Nilotic into clear-cut separate races, the Bushmen, insignificant as they are in numbers, do seem to constitute a distinct race. The Xam Bushmen are short—the men average less than four feet ten inches; they have exceedingly wrinkled skin of a light, yellowish-brown colour; little facial and body hair; short head-hair in tight 'peppercorn spirals'; they have an eyefold which is prominent, but distinct from the Mongoloid variety. In the women the phenomenon known as 'steatopygia' (prominent buttocks) is marked.

The Bushmen, Hottentot and Bergdama are related, the Hottentot differing culturally from the other two groups in that they became cattle herders after contact and miscegenation with the south-western Bantu. It is not known exactly what the numbers of these groups are, although it is certain they are diminishing every day. The Bushmen include the Hukwe, Korana, Korkoka, Kung, Nama, Namib and Xam sub-groups. Only a few of them still subsist exclusively by hunting and gathering, yet agriculture was totally unknown before the arrival of the Bantu and the Europeans, who forced them further and further into the inhospitable desert.

Bushmen types also once lived throughout the portion of East Africa which extends from the borders of the Transvaal north-eastward to southern Ethiopia. In some areas, hunters and gatherers—while basically Negroid in physique—are obviously the remnants of these inhabitants: they include the Boni of southern Somalia, the Dorobo of Kenya, the Kindiga and Sandawe of Northern Tanzania and the Hadza who still hunt and gather near Lake Eyasi.

Pygmies

The Pygmies also have a distinct appearance with their short stature, their pale skin covered with down hair, and their high, bulging foreheads. Many Pygmy groups, however, are darker in colour, because of miscegenation with Negro neighbours, whose language they speak. Once they roamed the equatorial forest undisturbed until their territory was penetrated by Bantu farmers. Today the great majority of Pygmies live in their ancient forest home. Among them four groups may be distinguished, which could be further divided into many sub-groups: they are the Binga, the central Twa, the Bagesera and the Mbuti. The Mbuti, to some extent, have preserved their unique culture and racial characteristics despite constant contact with farming neighbours who are both numerically and technologically superior. The Pygmies are nomadic and make their livelihood from hunting game and collecting wild fruit and roots. The forest is the Pygmies' home, a dark cathedral of gigantic trees, the ceiling a tracery of dripping foliage which forms a constant barrier against the sun. Negro farmers, living on the edges of this forest, find it a forbidding place and use their Pygmy 'slaves', as they regard them, to procure game and other forest foods for them. Such is the extent of their bond to the forest that attempts by well-meaning administrators and missionaries to free Pygmies from it, or even from their client relationship with the Negroes, have met with enormous difficulties. In the first place, the interdependence between Pygmy and Negro (in what is called a symbiotic relationship) is mutually advantageous, each providing the other with essential services while maintaining their separate cultural identities. Both Negro and Pygmy have a healthy contempt for each other's appearance. The Negroes pity the Pygmies for having to live in the forest, while the Pygmies laugh at the Negroes' fear of the spirits and mock the clumsy farmer when he tries to move about in it.

So far only a few Pygmies have been persuaded to leave the forest and set up camp beside their Negro 'masters', where they have become tourist attractions, posing in clothes they would never wear in the forest, and selling weapons which they got from the Negroes. The forest Pygmies pour scorn on these degenerate 'monkeys' who ape the real Pygmies for the benefit of passing white men. In the short space of one or two generations, Pygmies who have moved to the edges of the forest acquire Negro physical characteristics, values and behavioural patterns. There seems, in fact, no hope of Pygmy groups surviving either physically or culturally outside the forest.

Of the total of 150,000 remaining Pygmies, some 40,000 live in the Ituri Forest in north-east Zaire (former Congo-Kinshasa). In the Congo, before independence, Belgian policy had always been to leave these people as they were, mainly because they lived in an inaccessible and unprofitable part of the colonial domain. Recently, however, changes have come about. Large clearings have been made outside the forest and government-built Pygmy settlements have been organized.

Mbuti Pygmies, in the Ituri Forest of Zaire, smoking a banana stem pipe. They build their huts from saplings and the frame structure is covered with rainproof mongongo leaves hung like roof tiles.

The Pygmies at first reacted enthusiastically to the free tools, the seed corn, schoolhouses and dispensaries. But the plan failed; the Pygmies went back to the forest, ate the seed and sold the tools to the Negroes. They took the view, 'Why should we work our farms when we can steal from the villagers, anyway?' The problem will not become serious until the Pygmy environment totally disappears. They have survived for thousands of years and are certainly not going to give in now. Their life is in the forest and they are standing out against any merging of cultures, forced or otherwise. The older men preach a strong resistance to all changes. 'We are the people of the forest and we have no need to fear it. We are only afraid of what is outside the forest'. They know, and so do the administrators, that Pygmies cannot survive in the open lands outside the forest. They soon become ill from diseases which they have not met before; they cannot even drink water which is completely harmless to sedentary Negro farmers and Europeans. In one model village for Pygmies, twenty-nine died in a single day, primarily from exposure to the sun. It is the old, old story and any careless regimentation or too-eager plans for reform may bring further, like disasters.

West African Negroes

Unlike the Pygmies the Negro groups of West Africa are mostly found in large, tribal groups. In some cases chiefdoms or even empires ruled part of their lives. However, within such large groups and states the local community exists as an independent community, paying tax to the government today as it paid an irregular tribute to an overlord in the past, but retaining cultural elements, and dialectical variations which separate sub-groups and even villages from each other.

History reflected in a piece of Yoruba art from the end of the nineteenth century: this is a detail from the wooden doors of the palace of the Ogoga of Ikere-Ekiti; in the lower right-hand panel the colonial administrator comes to meet the Ogoga.

The universe is usually the village where work and play, politics and religion are focused. Witchcraft accusations are made against neighbours and special categories of kin; the village has its special protective deity; dance ceremonies and initiation rituals are performed there; and often the people down the river or over the hill are despised, feared or mocked.

The Negroid race has its heartland in the equatorial forest and western Sudan. They are tall, dark brown, with black, frizzy hair, broad nose, and everted lips. Towards the coast the stature is usually shorter. A solid block of Negro tribes along the coast and hinterland of the Ivory Coast and Liberia belong to the Kru branch of the Kwa languages. Among these Kru peoples can be numbered the Kran, Wobe and Kru proper. Their neighbours include the Kissi, Sherbro and Temne and Mande-speakers, such as the Dan, Guro, Kpelle, Mende and Vai. Throughout this area, the inhabitants are organised into village communities directed by a headman and a council of elders or petty chiefdoms. All tribes carry out intricate initiation rites involving circumcision and education in 'bush schools' which eventually give the neophytes the right to enter a secret society. Two such societies—one for males, called Poro, and another for women, called Sande or Bundu—occur widely throughout the area.

The Twi inhabit another cultural province of West Africa covering eastern Ivory Coast, Ghana, Togo and Dahomey. Twi-speakers include the Ewe, Fon and Ga of coastal Dahomey and Togo, the Kposo, Avatime and Krachi of the highlands of Central Togo, splinter tribes driven into the region by the expansion of powerful neighbours; the Akan, including the Anyi and Ashanti, the Baule, Brong and Fanti; and the Lagoon peoples—the Ajukru, Ari, Ebrie, etc. Until the nineteenth century the Akan were organized into large-scale chiefdoms, kingdoms and empires and the Fon were ruled by the king of Dahomey, an absolute monarch at the head of an elaborate bureaucracy. The Ashanti—along with all the societies of the Akan and Lagoon group—practise matrilineal inheritance and succession today, despite their assimilation into the modern industrial world.

The Negroes of Southern Nigeria speak languages of the Kwa family, although some groups in the south-east speak Bantoid, or semi-Bantu languages related to those of the Cameroon. Bantoid-speaking peoples include the Banyang and Ekoi,

Fon people drawing in nets in the lake dwelling-town of Ganvié, Dahomey.

the Mbembe and Yako; the Idoma group includes Igala and Iyala as well as Idoma; a large central cluster speak diverse languages of the same family and include the Edo or Bini, who number half a million, the well-known nation of the Ibo, the oastal fishermen, the Ijaw and the Itsekiri. The Yoruba, the main people of western Nigeria are divided into several cultural and linguistic blocks such as the Egba, Ekiti, Ife, Ijebu and the Yoruba 'proper', who include the Ibadan, Ilorin and Oyo.

The Nilotes of the eastern Sudan, mentioned on page 000, are sufficiently divergent in physical characteristics to warrant classification as a separate Negro group. The Nuer and the Dinka are very tall (five feet ten inches for adult males), with long slender limbs, dark skin, narrow head, broad nose and medium-to-everted lips. All the Nilotes speak languages of Sudanic stock and occupy a large territory extending from the border of Kordofan in the north-west through southern Sudan, northern Uganda and Western Kenya in the north-east to the border of Zaire in the south-west. They include the Beir, the Dinka, the Nuer, the Luo, the Bari, the Karamajong, Nandi, Masai and Didinga.

The Bantu

'Bantu' implies a linguistic grouping, nevertheless Bantu-speakers tend to be somewhat shorter, lighter and less prognathous than Negroes of other parts of Africa, West Africa for example. Today, they occupy approximately one third of the African continent, and may be grouped into the following cultural areas.

The north-west Bantu of Cameroon and Gabon include the Duala, Kossi, Bakwere along with the Mpongwe and Teke. The Equatorial Bantu are vast congeries of peoples with no notable cultural differences. The main tribes are the Amba, the Fang or Pangwe, the Kota and the Ngala. In the heart of the equatorial rain forest, in the source of the Congo River, live the tribes which constitute the Mongo nation. South-east of the Mongo, in the adjacent highland and savannah territory live quite different peoples, mainly Luba and related groups, such as the

A young Fang woman decorated in accordance with ceremonial custom.

Lulua. The Central Bantu include the Kongo, Kimbundu, Kwango, Kuba, Tshokwe and Lunda, Bemba and Yao. The economy of the Central Bantu rests primarily upon swidden agriculture, growing manioc and sweet potatoes, bananas and yams.

The Tanzanian Bantu include the Gogo, the Turu, the Nyamwezi, the Fipa, the Nyakyusa. The Nyakyusa exhibit a distinctive type of social organization. At the age of twelve or thereabouts all the boys of a village leave their homes and start up a village of their own. Until they marry they return daily to eat with their mothers and farm with their fathers. Ultimately their wives join them in the village, so that local groups among the Nyakyusa consist of age-mates, rather than kinsmen. Each village has a headman, who is selected by the paramount chief. The chief is succeeded by two sons, the firstborn of his two 'great wives'. Some years before his death when these sons are about thirty-five, he retires at a great 'coming out' ceremony, dividing his territory between his two sons and assigning definite tracts of land to each recently established age-village.

The Zambesi Bantu include the Ila, the Lozi, the Tonga and Matotela. Many of these sub-groups still gather a large amount of their food. The Koba and Subia collect water roots and aquatic animals. The Nkoya are more hunters than farmers.

The south-west Bantu include the Ovambo, the Herero and the Nyaneka. Two great Bantu nations occupy Rhodesia and the southern half of Mozambique: they are the Shona and the Thonga, while the Nguni (including the Zulu), the Ngoni and the Ndebele constitute the southernmost extension of the Bantu. The last wave of Bantu expansion carried the Tswana branch of the Sotho tribes westwards into the country known as Botswana, where they took over from the indigenous Bushmen. Sotho peoples now occupy Basutoland and a considerable area in the interior of the Union of South Africa.

A Zulu woman covered in carefully made bead necklaces.

The Bamileke

These peoples occupy a zone midway between tropical forest and savannah. Their language is also said to be midway between the Sudanic and Bantu languages and their racial characteristics are also mixed. The Bamileke had remained isolated from European contact until the nineteenth century when German explorers, traders and labour agents stumbled out of the Cameroon forest into the romantic world of princes and queens, palaces and royal harems, wide vistas of exquisitely cultivated gardens and farms, the world of the Bamileke peoples. Everything went smoothly for the German agents; instead of using their whips, their Mauser guns and their soldiers to persuade the local chief to provide them with food, sleeping quarters and a safe passage, they were overwhelmed with hospitality and gifts. Moreover, the chiefs in the Bamileke grasslands were not emaciated old men, who sat in the corner of a wattle and daub hut and lacked real political power, but powerful lords with a huge complement of retainers, slaves, warriors and wives, as well as common subjects who obeyed them as living gods.

The chief's palace is quite an appropriate word for the Bamileke ruler's home. In the past ten to twenty years, revolution, insurrection and reprisals have completely changed most of the traditional Bamileke landscape but the area where I stayed for two years escaped these recent, as well as more long-term, changes. The chiefs still lived in their splendid compounds, served by retainers and surrounded by wives, fifty not being considered an excessive number. Since there are no villages, the centre of his country is the market with its great drums and sacred copse, and the palace itself. A Bamileke market is an open space, divided into

The paramount chief of the Bamileke standing in front of his palace. Palaces are elaborately carved and painted contributing to the glory of a chief.

sections for selling livestock, foodstuffs, oil, mats, carved objects, European cloth, palm wine, and comes to life once during their eight-day week when the people pour in from every corner of the country to buy and sell, bargain and barter, chat and quarrel, settle disputes, get a little drunk. The rest of the week the only inhabitants of the market are the chief's dwarf cattle—of ritual significance, his sheep and goats, and his children. Between the market and the palace is a dancing green where public ceremonies take place, shaded by a patch of forest trees. A sacred copse, where certain secret societies meet, is also the burial place for royal children. The palace entrance itself is flanked by a row of servants' huts. These are linked by a verandah where people congregate and gossip, waiting to visit the palace or to speak to the chief or his second-in-command, the court chamberlain. Inside the porch and behind the high fern-pole fences the chief lives with his wives. He is left strictly alone from dusk to dawn, but during the daylight hours he is always in the company of his councillors, subchiefs, servants and subjects.

This architectural grandeur is found in the same country where simple hunters and pastoralists roam without even a permanent shelter. Yet these Bamileke kingdoms are also small-scale in their way: everything is in miniature. In the region where I lived there were nine kingdoms, the most important having a population of 15,000 (and many less in the nineteenth century) and the smallest—still a fully-fledged chiefdom—only a few hundred. In these statelets a chief would know personally all his adult subjects; he was not only a splendidly dressed, wealthy figure whom his subjects adored from a distance, but a friend and councillor, an in-law or relative. If, as occurred in one case, the chief has fifty wives, a corresponding number of children and only a hundred or so male subjects, the percentage of collateral royals—and hence kinsfolk—among the latter must be very high indeed.

The chief and his queen, his two titled wives (the 'first wife' and the 'favourite' wife), and the court chamberlain formed the palace nucleus. The chamberlain was usually the head of a long line of 'civil servants', who had become associated with the royal family in the government of the country. Together, he and the chief settled disputes between subjects, took political decisions, celebrated ceremonies, protected the palace and the people from the plague of witchcraft and sorcery and worshipped the ancestors for the benefit of the royal family and the general public.

In administering their chiefdom the chief and his chamberlain depend on subchiefs and local notables who settle disputes in their hamlets, collect tributes and round up warriors in wartime—all on behalf of the central power. They depend even more on the servants and pages who inhabit the palace precincts. The origins of these retainers vary: some are slaves and descendants of slaves, but even free men could choose to become a servant, since working at the palace entailed material advantages. Sometimes, this even included the gift of a wife—a very expensive person—at the end of a period of service. Pages are recruited from the sons of subchiefs. Palace retainers are ranked; the greatest of them all is the chamberlain, whose powers approximate to those of a prime minister and his servant status is not obvious. Other servants are distinguished according to their work or rank and wear special necklaces, caps and wristlets in token of these positions. Some work around the palace, others supervise community labour, collect dues and bridewealth or arrange the marriage of princesses. Menial work is done by lower ranks in the chief's palm oil plantations. A chief often trusts these ex-slaves and palace retainers more than his wealthy brothers or powerful subchiefs since they are more beholden to him; like the chamberlain they may acquire political influence through their close intimacy with the chief.

Bamileke chiefs are wealthy men, a wealth primarily concentrated in women and, formerly, slaves. Women as wives are a source of prestige, children and labour, consequently polygamy is practised by most of the men who can afford it. Bridewealth is high and bachelors take many years to accumulate sufficient money to marry. Wealth is also stored in livestock (cows, goats and sheep), currency (now Cameroon francs, but formerly all kinds of beads, cowrie shells, iron bars, copper rods) and works of art. The Bamileke are renowned as carvers, beadworkers, featherworkers and blacksmiths and their work contributes to the glory and wealth of the chiefs. Compounds of rich men are ornately painted and embellished

The costume of this Bamileke dancer is trimmed with animal fur and he wears a special mask for this dance.

with carving. Masks are painted and covered in skins or copper plating. Statues in the likeness of the ancestors are sometimes covered with beads. Fetishes are fashioned in grotesque forms to frighten witches and hunt out sorcerers. The chiefs wear carved ivory bracelets and rings, eat from intricately worked bowls, keep off flies with beaded and carved flywhisks, and wear elaborate costumes of local stuffs.

In many ways these little grasslands kingdoms are quite miraculous in the elaboration of their material culture, not to speak of their social organisation and cosmology which is no less complex than that of the Dogon. How did it happen? Whence the refinements, the wealth, the elegant political system? The Bamileke chief can hardly be compared to the kings of Ashanti, Benin, Yoruba or the Congolese potentates in terms of power and grandeur; their kingdoms are small, their subjects few and their autocracy limited. Their wealth was derived from 'exploitation' but it did not imply degradation of their subjects: slaves were only slaves in the matter-of-fact sense of their having been bought. Children of slaves were as free as the son of a chief and could obtain power and influence themselves and even have their own slaves. Free men married slaves and it almost became the rule that a king's successor should be the son of a slave. Princesses also married slaves. Nor did the chiefs depend on forced labour from their subjects or taxation, although a certain amount of wealth derived from annual gifts of wine, oil and foodstuffs.

It was commercial enterprise which provided the Bamileke with the wherewithal to develop their unique and fascinating culture. Agriculture is a minor activity; the men rarely help their wives in the yam and corn fields. Men's occupations were trading, governing and war. Every chief and subchief worthy of the name clears a space, plants a shade tree and starts a market where local goods and European articles are exchanged. However, the prime source of wealth for these chiefs, a source which has well and truly dried up now, was the slave trade. Slaves were bought or captured elsewhere in the grassfields, channelled to forest

The Bamileke preserve a complex 'feudal' hierarchy. This is a Bamileke servant. Addressing superiors calls for an attitude of respect.

trading partners and sold to the white man at the coast or wealthy African plantation owners. A few of the male slaves and most of the women were kept to stock the ever-growing palaces as servants and wives. With their wealth the chiefs built their fine houses and assembly halls, encouraged carving and iron-working and enjoyed a standard of living which they shared, more or less, with their subjects.

This brief description of an African state, with its kings and queens, chamberlains and retainers, pages and slaves, ritual and etiquette, shows an exotic world, far from our own where many kings ride bicycles, and government is a distant concept which has reality only in tax forms and driving licences. In the Cameroon the palace is the centre of the state and the centre of the world. There, people come to enjoy the chief's munificence, eat at his table, seek his advice and protection and join in dances on special occasions. However, this world is not so exotic—I find the flavour of the Bamileke court in accounts of early medieval Europe. Like the Bamileke kings, Clovis and his descendants, for example, were theoretically absolute monarchs, supreme judges, makers of war and peace, their treasuries filled with war booty, profits from royal estates, fines, death duties and tribute. An elaborate palace organization grew up around the Frankish kings; retainers, often their slaves, ran their domestic establishment, acting as spies and agents throughout the kingdom just as Bamileke servants, in their hooded costumes, supervised the administration of the chiefdom. In Merovingian times, royal charters were signed by the king's bedroom servants and scribes and the palace provided military chiefs and councillors of states. In both African and

A Bamileke market where people from the grassland kingdoms congregate to trade goods and gossip.

European situations, political power was as far as possible denied to royal relatives in favour of members of the king's household who were slaves or descendants of slaves. In Africa, we have the not uncommon anomaly of free-born territorial chiefs who bow low to a royal pipe-bearer or chief eunuch who had the king's favour. In Europe, when the count of the stables became commander-in-chief of the Carolingian armed forces, he was still termed 'constable', while a bedroom servant could achieve the rank of 'chamberlain'. In some cases the chamberlain acquired such wealth and influence that he became the most powerful figure in the kingdom. In exactly the same way as many Bamileke chamberlains, the Merovingian mayor of the palace influenced all political decisions, gained control of wealth and acted as regent during the king's minority. In the Bamileke case such a rise to power might be stopped by summary banishment or a trumped-up charge of witchcraft and subsequent execution. In France less than one hundred and fifty years after the death of Clovis his descendants were do-nothing kings, long-haired recluses and in 751, Pippin the Short, mayor of the palace, became king of France and began the Carolingian dynasty.

South America

The arrival of man in the continent of South America certainly took place in relatively recent times: he came south from North America in the main, although scattered groups may have arrived across the Pacific Ocean from the Malayo-Polynesian regions. In the pre-Columbian era great empires flourished in places along the west coast and in the mountainous regions; here, living conditions were often difficult, but commerce easy and farming techniques advanced. Other parts of South America were only thinly settled by people of less advanced techniques and simpler social structure. In the Andean regions there existed many peoples who lay in the main path of the Spanish conquistadores and who were overwhelmed by them. The Spaniards were attracted by the abundance of gold ornaments and religious objects displayed in the native villages and were excessive and violent in their search for greater wealth. In modern times immigrants of Spanish, Portuguese, English and Italian origin have introduced Western European culture throughout the continent. And the descendants of African Negroes who originated as slaves now constitute a substantial part of the population of some countries, especially Brazil and the Guianas.

In South America it has been estimated that 15% of the population is Negro or Mulatto (of mixed Negro and European blood) and 13–15% are Indians. Of the remainder, the overwhelming majority, as in Central America and Meso-America, is undoubtedly *mestizo,* that is, a mixture of Indian and European elements in varying proportions. Colombia, Venezuela, Ecuador, Peru, Bolivia, Chile and Paraguay are all predominantly mestizo, either racially or culturally, but all have extant Indian minorities. These countries were all originally colonized by Spain and Spanish is the official language. Apart from these major groups—Indian, *mestizo,* White and Negro—there are other cultural enclaves. East Indians from Asia, for example, form 40% of the population of Guyana, descendants of the indentured labourers brought between 1837 and 1917 to work the sugar plantations. The same applies to Surinam. Then we have groups of English in Argentina, Welsh in Patagonia, Germans throughout the continent, Italians in Uruguay and Argentina, the Japanese of Brazil and the Javanese of Surinam.

It would be feasible to discuss in detail the cultures and traditions of many of the communities of Spanish and Portuguese origin, many of whom have established specifically Latin-American ways of life. I have been forced to be selective, concentrating mainly on the Indian cultures, due to the enormous numbers and the variety of peoples involved. In another sense the peoples of Hispanic culture share common values and customs based on Spanish traditions, particularly on the Roman Catholic church and the Spanish and Portuguese languages; while the various Indian tribes—only a fraction of whom I cover here—have extraordinarily diverse ways of behaving, looking at the world and speaking. Moreover it is the Indian culture which is on the wane and is therefore perhaps the more deserving of our attention; that of the *ladino* is not threatened.

South American Indians

Estimates as to the total number of Indians in the various South American countries vary considerably. Today there remain perhaps 800,000 Indians in the Amazon basin and adjoining lowlands. Any accurate count of numbers is made difficult by the fact that there is no general consensus as to what is an 'Indian'. Nevertheless the national censuses of the various countries provide the following general statistics. In Peru, the Ministry of Agriculture puts the total number of Indians as a quarter of a million in 64 different reserves. In other estimates the figures are much higher, probably due to the fact that Indians who speak some Spanish and have been absorbed into Latin cultures have been classified as 'White' or *'mestizo'*. In Brazil, native indigenes could number up to 100,000. In Colombia the figure is about 150,000. The Paraguayan Department of Indigenous Affairs, an arm of the Ministry of Defence, estimates the total of tribal peoples at roughly 60,000. Nevertheless, in Paraguay, there could be a case for calling three-quarters of the population 'indigenous', since they are predominantly of Guarani descent and the Guarani language is the lingua franca over much of the country. In Bolivia the number of Indians is estimated at 83,000—the largest group being the Chiquitanos. Venezuelan Indians amount to more than 100,000, the largest number being the Guajiro living in the Maracaibo and Orinoco regions. In Ecuador there may be 50,000 Indians; in Guyana some 33,000, while in Northern Argentina along the border with Paraguay there are possibly 50,000 more. Importantly, all these statistics exclude the Aymaras and Quechuas of the Andes who total 2,000,000 in Bolivia alone, and who are also the most important tribal groups in Peru and Ecuador. As always, however, these figures may only serve as a rough guide. Other statistics give quite different, usually much higher, results.

The way of life of every full-blooded Indian community may be said to be threatened in the twentieth century. Some have been assimilated and have settled beside mission stations, large farms, towns and outposts. Others live in reserves where settlers have taken root. In many of these areas there is no work and total depression has resulted from plans for enforced settlement. In many cases the sole protectors of the Indians against the ravages of land-grabbers are the missionaries, although some anthropologists and observers credit the rapid deterioration of the Indian morale to the blind attitudes of missionaries whose simple promise that the Christian God is the only true God may not be the answer to the 'Indian problem'.

A limited number of Indians live in happier circumstances, particularly in the huge protected Xingu part of Brazil administered by the Villas Boas brothers. This is an area of about 22,500 square kilometres, in which there live approximately 1500 Indians from 15 tribes, the remnants of hard-pressed Indian groups who are allowed to live according to their own ways, protected more or less successfully from the dangers of the outside world—oppression, illnesses, exploitation. This experiment has been a success; the Indian population is rising and the administration has been convinced that by this way Indians can be successfully blended into the modern world. Their plan includes a period of acclimatization for the Indian in which he is protected from the full shock of 'civilization', followed by a stage in which he adapts to the modern way of life at his own speed.

What is an Indian? On the whole Indians are recognized by cultural and not racial traits, i.e. by the very simple criteria of whether they speak an Indian language, wear Indian clothes and practise Indian traditions. In Peru and Bolivia, where roughly half the population is Indian, an Indian is a person who wears sandals, lives in a mud-walled, thatch-covered house, believes in a 'non-Christian' religion. A *mestizo* or *ladino* wears shoes, eats bread and lives in a tile-roofed house, practises Christianity and exhibits other features of Hispanic culture. If he has light skin or is of near-white descent from well-to-do 'criollos', mulattos of Spanish culture, he is White. Unlike the Indian, the Negro of South America can be distinguished physically. In the Guianas, Negroes inhabit an area including British-, French-, Dutch- and Portuguese-speaking Guiana and part of Venezuela. The indigenous Indian cultures have largely disappeared owing to the settlement in the country near and along the coast by Bush Negroes and escaped Negro slaves, who introduced an African culture which is maintained up till the present day. The Indians who remain include those of the Barama River Carib, the Camaracoto groups which tend to be matrilineal in social structure, with a religion centred on nature spirits, group ceremonies and shamanism, involving elaborate curing rites;

Quechua woman weaving by the old Inca method. The Quechua wear full skirts and varied styles of hats.

they also practise the couvade, an institution whereby the husband of a woman in childbirth undergoes a parallel, ritual suffering, thereby establishing his status as father of the child in a physical and social context.

Shamanism, involving spirit possession and curing rites, is basic to the religious beliefs of most of the South American Indians. 'Shaman', as a word, came into usage from the Russian, but was originally derived from the dialect of the Tungus of Siberia. Although found in classical form in Siberia, shamanism occurs throughout the world, mainly among nomads and hunters in the Americas, Asia, the Arctic, India and Indonesia. Shamanism, in South America, is frequently associated with the taking of stimulants and narcotics. The Tupinamba shaman, for example, fumigates his rattle with tobacco which is believed to contain an animating principle that confers on the rattle the facility of speaking, that is, of revealing the future.

Alcoholic beverages are consumed mainly during the religious festivals and obtained by fermenting manioc, corn and other plants. Coca leaves are chewed especially in the sub-Andean regions, and an infusion of maté is taken in Paraguay as well as by the Jivaro and other groups of Ecuador. Hallucinogens are used mainly in the Amazon-Orinoco region: they include banisteropsis, a species of tropical liana, from which is made a potion inducing visions. In certain tribes, the use of this drug is reserved to shamans; in others, as in the Uaupés river area, it is an essential element in religious festivals in which the community revives its mythic traditions. Other narcotics in ritual use, amongst which is the yopo (Piptadenia) known in northern groups, are often breathed in the form of snuff which partners blow into one another's nostrils. The Omagua of the Upper Amazon use it as an enema.

Some magical practices are reserved for the shaman, who acquires his status by natural endowment, by inspiration, by apprenticeship or by painful initiation. The shaman may practise medicine, perform magic rites and lead religious ceremonies. Rarely, however, is he a priest in the usual sense of the term. In many groups, his influence is superior to that of the political chief. In some, as among the Guarani, the two roles may coincide. Not uncommonly, his influence continues after death. In the Guianas, his soul becomes an auxiliary spirit of his living colleagues, helping them in their curing practices and in the control of harmful spirits.

In curing the sick, the shaman must remove the object causing the sickness—a small stone, a leaf, an insect, any substance that has been sent through the black

A Guarani-speaker in the southern Mato Grosso thatching his house.

magic of an evil doer. The cure consists of massages, suction and blowing and fumigation. If the illness comes from loss of the soul, the shaman must search for and recover it. If it comes from a bad spirit he tries to overcome the evil influence with the help of one or more auxiliary spirits.

Anthropologists have divided South America into cultural zones based on a variety of criteria—linguistic, geographical, or according to the mode of livelihood of the indigenous populations. Linguists have reduced the hundreds of languages and dialects into three very general groupings: the 'Andean-Equatorial' languages distributed from northern Peru southward through most of the Andes and the Chilean archipelago to Terra del Fuego and east of the Andes and the Chilean archipelago. The distribution of this language group shows a general picture of population movements along the Andes from north to south. The 'Macro-Chibchan' family of the northern Andes of Ecuador and Colombia (as well as Central America) was localized in an area of traditional chiefdoms which expanded from south to north—from South America to North America. The 'Ge-Pano-Carib' group is confined largely to tropical forest peoples of the Amazon and East-Brazilian highlands and the Brazilian coast.

The continent may also be categorized according to cultural-geographical criteria—the Chibchan, Andean, Antillean, Amazon, Eastern Brazilian Highland, Chaco, Patagonian (Pampan), Araucanian and Southern (Fuegian) areas.

For our purposes it is most convenient to consider the area as being divided into four very general cultural zones: the Central Andean irrigation cultures; the former chiefdoms of the northern Andes; the tropical forest farming villages; and the nomadic hunters and gatherers. It should be mentioned that the first two regions, while still maintaining flourishing Indian populations, have long lost their ancient cultures based on centralized state systems and striking class distinctions.

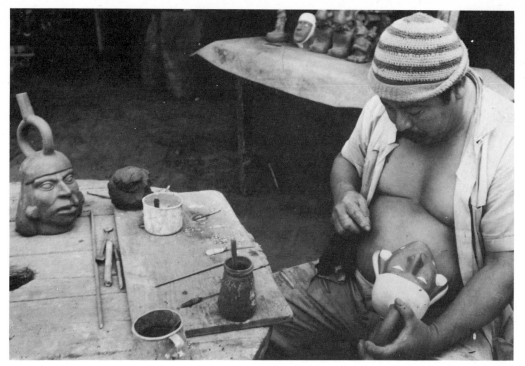

A Moche descendant making a replica Moche pot in Peru. Tribes are being encouraged to preserve ancient crafts.

The Central Andean irrigation civilizations

In the Central Andean Region, in Peru and Bolivia, almost half of the population is Indian, some of them descendants of the legendary Inca. Although most Indians now work on modernized plantations, one of the genuinely Indian of the coastal cultures is that of Moche, a community which differs from its neighbours, not so much in retaining a pre-Columbian culture as in the presence of such sixteenth-century Spanish features as witchcraft ritual and household ceremonies. On the whole the Indian populations of the mountains have been migrating to the lower valleys and the coast. However the population that remains is still strongly Indian and they still speak the Quechua and Aymara languages. The traditional culture survives—the family sod or stone huts, pottery, llama wool ponchos being distinctive characteristics of the Indian. Other groups live in self-contained 'closed' villages. The community usually consists of several extended patrilineal families related to one another through marriage. Their religion is a tangle of Catholic and Pagan beliefs which entail ritual celebrations geared to a Christian church calendar. Religion is integrally a part of the political, social and economic life of the community and has only a tenuous connexion with the Catholic church. Nearly all the communities have land set aside for the support of elaborate religious ceremonies.

The Buca is a group which includes a very large number of tribes inhabiting the Andean highlands and the Pacific coast of Peru, peoples once part of the Inca empire. They practise intensive agriculture with irrigation and terraced fields. They hunt and herd llamas.

The Aymara practise their ancient Indian culture, some living on floating islands of totora reeds, fishing from reed boats which still have reed sails and have

not changed noticeably in two thousand years. The Aymara Indians number about 600,000 and live predominantly in the Titicaca Basin in Peru and Bolivia in villages. Nowadays they grow crops for sale in the market, like onion, potatoes, beans and guinea corn. Chicha, a maize beer, is drunk and coca—a drug—is chewed.

The Northern Andes

In the Northern Andes, an extensive and geographically varied region, many Indians were unable to hold out against the avaricious Spanish conquistadores. Among the chiefdoms were the Chibcha of highland Ecuador (the greatest of them all) and the Coconuco, Pijao, Paez, Puruha, Cana and Palta of the northern Andes; the Jirajara and their neighbours, the Caequetio, Palenque and Cumanagoto of northern Venezuela.

The Guajiro Indians, speaking an Arawak language, still live at the northern end of the continent on the Guajiro peninsula, and practise a successful nomadic economy based on horses and cattle. As well as herding, they trade skins and salt with Columbian and Venezuelan traders for spirits, ammunition and other western products. They have matrilineal kinship groups and combine a form of shamanism with Catholicism. The Guajiro culture has survived well into the twentieth century despite the fact that they were driven by the Spaniards into a very arid peninsula. From being hunters and gatherers they became herdsmen and even work their own mines. The women still gather wild vegetables and the men sometimes hunt.

Further south, other farmers and pastoralists include the Atacama of the desert oases, the Diaguita farmers of the semi-deserts and the Araucanian Indians, numbering 300,000, who once covered a vast area in Chile, but nowadays live restricted to the south. The best known tribes are the Picunche, Mapuche and Huilliche. They live in reservations and grow wheat and potatoes as well as herding sheep and cattle.

The tropical forest farmers

The Indians we know most about and who still maintain their traditional style of life to the greatest extent are all mainly tropical forest dwellers. These Indians live in villages of thatched houses, sleep in hammocks, use dug-out canoes, make pottery and live on root crops such as manioc and sweet potatoes supplemented by

Aymaras living on the floating reed island on Lake Titicaca. Fish, the staple diet, are drying in the foreground.

fish and game. Unlike the peoples of the Andes, these groups lacked chiefdoms, social classes, and temple-idol cults. The distribution of this homogeneous type of culture coincides to a remarkable degree with that of the tropical rain forests as defined in geographical terms, through most of the Amazon basin, and down the coastal Brazil strip; it is also found in Paraguay and a part of Bolivia.

The tropical forest dwellers may be divided into linguistic families. Caribans inhabit the Lesser Antilles, Arawaks and Caribans are found in the Guianas and lowland Venezuela. Tupian-speaking peoples predominate on the lower Amazon (Mundurucu, Parintintin, Arua, Omagua, Cayabi, etc.). The Mundurucu are the best known group living in villages of up to thirty, dwelling in matrilineal households, based on women, but are also divided into patrilineal clans and dual divisions known as moieties, based on men. This is known as a double-descent system. Their culture, particularly their elaborate fertility rites, was violently affected by the rubber trade. On the coast of Brazil there are the Tupinamba and in Paraguay the Guarani. The Guarani constitute most of the million or so peoples of nuclear Paraguay. While many of these people also speak Spanish, popular belief holds that Guarani culture as well as language has been perpetuated in Paraguay. In fact there is little left of Guarani culture and Paraguayan-Guarani social organization and religion is typical of lower-class Spanish culture.

Also sharing this culture were the Panoans, and the Kawapanans living in the foothills of the Andes above the Amazon basin; and the Catukinans on the Jurua and Purus rivers. Arawak and Cariban groups are also found in eastern Colombia, the best known of which are the Motilon who still avoid contact with Europeans. On the lower west coast of Colombia and the southern coast of Panama,

Guajiro Indian women, their faces covered with mud masks to protect them against the sun, ride donkeys across the arid peninsula in Colombia.

OPPOSITE:
Dinka tribesmen standing smoking clay pipes at dusk in Juba, Sudan. The Dinka are cattle herders, and use cattle as part of dowries as well.

the Choco retain much of their traditional way of life. The Chuncho, a collective name for a large group, inhabit the eastern flank of the Andes from Ecuador to Bolivia.

In eastern Bolivia we have an even greater cultural diversity with people including the Sinabo, Chacobo, Caripuna and Pacaguara linguistic groups and the Tiatinagua, Leko, Yuracare and Chapakura.

Along the north-west Amazon, the best known of many groups are the Tucuna and the Witoto. In the eastern Colombian lowlands there are the Guayape and Sae, the Achagua and Saliva, along with the Caribbean groups—the Betoi, Patangoro, Guajiro and Mosquito.

In the Amazon area we find groups of warlike peoples who once practised headhunting, their religious ceremonies honouring the ghosts. In the highland plateau of eastern Brazil is a block of Ge-speaking peoples. The majority of these Ge-speakers were formerly nomadic hunters and include the north-western Ge, the Timbira, southern and northern Cayapo, and the Suya. The Shavante and the Sherente form the central Ge. Other groups of the eastern Brazilian highlands are the Caingang and Bororo.

The Ge and the Bororo live in villages whose house arrangements reflect certain features of their social organization. The Ge village contains several hundred persons whose houses are characteristically placed in a circle or semi-circle around a central plaza in which the men's or bachelors' house stands. The dwellings moreover are grouped according to moiety membership of their occupants. The Bororo houses are also arranged in northern and southern halves which are cross-cut by moiety membership referred to as 'Upstream and Downstream' divisions. The Bororo dwelling is built by men but following matrilineal principles, it is owned by the women of the several families who are related through a female lineage in the clan. In the house each nuclear family has its own fireplace and

OPPOSITE:
A Bamileke man from the Cameroon in the elaborately carved doorway of his house.

Despite being discovered as early as the 18th century, the Bororo cling proudly to their culture. This is a Bororo chief.

platform beds. The Bororo men's house is the centre of the village and the worship and ceremonial centre for all men of the community as well as a dormitory for bachelors; women are strictly excluded.

The Yanoama constitute one of the largest Indian tribes of South America and a linguistic subgroup has recently been described in some detail by Napoleon Chagnon, an American anthropologist. The Yanomamö live in Southern Venezuela and the adjacent portions of Northern Brazil and number more than 10,000. Their interest stems primarily from the fact that they were still warring in traditional fashion when observed by Chagnon in the sixties. Aggression is expressed in their culture in a very positive way—in wife-beating, chest-pounding, duelling and organized raiding by parties that set out with the intention of ambushing and killing men from enemy villages. This chronic state of warfare is reflected in their mythology, values, settlement pattern, political behaviour and marriage practices. Their fierceness is often stimulated by drugs, wads of green tobacco stuck between their lower teeth and lips. The drug is fabricated by scraping the bark of a tree, mixing this with ashes and making it into a wad, ground into powder and dried. It is taken by blowing into the nostrils through a cane tube. The recipient usually vomits and develops a green runny nose—within minutes he starts acting intoxicated and the drug produces coloured visions and permits the user to enter into contact with his particular spirit who lives under rocks and in the mountains.

The Yanomamö explain and justify the nature of their constant ferocity towards each other and their neighbours in myths and legends. They also indulge in competitive aggressive feasts where hospitality is often rewarded by hostility in the form of chest-pounding competitions. Here in the village, with visitors and

Yanomamö hut on the Catrimani reservation in Brazil, built with vines and leaves, and poles for the frame.

hosts divided into two arenas, the two champions, one from each side, confront one another. One steps up, legs apart, bared chest, and dares the other to hit him, which he does delivering a close-fisted blow on the chest and putting all his weight into the blow. Punishment is accepted willingly, but the only reward is status and the reputation of being strong and fierce. Often these individual contests develop into fights involving stones or axe duels resulting in bloodshed.

During religious rites as well, aggression is a marked aspect of the proceedings. In a ceremony to ward off evil spirits, a score of men, streaked with their green nasal mucus, grow aggressive and violent as the combined effect of magic and drugs hits them. The fierce ones of the village are driving out the imagined illnesses that the shaman has said were sent by enemies from a nearby village. Their behaviour is unpredictable and very violent, due to the ecstacy induced by the drugs. The rules of the rite allow the men to frighten women and children and discharge a few arrows.

Yanomamö woman and children outside a hut. The woman's duty lies traditionally in the house; she has to look after children, keeping them close at all times in case of abduction by rival tribes. She is decorated with red pigment and sticks inserted at the corners of her mouth in childhood. Her leather strap is a versatile means of carrying articles.

Amongst the Yanomamö, violence and war are valued cultural institutions. Aggression is even associated with trade and friendship; fighting permits allies to display the fact that they are friendly but capable of defending their sovereignty. Two fierce chest-pounders, for example, may embrace each other intimately, vow eternal friendship and ask each other for specific trade goods. It is merely that Yanomamö values demand a display of ferocity, a display which reduces the possibility of neighbours constantly fighting at a more serious level. Duelling, although violent, is innocuous and has rules, and even the club fights are between groups which remain on the whole peaceful; these usually arise from arguments over women. Clubs over two metres long are used and aimed at the opponent's head. The tops of most men's heads are covered with proud scars kept cleanly shaved to show them off.

The Yanomamö fight wars constantly, not for land or other goods: the chronic disposition to do battle, to oppose and dispose of one's independent neighbours is part and parcel of their way of life and political organization. The objective of a 'raid'—the basis of Yanomamö warfare—is to kill one or more of the enemy and flee without being discovered. Women are captured and are raped by all the men in the raiding party and later in the village, and then given to one of the men as a wife. Apart from women, most wars are a prolongation of earlier hostilities stimulated by revenge motives. The causes may originally have been sorcery, a murder or a club fight resulting in death. The raids are self-perpetuating and continue over the years.

Mosquito

Carib
Caequetio
Guanahably
Guajiro
Jirajara
Palenque
Warrau
Betoi
Chibcha
Yaruro
Camaracoto
Carib
Choco
Chiricoa
VENEZUELA
COLOMBIA
Macu
Arawak
Patangoro
Achagua
GUYANA
SURINAM
FRENCH
GUIANA
Coconuco
Sae
Saliva
Guayupe
Yanoama
Paez
Pijao
Motilon
Quaharibo
Witoto
Shiriana
Puruha
Tupinamba
Quecha
ECUADOR
Tucuna
Jivaro
Palta
Omagua
Mura
Mundurucu
Ge-speaking
peoples
Parintintin
P E R U
B R A Z I L
Cana
Nambicuara
Aymara
Siriono
BOLIVIA
Bororo
Chiquitano
Guato
Atacama
Guaitaca
PARAGUAY
Puri-Coroado
Diaguita
CHILE
Guarani
Guaycumuan
Caingang
Araucanian
A R G E N T I N A
URUGUAY

SOUTH AMERICA
some names mentioned in the text

Chono

Alacaluf

Yaghan

The pursuit of political goals by means of violence results in an attempt to keep as much space as possible between one's group and that of neighbours—known and feared as sorcerers and witches. Much of the fighting also has to do with the acquisition and raping of women who are in short supply. The Yanomamö, like many simple peoples, marry those whom they fight.

The intensity of warfare is very variable, although it is constant. Wars wax and wane from one decade to the next. Nevertheless, the simple statistic, observed by Chagnon, that out of fifty-nine men only seven died in their beds, the rest dying in war, makes the significance of violent attack for the Yanomamö quite clear.

Hunters and gatherers

Hunters and gatherers, through South America, inhabit or inhabited marginal lands, peripheral to centres of great cultural development. All of Argentina and the archipelagic zone of southern Chile once comprised the habitat of such hunters and gatherers as the Chono, the Alacaluf, the Yaghan. In the Gran Chaco region there were the Guaycuruan Indians (Abipon, Mataco, Vilela and others) who were migratory peoples roaming the grassy plains of their small territories in search of rhea, guanaco, peccary and jaguar. At the time of their discovery by European colonialists, the nomads lived in regions that were economically marginal, avoiding their more powerful and warlike neighbours who inhabited the arable lands along the principle river systems. These hunting groups are—or mostly were—of different types: the shellfish gatherers of southern Chile, the plains hunting bands of Argentina and Patagonia, the forest hunters and gatherers of Brazil. They all inhabited areas of the sparsest population and their social structure strongly reflects the demands of the food quest—individualistic and competitive in the collection of food and co-operation in hunting and fishing. Hunting bands are either patrilineally or matrilineally organized, but some bands such as the Chono, the Alacaluf and western Yaghan of the Chilean archipelago have only the elementary family as their basic unit. The Nambicuara of the southern Mato Grosso reasonably disperse into individual family groups. The Ona, Haush and eastern Yaghan are organized into patrilineal bands, while the Guaki and Siriono are matrilineal. The Gran Chaco peoples lived in composite matrilineal bands.

Other little-known groups include the southern Cayapo, Mura, Shiriana, and the Chiricoa. With the notable exception of the Mura, none of these bands was warlike. The Mura were famous predators who spent much of their time stealing food from their farming neighbours. They were good canoemen and fully exploited the rivers for fish, mammals and turtle eggs. They used bark canoes. Today, with their pacification, the Mura have tended to merge with the Neo-Brazilian population.

The hunters and gatherers usually known as 'foot nomads', include the Siriono of Bolivia, the Guaka of Paraguay, the Nambicuara of the Mato Grosso, the Puri-Coroado and Guaitaca of the Brazilian coast. Also belonging to this general classification are the Macu of the Amazon jungles, the Quaharibo and Chiricoa of eastern Columbia and the Guanahatably of the Western Antilles. There are other nomads known as the 'Aquatic nomads' and these include the Guato of the Upper Paraguay river, where they live for most of the year in dug-out canoes, the Mura, already mentioned, the Yaruro of the Orinoco tributaries, and the Warrau of the Orinoco Delta.

Only the Siriono, however, are at all well known. They occupy the dense tropical forests of eastern Bolivia. Disease has decimated them in the past generation and they probably number less than 2000, living in widely scattered small bands. They hunt more than forty species of game and eat many varieties of wild plants, especially the palm cabbage. Hunting is rarely co-operative as among the Ge; individuals stalk and shoot game with bows, seven to eight feet long, and arrows even longer. The animal food quest follows a regular pattern. During the dry season the Siriono may clear a patch of forest, plant maize and manioc and sweet potatoes, and then move off in search of game and wild plant foods, visiting the clearing from time to time only long enough to care for the field. They return to harvest and store the crops in large palm baskets and then resume their travels. They cross rivers on felled trees or by swimming and carrying a firebrand with them from one camp to another, since they say they have forgotten how to make fire. They build large, flimsy huts which shelter the whole band of from thirty to a hundred people. Each band is matrilineal and is composed of elementary families related through women. The different Siriono bands are seldom in contact and the band leader has minimal authority. Their precarious lives and constant movement allow for little elaboration of ceremony and rite, although they dance and enjoy drinking bouts which frequently end in fighting. They consider the moon as a culture hero who gave them maize and manioc. The Siriono fear the spirits of the dead as evil and in order to ward off the spirits' malevolence while curing illnesses, they rub and chant over the skull of a dead person.

Central and Meso America and the Caribbean

Central America may be defined as the area from Panama to approximately the Ulua River in Honduras. This river marks the Maya frontier, a rather sharp boundary north of which were the great Meso-American cultures. Central America as a culture area then includes the prevailing indigenous peoples of Latin America south of Guatemala, as well as those of the northern coast of southern America. It also customarily includes the West Indies.

Most indigenous cultures in the area did not survive the arrival of the Europeans, and those that did are little more than 'relics'. The Cuna of Panama, a once important group, has become largely Hispanicized, although their colourful dress still makes them distinctive. The Lenca are the northernmost of the Indians of Central America. Their culture is Meso-American in character but their language is Chibchan. The Lenca are nominally of Roman Catholic faith, but maintain traditional religious features such as a reverent attitude towards the sun. Shamans still serve them as curers.

While Central America is culturally diversified, with enclaves of tropical-forest farmers who once lived a simple village life among militaristic chiefdoms, it is, apart from the Lenca, culturally affiliated more with South America than Meso-America. The Chibchan languages of most of the Indians have their origins in South America, and so did most of the cultural features of their lives.

The Chibchan dialects are mostly mutually unintelligible and the societies speaking them had no overall political unity. (The Chibchan proper, or Muisca, lived in the Cordillera Oriental east of the Upper Magdalena River.) Also Chibchan-speaking are the Guaymi, Bribri, Cabecar, Chanquena, Guetar, Rama who live in the Caribbean lowlands of western Panama and Costa Rica. Today, they farm with slash-and-burn techniques, the men clearing and the women planting and cultivating. They also continue to hunt where possible, using traditional techniques. Social structure is showing the effects of modern economic changes;

Cuna women wearing molas, blouses made with a cut-out cloth base and sewn with tiny pieces of variegated cottons. Cuna women tend to wear gold nose ornaments and favour gold pendants as their ancestors did centuries ago.

and the enhanced importance of the individual, particularly in property-owning, has weakened kin groups. Descent is matrilineal, but private property tends to be inherited patrilineally. Chiefs today, if they exist, are only titular leaders without authority, but with some relics of their former prestige.

Since 1797, there has been living on the Carib coast of Central America a group of people known as the Black Caribs, descendants of the Red Caribs, who occupied the Lesser Antilles at the time of Columbus and when Africans were brought to the New World as slaves. These people having spread up and down the coast now live in a series of towns and villages from Stann Creek, British Honduras, to the Black River in Honduras.

There are no Amerindians in the West Indies, apart from a pitiful remnant of Caribs in Dominica. An early consequence of European colonization was the almost total destruction of local groups by the Spaniards, English, Dutch, Scots, Bretons and French. Then came African Negroes in their millions, captured, sold, and enslaved on the New World estates of the same European invaders. The slave-based plantation system effectively blocked white immigration, for the potential migrant could not sustain the capital expense to acquire land, labour and machinery for the cultivation of cane and the production of sugar. Slavery was abolished everywhere in the nineteenth century and in a number of places, new immigrants arrived—indentured labourers from India, Africa and China.

The distribution of persons of African origin is heavier in some Caribbean islands and countries than in others. In many islands, such as Jamaica, rural communities of European extraction survived only as tiny enclaves within populations of mainly African origin. In the ex-Spanish colonies of Puerto Rico, Cuba and Santa Domingo, large European populations were stabilized before the re-expansion of the plantation system in the late eighteenth century and this is reflected in the population and character of these people.

The African origin of the populations of many Caribbean islands has had important cultural effects, particularly in Haiti, a fact which closely reflects plantation history. Creoles, who constitute the major population of Caribbean societies, represent the intermixing of Spanish, Amerindian and African elements.

The last of the race which once dominated the Caribbean is found on Dominica. Once warlike cannibals, they are now peaceful farmers, banana-growers and Roman Catholics. When Columbus arrived in Dominica (on a Sunday!), he found the island occupied by 'Caribs'. These fierce people, however, were not the original inhabitants of this island, since they were themselves immigrants who had come from the northern coast of South America, sailing from island to island in dug-out canoes. Nevertheless, the Caribs who survive in Dominica are probably the purest racial group to survive anywhere; they have high, wide cheekbones, the epicanthic fold and straight black hair, all of which clearly demonstrates their Mongoloid ancestry.

What about the linguistic position? In Guyana, the Caribbean and Louisiana, various new languages such as Sranan (Negro English), Saramakkan, Papiamentu, Negro Dutch, French Creole have emerged and for the most part prospered. These languages are peculiar in combining rather similar grammatical structures of a seeming African type with vocabularies that are predominantly European. Saramakkan is spoken by the Bush Negroes on the upper reaches of the Surinam River. Papiamentu is confined to the three Dutch islands of Curacao, Aruba and Bonaire. Sranan is spoken in Surinam.

'Meso-America', or 'Middle-America', is a term used primarily to indicate the general cultural zones of pre-Spanish, Mayan and Aztec civilisations. The northern border of Meso-America runs from a point on the Gulf coast of Mexico, just above the modern port of Tampico, then, dipping south to exclude much of the central desert of Highland Mexico, it ends up at the Pacific Coast opposite the tip of Lower California. Thus, Meso-America includes half of Mexico, all of Guatemala, British Honduras, El Salvador and parts of Honduras and Costa Rica.

The Indian cultures of these countries, from their agricultural beginnings around 6,500 BC, produced empires with elaborate political structures, an advanced agrarian technology, and monumental architecture; and they developed economic, social and religious systems—all elements of the most advanced world civilizations achieved at that time. The Mayans and Aztecs possessed cities, temples of stone, a form of writing, and a priesthood performing complex calendrical calculations. They had no metal, no wheel and no animal power.

After the Spanish conquest, the numbers of colonists increased and the Indians declined, due to disease, warfare, rebellion, etc. On the whole, the Indians were collected into communities and 'converted' to Christianity. Today, people are divided into Hispanic, or national cultures on the one hand (these are non-Indian whites and *mestizos*—or people of mixed blood), and Indians on the other. In a few

The Negro ancestry of this Black
Carib woman is apparent.

places, negroes remain ethnically distinct; examples are the Black Caribs of
Guatemala and the Belize Negroes of British Honduras. Mexico is basically *mestizo*
and there has been long and extensive interbreeding between Indians and non-
Indians.

The Indians of Meso-America

When Meso-America was conquered by the Spanish, this area was divided into
many kingdoms and tribes. Though all of Mongoloid stock, they varied in physical
type, language and cultural achievements. All of them, however, were descended
from Asiatic forebears who crossed the Bering Strait and moved southward across
northern America. Except in the isthmus of Tehuantepec, the Middle-American
Indian tends to be small in stature—not much over five feet or 155–160 cm—with
brown to coppery skin, straight black hair and dark brown eyes often above high
cheek bones, sometimes with epicanthic folds, the folds of skin over the eyes
characteristic of Mongoloid races. Mayan facial features are particularly
distinctive, being flatter than those of other groups: the Maya also have more
prominent noses and a tendency to rounder heads. Despite the distinctive
appearance of the Mayans and other Indian groups, it should be stressed that
'Indian' is not a racial term, but a social, economic, cultural or linguistic distinction.
The terms 'Indian' and *'ladino'* (Latin or European in culture) imply differences
between traditional, rural ways of life and the dominant Spanish culture, just as in
South America, which we looked at earlier.

The conquered Indians, who were forcibly baptized, did not lose their sense of
identity and many of them speak their distinct language and have distinct cultural
features. Nevertheless, the descendants of the Mayans and Aztecs have all been
Europeanized to an extent. Typical Indians, as opposed to *ladinos*, inhabit small
villages and look towards a common and usually Christian religious centre, the
image of the saint who is their patron. Villagers tend to intermarry and their way of
life is uniform without being politically unified. Most have the *compadrazgo*
institution described in more detail later, shamanism and festas, when the saints are

This is a Mayan calendar monument. For the Maya, time was an important matter in ritualistic, divinatory and social matters.

passionately celebrated. Only a few isolated groups have remained un-Christianized: the Lacandon, of the extreme south-east of Mexico, are a scattered people who number less than two hundred and live in smaller groups in a thickly-forested mountainous area, close to the Guatemalan frontier. Their habitation is almost 40,000 square miles of jungle with each village several days' journey from the next.

The census definition of an Indian is purely linguistic: if a person speaks Spanish, he is a national or Ladino. If he only speaks an Indian language, he is an Indian. In Mexico, there are two-and-a-half million speakers of Indian languages, living chiefly in the states of Oaxaca, Chiapas and Michoacan in the Yucatan Peninsula, although some Indian speakers are found in all states except Agua Scalinetes, Nuevo Leon and Tamaulipas. More than half the population of Guatemala speak Indian languages, over a million of them in the western highlands. Other Indian areas in Guatemala are the Verapaz and eastern Highlands. It has been estimated that six million Indians speak an indigenous language, even if not exclusively.

There is an extreme diversity of languages throughout the area, despite a long history of pro-Spanish activity and the use of Spanish in religious and government affairs. There are more than fifty distinct Indian languages, none of which

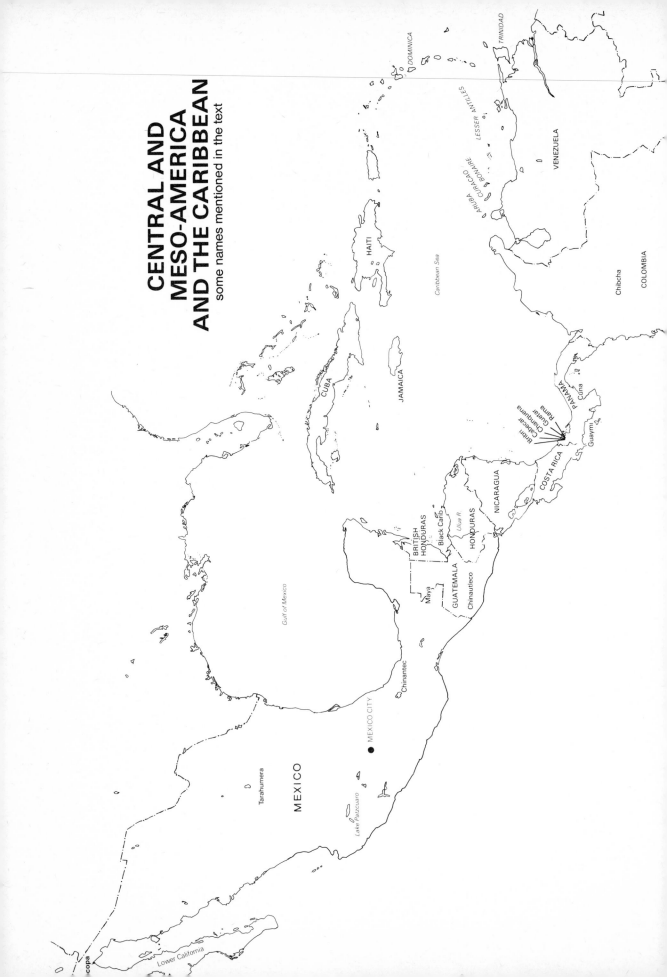

CENTRAL AND MESO-AMERICA AND THE CARIBBEAN

some names mentioned in the text

MEXICO

Tarahumera

Lower California

copa

Lake Patzcuaro

MEXICO CITY

Chinantec

Gulf of Mexico

CUBA

JAMAICA

HAITI

DOMINICA

TRINIDAD

LESSER ANTILLES

ARUBA
CURAÇAO
BONAIRE

VENEZUELA

COLOMBIA

Chibcha

Caribbean Sea

PANAMA

Cuna

Guaymi

COSTA RICA

Bribri
Cabecar
Chanquena
Guetar
Rama

NICARAGUA

HONDURAS

Ulua R.

Black Carib

BRITISH HONDURAS

Maya

GUATEMALA

Chinautleco

Lacandon Indians, descendants of the Maya, in the jungle of the Chiapas, Mexico.

unfortunately has a wide intelligibility for use as a *lingua franca*. These languages have been classified into three main language families: Uto-Aztecan, which includes a million Aztec speakers; Mayan, or Hokaltecan, which includes Yucatec, Quiche-Tzutuhil, Mam and Kekchi; and the Oto-Manguean family, comprising the Mixtec, Zapotec and Atomo languages.

The Maya constitute one of the largest remaining Indian groups: more than two million of them live in the Mexican states of Chiapas and Yucatan, in the Guatemalan highlands and British Honduras. In Guatemala, more than half the population speak Mayan and associated languages. In these regions, the Maya form a continuous territorial—and share a common historical—identity. They live much as they did generations ago. Mayan speakers include the Aguacatec, Cakchiquel, Chorti, Ixil, Jacaltec, Kanhobal, Kekchi, Pokoman, Pokonchi, Quiche, Chuh, Uspantec, Rabinal, Tzeltal, Mam, Lacandon, Tzotzil, Tojolabal, Tzutuhil, Solomec.

Let us look in more detail at how one Indian group has adopted to life with the *ladinos*. The Chinautleco are Indians of Mayan descent who have constituted a distinctive group for hundreds of years and live a few miles only from Guatemala City. In the early sixteenth century, the indigenous Mayan Indians of the area were defeated by the Spaniards whom they accepted as their 'conquerors'; they brought blankets, feathers and gold as tribute and since then, contact between the *ladino* (a person of Spanish culture) and Indian has been continuous, the *ladino* coming as priest, administrator, teacher and landowner. Today the Chinautleco Indians live alongside *ladinos*; the relationship between these two pervades Chinautleco life—Indians are proud of their descent from an ancient Mayan race, while *ladinos* consider the Spanish conquerors as their ancestors and see themselves as transmitters of the Spanish heritage. The Indian community maintains a suspicious attitude, not only to the small Spanish population, but to the whole outside world; envy and mistrust also mark the attitude of different Indian groups within the community. It is in the Catholic church and the bonds of friendship that individuals seek emotional fulfilment and an escape from the press of a hard life—marriage does not provide this release, since husband-and-wife relations are conducted on a businesslike and formal basis.

Apparently Chinautleco friendship—*camaradia*—reaches its highest intensity at that transition in life in which young men achieve adult status without acquiring its emotional rewards. Most adolescents and young men have 'best friends' with

Cultural continuity and stability are salient features of Chinautleco society; outsiders are viewed with suspicion.

whom they share secrets and ambitions and plan love affairs. The relationship is institutionalized in so far as the particular friendship between two men is publicly known and talked about: 'Yes, Miguel is Antonio's friend'. Friendships are made and broken almost with the ceremony and formality of a betrothal between a youth and his fiancée.

Among the Indians, friendships of all kinds play as important a role as kinship. One of these institutionalized friendship relations, found throughout Latin America, is the *compadrazgo*, or parent/god-parent, relationship. The christening ritual among the Chinautleco not only establishes a spiritual relationship between godparents and the child; in most cases it is the friendship which results between the parents of the child and the godparents which explains why this Christian institution flourishes in South America today. The christening ceremony sanctions friendly relations between friends and neighbours, with the child acting as a symbol of this friendship. And if there is no child handy, a couple of unrelated men, who want to become firm friends, will christen a tree or sponsor a shrine—thereby becoming the closest of *compadres,* or godparents (the old English word was godsib or gossip).

The *compadrazgo* institution is used to gain friends and allies or to impose a ceremonial relationship on an already established friendship. Chinautleco parents are careful to find the right person to accept sponsorship of their child. It is believed, for example that a *compadre* with 'good luck' can influence the course of his godchild's life. When an Indian chooses a superior *ladino* as godparent of his children, however, he is consciously using the institution as a means of building up materially advantageous relations for himself as well as for the child. *Ladinos* and Indians who are *compadres* address each other on equal terms—they use the *tu* form of address instead of the formal *usted*—and refer to each other as 'my compadre'. It is interesting that between villagers who are both Indian, i.e. native,

A Chinautleco family in Guatemala. The Chinautleco are professional charcoal-makers and potters. Their tools have not changed for centuries.

the term 'compadre' is not used, possibly because the notion of equality does not need to be stressed, as it does between the wealthier, Spanish-speaking *ladino* and the Indian.

In Chinautleco, in fact, many other institutions reinforce friendship, and *compadrazgo* is relatively insignificant. We have seen the institutionalized friendships between the young and in the *confradria*, the association which organises fiestas in honour of the saints, co-operative friendships are formed between individuals of both sexes. Nevertheless friends are bound together through the ritual sponsorship of baptisms, marriages, confirmation and even the blessing of a shrine or a saint. Relations between co-godparents are usually renewed when other children are born and it becomes an on-going relationship. When a woman becomes pregnant it is immediately known, therefore, that the godmother of her other children will become responsible for the coming child. In one case, reported by Reina, the child of a woman was born dead and the godmother—the woman's *commadre*—hurried to the house, made the sign of the cross over the face of the child, baptizing it in the name of the Father, the Son and the Holy Ghost. And by placing a grain of salt on his lips she further ensured its future life as an angel. She then made a shroud of bright crepe paper, fired rockets at the house and the cemetery, and headed the funeral procession, burning incense all the while. She brought one and a half quarts of beer, a dollar's worth of bread, a chicken and other food. In this relationship brought about through *compadrazgo*, a woman was able to depend on her friend, the godmother of her children, to help at the death of her baby, since a permanent alliance had been set up between them at the birth of her first child.

We must add a sad postscript to our account of the Chinautleco. Their area was severely affected by the Guatemalan earthquake of 1976. Let us hope that the Chinautleco way of life survives this severe test.

An old Chinautleco man in Guatemala.

Non-Mayan cultural zones

The highland peoples of Southern Mexico developed the Aztec traditions of Mixtec and Zapotec, while the coastal peoples seem to have remained isolated. The Central Mexican Highlands constitute the central area of the former Aztec empire. Mexico City is built on the ruins of the Aztec capital of Tenochtitlan and descendants of the Aztecs still live in the area. In the mountain chain around the high lake of Patzcuaro, Tarascan cattle-raisers live in isolation and work out their original culture patterns. North-west Mexico has three types of culture, basically Hispano-Indian in nature. The early population was taken over by the Jesuits who built mission communities. The relative isolation of the region, following the collapse of Spanish power, together with the weakness of the Mexican government, permitted the survival of a blend of Spanish and Indian cultures.

Tribal groups include the Chinantec on the forested north-facing slopes of the Oaxaca mountains in Mexico, the Cuitlatec of the Mexican state of Guerrero, the Mixtec, a million Nahua (Mexico's largest indigenous group), 375,000 Otomo, now *mestizo*, and the Tarahumara who live in the mountains of south-western Chihuahua.

Strictly outside the Meso-American area, the Cocopa were once a large tribe in Baya or Lower California, the few survivors now living in poverty around San Luis in Sonora State. They live in reservations, supplementing their diet of maize by hunting deer and rabbits. There are only a score or two Kiliwa, speakers of an Aztecan language, who have lost their land and work as ranchers; their favourite occupation—as with many dispossessed peoples—is gambling.

North America

The North American 'melting pot' has not been a completely thorough one. The rapid transformation of Russians, Germans, Swedes, Japanese, and other immigrants into conforming 'Americans' over a phenomenally brief period has not been universal. Apart from the groups of American Indians who have been able to survive into the twentieth century—the Navahos are an example mentioned in this chapter—other ethnic groups have clung to their ancient traditions and even languages. Italo-Americans are an example. The Mormons may be American-speaking citizens of America, but their special way of life, their religion, their attitudes to non-Mormon America may justify their treatment as an 'ethnic group' within the American nation, composed of countless other ethnic communities. The innumerable communes distributed down the Californian coast and throughout America would also be more than happy to be considered in a book devoted in major part to communities considered primitive in some sense. Anthropologists who have studied in New Guinea and Africa have often returned to America and found rich ethnography in the ghettoes of New York or the suburbs of this or other American cities.

In this section I have concentrated on two aspects of this diversity within life in North America: there is a survey of Indian groups, in many ways a sad story as many of them are either extinct, dispersed, or tragically reduced to a few surviving members; and also included are some white American groups, who by force of circumstance (their poverty and their isolation) have remained outside the mainstream of American civilisation.

Columbus called the original inhabitants of North America 'Indians' in the mistaken belief that he had arrived at an island off the mainland of Asia, or even the fabled Indies themselves, and this name has remained in use until today. Among themselves, of course, the American Indians had no name distinguishing their race from any other, having no knowledge that any non-'American Indian' peoples existed. Throughout the continent, the Spanish found a bewildering variety of peoples, some in small bands, some in chiefdoms and federations.

The Medicine man of the Sioux in full ceremonial dress.

Since the discovery of America almost, the European invader has attempted to classify the Indian: by his position on a hypothetical evolutionary scale, by the language he speaks, by the type of social structure he enjoys, by his means of livelihood. More is known about the American Indian than any aboriginal group in the world and he has been observed, described and catalogued endlessly. In this brief survey, I have only attempted to divide up the Indians according to a very general geographical-cultural system worked out by American anthropologists.

The south-eastern farming Indians

The tribes and confederacies of the south-eastern culture area may be characterized as possessing productive farming techniques of an advanced nature. They had relatively complex social and political institutions and elaborate ceremonial and ritual lives. Most of the tribes were soon destroyed or dramatically changed after contact with the European invaders. On the whole, they were sedentary farmers living in palissaded villages with important ceremonial centres—earthern mounds serving as platforms on which the great ceremonial activities took place. Culture traits include cranial deformation, matrilineal descent, clans named after animals and plants, tribes divided into halves (known as moieties), sometimes a hereditary class system. War was everywhere important and ceremonialized, and successful warriors were given great honours.

Cherokee woman weaving baskets of honeysuckle vine on a white oak base. Colours are achieved with natural dyes made from formulas passed down the generations.

The south-eastern tribes includes the Catawba, Creek, Natchez, Timucua, Koasati, Chickasaw, Alabama, Chatot, Apalachee, Pensacola, Mobile, Biloxi, Chitimacha, Atakapa, Avoyel, Choctaw, Tunica, Quapaw, Yuchi, Cherokee, Calusa, Caddo, Hichiti.

Many different languages were spoken, the most widespread being the Muskogean language family in Georgia, Alabama, Mississippi and parts of Louisiana and Tennessee. The Muskogeans once numbered over 50,000 people and included the Creek and Natchez who occupied a number of villages in the vicinity of the present-day city of Natchez, Mississippi.

The Natchez were organized into an elaborate chiefdom; the chief was the 'Great Sun' and important nobles 'suns', and all aristocrats were treated with extreme deference. The Great Sun was the symbol for the entire chiefdom. His succession and funeral rites were spectacular, and in the latter case, wives, guards and retainers died with him. The Great Sun was the eldest son of 'White Woman' (descent was matrilineal), and his next brother was 'Little Sun and Great War Chief'. All the remaining brothers were 'Suns'. Then came nobles and honoured people and, lastly, 'Stinkards', the lowest caste. Although, in 1940, two old people of Natchez ancestry were discovered among the Cherokee, and still spoke the old language, all that remains of Natchez blood today flows in the veins of some Chickasaw, Creek or Cherokee, and the only memorial to its fine culture, the mere name of a riverside, white-American town.

North-eastern hunting and farming Indians

This involves a heterogeneous area, which cannot be summarised glibly. It contains groups I have already included in the Sub-Arctic Indian groupings in the section on Circumpolar peoples—the Algonquian peoples, such as the Ojibway. The important language group is that of the Iroquoian. In the central and southern zones slash-and-burn agriculture was practised everywhere to raise corn, beans, squash, pumpkins and sunflowers and tobacco. The Indians lived mostly in villages which may have been deserted during the winter-hunting periods. Both long-houses and wigwams were used. Among the matrilineal and warlike Iroquois, groups were organized into confederations.

The Iroquois, so different from the neighbouring Algonquian bands, ravaged their neighbours. The fiercest of them were the Mohawks, the Oneida and the

Seneca. The warriors carried bows and arrows, but these were used only for ambushes, the Iroquois preferring close-in fighting with the club, called a 'tomahawk' by the Algonquians. Their method of attack was to sneak up on the enemy 'like foxes', fight 'like lions' and disappear again 'like birds', taking captives with them who were either adopted into the tribe or reserved for orgies and torture.

A listing of 'north-eastern' Algonquian and Iroquois peoples, many of them extinct, includes the Beothuk, Micmac, Malecite, Passamaquoddy, Penobscot, Wawenock, Norridgewock, Abnaki, Algonkin, Ottawa, Tobacco, Huron, Neutral, Potawatomi, Missisauga, Ojibway, Menomini, Winnebago, Sauk, Fox, Kickapoo, Illinois, Miami, Erie, Shawnee, Wenro, Seneca, Tutelo, Powhatan, Nottoway, Tuscarora, Nanticoke, Delaware, Conoy, Montauk, Wappinger, Nipmuc, Massachuset, Pennacook, Nauset, Wampanoag, Narraganset, Pequot, Mohegan, Mahican, Pocumtuc, Cayuga, Onondaga, Oneida, Mohawk, Susquehanna.

The Plains bison-hunting Indians

The Plains bison-hunters are perhaps the best known of America's Indians. War-bonneted Plains warriors are the epitome of Indians everywhere. Horsemen and warriors, the acquisition of the horse (from the Spaniards) transformed their life from one of scarcity and near-famine to one in which food (the bison or buffalo) was assured. They hunted antelope and cultivated corn, beans, squash and sunflowers. Virtually all the nomadic Plains' tribes held some version of the Sun Dance, which originated with the Arapaho and Cheyenne.

The Plains bison or 'buffalo' lived in migratory herds along with the Indians and the European wild horse from the sixteenth century. Typical hunting tribes are the Blackfoot, the Crow, and the Cheyenne, who formed effective units for annual hunts, driving the buffalo into pounds large enough to hold a hundred or more head. The strategy of the hunt was to frighten the buffalo and drive them down a prepared lane to stampede over a cliff, where they fell injured into the pound below. With the horse available, herds could be brought to the pounds from several miles distant and large massacres took place, after which the entire camp flayed and cut up the animals, leaving nothing behind but a pile of surplus horns.

A complete list of the various Plains peoples includes the Sarsi, Plains Cree, Blackfoot, Gros Ventre, Assiniboin, Plains Ojibway, Crow, Hidatsa, Mandan, Yanktonai, Teton Dakota, Wind River Shoshoni, Cheyenne, Arikara, Santee

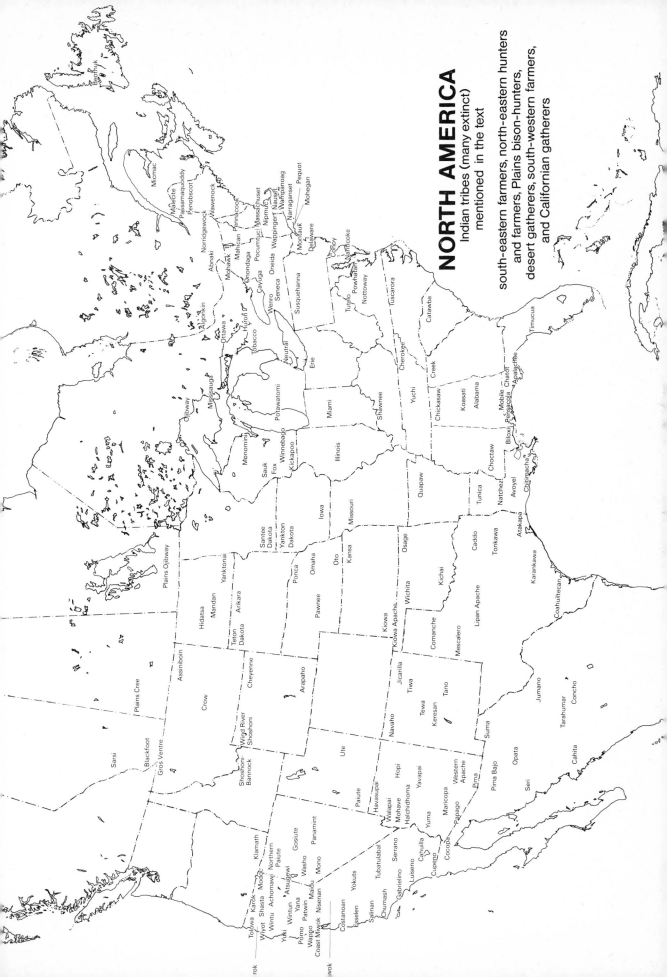

NORTH AMERICA

Indian tribes (many extinct)
mentioned in the text

south-eastern farmers, north-eastern hunters
and farmers, Plains bison-hunters,
desert gatherers, south-western farmers,
and Californian gatherers

Beothuk

Micmac

Malécite
Passamaquoddy
Penobscot
Wawenock
Norridgewock
Abnaki
Mohawk
Onondaga
Cayuga
Seneca
Oneida
Wenro
Mahican
Pennacook
Massachuset
Nipmuc
Wappinger Nauset
Pocumtuc Wampanoag
Narraganset
Montauk
Delaware
Pequot
Mohegan
Conoy
Nanticoke
Tutelo
Powhatan
Nottoway
Tuscarora
Catawba
Timucua

Ottawa
Huron
Tobacco
Neutral
Erie
Susquehanna

Algonkin

Ojibway

Mississauga

Monomini

Sauk
Fox
Winnebago
Kickapoo

Potawatomi

Miami

Illinois

Shawnee

Cherokee

Creek

Yuchi

Chickasaw

Koasati
Alabama
Mobile
Biloxi Pensacola
Natchez
Avoyel
Chitimacha
Chatot
Apalachee

Tunica

Choctaw

Quapaw

Iowa
Missouri
Oto
Kansa

Omaha
Ponca

Osage

Caddo

Tonkawa

Karankawa

Atakapa

Coahuiltecan

Pawnee

Wichita
Kichai

Lipan Apache

Comanche

Mescalero

Kiowa
Kiowa Apache

Jicarilla

Tiwa
Tewa
Keresan
Tano

Western
Apache

Jumano

Tarahumar
Concho

Santee
Dakota
Yankton
Dakota

Yanktonai

Hidatsa
Mandan
Arikara

Teton
Dakota

Assiniboin

Plains Ojibway

Plains Cree

Sarsi

Blackfoot
Gros Ventre

Crow

Cheyenne

Arapaho

Wind River
Shoshoni

Shoshoni-
Bannock

Ute

Paiute

Navaho

Hopi
Walapai
Havasupai
Mohave
Halchidhoma

Yavapai

Maricopa

Western
Apache

Pima

Papago

Pima Bajo

Opata

Seri

Suma

Taos

Coahuiltecan

Tarahumar
Concho

Cahita

Northern
Paiute

Klamath
Modoc
Shasta
Achomawi

Atsugewi
Yana
Washo
Patwin
Maidu
Nisenan
Mono

Panamint

Gosiute

Wintu
Wiyot
Karok
Tolowa

Yuki
Pomo
Wappo
Coast Miwok

Costanoan
Esselen
Salinan
Chumash

Gabrielino
Luiseno
Cupeno
Serrano
Cahuilla

Tubatulabal

Yokuts

Yuma
Cocopa

rok

wok

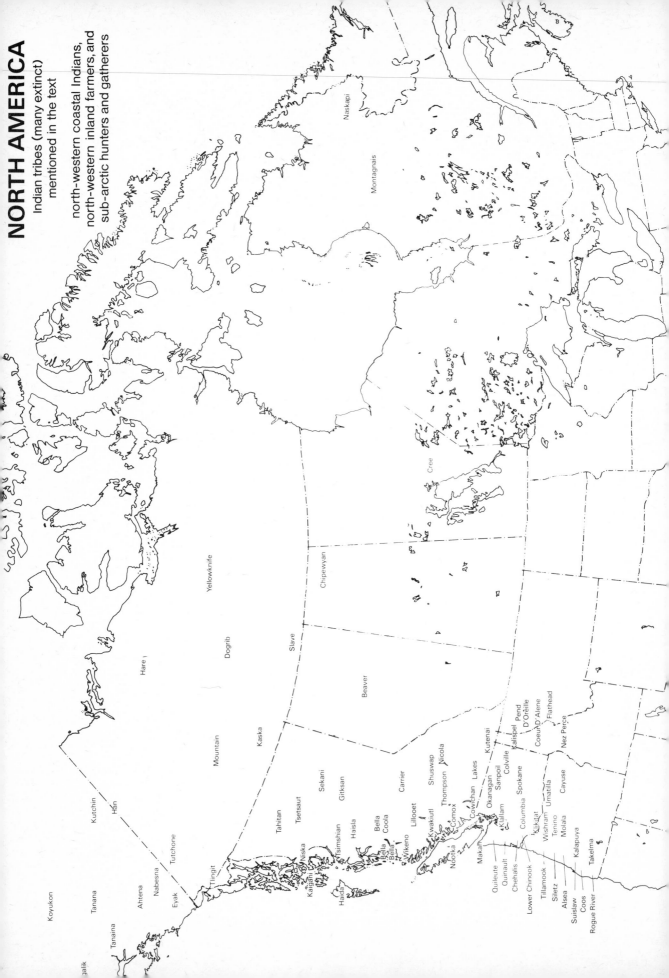

NORTH AMERICA
Indian tribes (many extinct)
mentioned in the text

north-western coastal Indians,
north-western inland farmers, and
sub-arctic hunters and gatherers

Naskapi

Montagnais

Cree

Chipewyan

Yellowknife

Slave

Dogrib

Hare

Beaver

Mountain

Kaska

Koyukon

Tanana

Ahtena

Nabesna

Tutchone

Kutchin

Hän

Eyak

Tlingit

Tanaina

balik

Tanana

Sekani

Tahitan

Tsetsaut

Gitksan

Carrier

Shuswap

Nicola

Thompson

Lakes

Kutenai

Pend
D'Oreille
Flathead
Kalispel
Coeur
D'Alene
Nez Perce

Cowichan

Okanagan
Sanpoil
Colville
Columbia
Spokane

Niska

Tsimshian

Haisla

Bella
Coola

Bella
Bella

Lillooet

Kwakiutl

Comox

Wikeno

Nootka

Makah

Haida

Kaigani

Umatilla
Cayuse

Klikitat
Wishram
Molala

Tenno
Kalapuya

Takelma

Quileute
Quinault
Chehalis
Lower Chinook
Tillamook
Siletz
Alsea
Suislaw
Coos
Rogue River

Klallam

A medicine man of the Blackfoot explaining a pictograph. The importance of ritual practices, especially those concerned with magic, still exists for many Indian peoples.

Dakota, Yankton Dakota, Iowa, Ponca, Omaha, Pawnee, Oto, Kansa, Mescalero, Missouri, Osage, Kichai, Tonkawa, Lipan Apache, Comanche, Wichita, Kiowa and Kiowa Apache, Arapaho.

Desert gathering Indians

The most inhospitable areas of North America are two desert regions, where wandering, gathering peoples subsisted on wild plants and animals, while a few groups of sedentary farmers scratched a living from the poor soil. These gatherers utilized over a hundred different kinds of plants, the pinon nut being the most important. The Shoshoni, Ute and Paiute lived in temporary dwellings and in small self-sufficient bands. Usually they were peaceful, with simple religious beliefs based on guardian spirits, dreams and the curing powers of shamans. The Paiute of the arid plateaus of the Great Basin in western North America, occupied a territory of fifty to a hundred square miles, hunting both spring and summer in individual families. In the winter, the band congregated on one or two fairly large and semi-permanent settlements, the commonest form of winter dwelling being a conical structure built of juniper branches with a central fire-pit and smoke-hole, near a stream. In these sweat houses, hot stones were placed and water poured over them to produce a hot, steamy atmosphere in which men sweated before plunging into the river. This was the Paiute meeting-house for men and dormitory for youths. Sweating was believed to have medicinal value and also had strong religious associations.

Along with the Paiute, peoples of the desert include the Klamath, Shoshoni-Bannock, Northern Paiute (Paviotso), Gosiute, Washo, Mono, Panamint, Ute, Coahuiltecan and Karankawa.

South-west farming Indians

Unlike in many other parts of 'Indian' North America, many of the descendants of ancient Indians of the South-west survive, the most important being the Navaho and Pueblo groups. The colourful Pueblo live scattered from the Rio Grande valleys in New Mexico to Arizona and still cling to their old way of life. The Pueblo Indians are skilful and resourceful farmers, depending on a very scarce rainfall. They live in towns or pueblos, in stone and adobe dwellings built in compact clusters. In the past their irrigation system of farming required a fairly complicated government organization, centring on religious leaders and a matrilineal clan system.

With the Navaho we can use the present tense with confidence. They are alive and flourishing. They are relative newcomers to their area, but are the largest Indian tribe in the United States. During the seventeenth and eighteenth centuries the Navaho came to occupy the scenically magnificent plateau country known as the 'Four Corners'. At first wandering hunters and gatherers with a limited knowledge of farming, they were taught by the local Pueblo people to farm properly and they consequently came to subsist on the agricultural produce of small gardens — corn, beans and squash, then with the arrival of the Spaniards, wheat, oats and fruits. They also acquired sheep and goats as well as cattle and horses, and became semi-pastoral people, moving seasonally with their flocks in search of pasturage. In terms of ecological destruction, however, the sheep and goats were the most insidious acquisition, stripping large areas of the ground cover. As a result, large parts of the huge Navaho reserve are barren and unproductive — sixteen million acres are not sufficient to support the population of 100,000.

In the past, farming and herding provided sufficient livelihood, while trading posts offered a market for their products, such as rugs and silverware. Now, surrounded by a constantly growing white population, they have to confront the 'threat' of the American way of life and attempt to enter the modern American economy. Change is not new to the Navaho, however. During World War II, Navaho men went to the army and the women worked in defence plants. Then, the discovery of uranium deposits brought money to the Tribal Fund and work for the young men. Later came the development of new oil fields. With the money, the Tribal Council provides new roads, water supplies, irrigation projects, etc. Since Navaho country abounds in interesting sights, such as the remains of walled cities and the Chaco Canyon monument, tourism is an important industry in the area.

The Navaho, almost miraculously, have retained much of their Indian culture and have their own tribal government. Prior to the occupation of the southwest by the United States, they existed as small bands united in clans, but there was no government. On their return to the reservation after an enforced exodus in 1868, changes were begun and by 1901, the Bureau of Indian Affairs divided the country into six districts, along with another tribe, the Hopi. However, it was the discovery of oil in 1921 that brought into focus the need for a Navaho tribal government. A council was elected and it was ruled that the oil leases should be for the benefit of

Navaho sheep-breeders in Monument Valley, Utah, search for water and fodder for their animals. Flocks still spell status, bringing increased wealth from wool and weaving.

the tribe. In 1940 when the Tribal Council voted to establish a Department of Resources, the first developments were the Sawmill Project and the Arts and Crafts Guild. Two hundred Navaho men were trained in the best methods of handling lumber and in the concept of sustained-yield forestry. Strip coal-mining was also begun. On the whole, the rich earnings from the Department of Resources is being wisely used. Money is never distributed to individuals, but is widely invested.

The Navaho way of life, in the face of these twentieth century innovations, has changed a good deal, but much remains. The basic unit of Navaho society is still an extended family of parents and daughters with their husbands and children, that is, it is matrilineally organized. Women still play an important role, as children grow up among their maternal relatives and much property, including livestock, passes through the female line. A man, when he marries, does not acquire his wife's property, but retains his interest in his mother's extended family and, as in many other matrilineal societies, the maternal uncle has many responsibilities for his nephew—his sister's son—as a disciplinarian, for example. The father is free to be his children's confidant and friend. Navaho men observe a strong avoidance relationship with their mother-in-law, and though friendly with sisters, they may have no physical contact with them.

Religious ceremonies still take place, particularly during the transition from childhood to adulthood. A girl's first menstruation ceremony lasts four nights during which she undergoes dietary and other restrictions: she races towards the rising sun each morning, grinds corn and has her hair ceremonially washed. The Navaho, terrified of the ghosts of the dead who may return and harm people, burn corpses as quickly as possible and without ceremony; the job is done by a non-Navaho if possible. If death occurs inside the 'hogan'—the Navaho house—the body is removed through the hole in the north side and the hogan abandoned, often burned.

The Navaho hogans are scattered far and wide over the reservation in order to obtain adequate pasturage for sheep. The hogan is a practical affair, heated with a minimum amount of fire, and cool in summer; it has no windows and is a retreat from the frequent winds in early spring. Round, or nearly round, in shape and with a dome-like roof, hogans always face east, to the rising sun. They are mainly built of mats, or with logs and stone, if available. On entering a hogan one must move from left to right, circling the fire in the centre of the room. On the west side, sheepskins,

Navaho woman at the Gallup Ceremonial, an Indian gathering. The abundance of silver jewellery she wears is to demonstrate wealth status as well as to achieve decorative effect. The Navaho now produce silver for commercial purposes, both touristic and tribal.

which serve as beds at night, are rolled up and stacked away. There is a place—almost ceremonial in importance—for everything. Near the winter hogan, there is always a summer shelter, for the Navaho live chiefly out of doors during the summer months. Built of upright poles, the shelter has a roof of fresh green boughs. The women set up their looms there and work their marvellous blankets, while the children watch the flocks and the men haul water and wood and tend the fields.

The south-western farmers have been catalogued by American anthropologists thus: the Navaho, Havasupai, Nalapai, Mohave, Halchidhoma, Hopi, Yavapai, Western Apache, Yuma, Maricopa, Cocopa, Papago, Pima, Pima Bajo, Opata, Seri, Tarahumar, Cahita, Concho, Jumano, Suma, Tano, Eastern Keresan, Western Keresan, Tewa, Tiwa, Jicarilla.

Californian gathering Indians

This group of hunters and gatherers, living in bands, is linguistically diverse, but culturally similar—wild-food gathering was their prime activity. They lived in a bountiful environment and had a basic reliance on acorns, which allows a relatively dense and settled population. Acorns are plentiful, dependable, easily secured, storable and nutritious. All these groups of Indians lived in small bands, divided into moieties, and were on the whole peaceful. Their shamans received their powers during dreams or trances. The most well-known of these Californian collectors are the Yurok and the Miwok. Other groups include the Tolowa, Karok, Modoc, Shasta, Wiyot, Wintu, Achomawi, Yuki, Wintun, Yana, Atsugewi, Patwin, Pomo, Wappo, Coast Miwok, Maidu, Nisenan, Costanoan, Esselen, Yokuts, Salinan, Tubatulabal, Chumash, Gabrielino, Luiseno, Serrano, Cahuilla, Cupeno.

North-western Indians

Among the north-western Indians, the fishermen of the coast are one of the most distinctive and singular cultures of America. Its affinities, however, are with the orient and not with Meso-America, like the Pueblo Indians and the Navaho. They inhabit a rich and bountiful coastline, well endowed with animal life. The tribes who live in this zone have a uniform culture with some interesting divergencies and considerable linguistic variation. The coastal Indians such as the Tlingit and Kwakiutl made their living primarily from the sea and the rivers that run into it — fish, clams, abalones and oysters were particularly plentiful. The Nootkas even hunted whales in the open, like the Chukchi of Siberia. The Tlingit hunted caribou. They preserved fish by smoking. They were skilful workers of wood and stone and make spectacular totem poles. The tribes were mostly hierarchically organized with ceremonies, known as potlatches, associated with the validation of statuses. Among the Kwakiutl of British Columbia, wealthy groups of Indians were divided into classes, with rank and status playing a vital part in social organization. The maintenance of rank depended not on heredity and succession, but also on the giving of large feasts, lavish display and gift-making. These famous competitive ceremonial feasts — the potlatches — between nobles and wealthy men centred around large stores of food and gifts accumulated in advance such as carvings and woven blankets. The giver of a potlatch made presents to invited guests according to their rank and these gifts always implied repayment obligations. Property was also destroyed. Canoes and coppers were often deliberately broken, slaves were killed and valuable fish-oil squandered by pouring it on the fire until the flames set the carved roof timbers ablaze.

The coastal Indians can be catalogued thus: the Eyak, Tlingit, Kaigani, Niska, Haida, Tsimshian, Haisla, Gitksan, Bella Bella, Bella Coola, Wikeno, Kwakiutl, Nootka, Comox, Cowichan, Klallam, Makah, Quileute, Quinault, Chehalis, Lower Chinook, Tillamook, Siletz, Alsea, Coos, Rogue River, Takelma, Kalapuya, Suislaw.

Further inland, the north-western Indian farmers are: the Lillooet, Thompson, Shuswap, Nicola, Okanagan, Lakes, Kutenai, Tenino, Sanpoil, Colville, Spokane, Columbia, Klikitat, Wishram, Molala, Umatilla, Cayuse, Nez Perce, Flathead, Coeur D'Alene, Kalispel, Pend D'Oreille.

Sub-Arctic hunters and fishermen

To complete the picture of the Indians of North America, I include the caribou hunters of Canada and Alaska, some of whom have already been mentioned in the section on the circumpolar regions. These groups of Indians are scattered through the austere inhospitable land of the sub-arctic. They have a simple, un-differentiated social organization living in small composite bands where individual families are the most important unit. They are the Koyukon, Ingalik, Tanaina,

Kwakiutl Indians salmon-fishing
in Thompson river, Canada.

Tanana, Kutchin, Han, Ahtena, Nabesna, Tutchone, Hare, Mountain, Kaska, Dogrib, Yellowknife, Slave, Beaver, Chipewyan, Cree, Carrier, Tsetsaut, Tahltan, Montagnais, Naskapi, Sekani.

White 'primitives'

In many parts of America, small tight-knit communities, isolated from the mainstream of our atomic age, pursue a way of life which is as 'primitive' as many of the Indian, or African societies described elsewhere in this book. Of the white ethnic minorities, most have, more or less reluctantly, melted into the American pot, sometimes taking several generations to do so. Other groups have retained their folk ways, special religious and taboos, and linguistic separateness over the centuries. Here, I am thinking of groups such as the Amish and Mennonites and also the lost communities of almost self-sufficient subsistence farmers, such as the inhabitants of the poverty-stricken Appalachians.

The Amish take their name from their original leader, one Jakob Amman. They are descendants of a religious sect that grew up among Swiss Anabaptists in the period 1693–97. In Europe, the sectarian Amish did not develop along the lines of a folk model, but when they came to America in the eighteenth century, they found they could live near to each other on family farms and maintain relatively self-sufficient, closely knit communities. An integrated folk culture developed and maintained itself, surviving in the New World as distinctive, small, self-governing communities.

The Amish society has so far rejected modern American values and know-how, in order to live their traditional way of life. Attachment to their ways, their religion and to the community itself is desirable and necessary to them, despite attacks from outside that any 'incestuous' attachment to ethnic-oriented groups is undesirable and un-American. The Amish are only one of many traditional, cohesive, farming groups whose way of life is being challenged by the technology and urban seductions of the outside world. Most of them are losing their distinctive languages, race, customs and ways of thinking and are merging into the dominant culture.

An Amish farmer with his pack horse in the Great Smoky Mountain. The Amish groups form a part of the Mennonite sect of Protestantism.

Amish society is a primitive or folk society—small, isolated, traditionalist, simple and homogeneous, where oral communication and conventionalized ways are all important in integrating the life of the community. Shared, practical knowledge is as important for the Amish as for the Navaho and, as with most other primitive peoples, association is personal and emotional rather than abstract and categoric. The Amish, like the Navaho communities, have a strong sense of belonging together and can communicate by shared symbols.

The Amish for centuries have conformed to traditions based on biblical teachings, traditions which stress again and again separation from the outside world. Neighbours of African pastoralists are thought to walk on their heads; the neighbours of the Bangwa in Cameroon are all witches; and American outsiders in Amish society are considered equally beyond the pale—they do not marry them or have social intercourse with them. Yankees visit Amish communities, as whites visit African compounds—as tourists. The Amish are not in spirit Americans, they are a distinctive ethnic group, speaking their own language, practising their own religion, using teams of horses and carriages on the highway, dressing differently, living in distinctive houses. According to the Amish charter, they should not engage in war, in politics or in business with an outsider-partner. They have restrictions against telephones and electricity. They have a distinct language, a common occupation, intimate knowledge of other members of the community and regular religious ceremonies which only they may attend.

Amish life, like Polynesian life, is pervasively religious. A great source of sacred tradition—the Amish myth—is the 'suffering of the faithful': *The Bloody Theatre of Martyrs* is an enormous tract of over 1500 pages in which there are accounts of Christians who were condemned to death for their steadfast faith. It is full of primitive burnings and stonings, crucifixions and live burials.

Four important qualities are shared by all so-called primitive peoples—distinctiveness, smallness, homogeneity and self-sufficiency. The values of the Amish resemble the values of other primitive peoples: they are taught to revere aged relations, glorify their own religion, despise outsiders, admire hard manual work. Families were traditionally thought to have special 'looks' and their own particular ways. Within his family a man is protected and at the same time cut

Pouring sorghum mash into a bucket in Cades Cove in the Smoky Mountain area. The essential key to Amish life is simplicity and rejection of worldly values.

off from the outside world. There is strict division of labour between men and women. Feasts are important. They live in *small* groups. The basic Amish unit is the 'church district', centring on a religious ceremony, which takes place within a household attended by thirty to forty other householders. As in primitive communities, virtually the whole society forms a body of relatives and the relationship of man to man and the persons who make up society are dependent on their genealogical position. They co-operate, farming together, sharing their specializations, shoeing mules, carpentering, hog-killing. Amish society, importantly, is homogeneous in the totality of its culture and psychology. They even believe they are racially pure. Psychologically, they are homogeneous in their opposition to new technology, wealth and outside influences.

Within the community, the elderly have the function of holding the group together and constantly stressing family values. The family, with the elders at the top, is thus the main unit of social control. An individual's action reflects honour or shame on the rest of the family, which is responsible for socializing the young.

Another group of American white primitives survives in the Appalachian mountains, not because of a stubborn Protestant faith, but through isolation and poverty. Today, in the Appalachian regions of America, the rural population contains the hardcore of America's distressed farmers. About their cabins they maintain a difficult subsistence by basic farming and hunting. The majority of the old farmers have left the hills; those who remain do so merely because 'the hills are our home'. The American government maintain that no farmer can make a 'respectable' living in the area; in fact, the Appalachians hold the highest concentration of low income farms in the United States. In what was once a sanctuary for hard-working small farmers, these hill-billies have missed or resisted progress exalting their isolation to the level of a mystique.

The Appalachians are, therefore, a United States problem area, 'suffering' from declining population, emigration, and isolation from the mainstream of American culture. American norms—progress, suburban morality, plumbing, conspicuous consumption—here, they go by the board. Like an African region, the Appalachians have even become a mission field; voluntary Christian agencies and churches are subsidizing ministers' salaries, building churches and establishing private academies for the 'poor people' of the mountains. Frontier nurses visit distant homesteads on horseback, delivering babies in isolated homes. Sentimental writers tell of their hard life and stubborn ways. Journalists write of incestuous families, feuding clans and primitive ways of living, and even anthropologists find them grist to their mill, as this book testifies!

Most of the original families of the Appalachians were of British origin when they settled in the mountain regions about 1800. They brought with them a culture that was predominantly British and a belief system that was, for the most part, derived from Protestant fundamentalism. They originally set up in villages, but with the end of the Indian threat, they lived in dispersed farms and settlements stretching for miles along relatively fertile river valleys. Over the years, much of the steep hillsides have been subdivided and handed down from one generation to the next and younger sons and newcomers moved up into coves and hollows of less fertility.

The Appalachian community has remained tight-knit; land is farmed by families and home and economic enterprises are combined into an inter-related whole. The family is the main unit of production, as in most primitive groups—90% of the total farm product being consumed at home. Corn is the main crop, while a third of the fields is devoted to tobacco—the only major cash crop. Like the African, in the twentieth century, faced with growing demands for cash to pay taxes and buy consumer goods, the Appalachian farmer has been forced out of his self-sufficient farm to seek work in forest projects, mines and factories. Poverty is now the continual threat of these one-time farmers: either the coal mines will close down, or the crops will fail.

Throughout the zone, in one of the principal tourist areas of the nation—the Great Smoky Mountains National Park has more visitors than any other national park—changes are coming thick and fast. There are even museums depicting the 'lost' way of life of the Appalachians. Yet numbers of the people still live in

An Appalachian woman on her
simple farm in the hills of West
Virginia. The quilt she is making
is sewn according to local custom
and long-standing tradition.

inaccessible areas, hostile to the foreigners (Americans!)—desperately clinging to
their isolated way of life. They resent administrative interference as much as the
Amish; and most of the older people—living in coves connected to major highways
by roads which may be impassable part of the year or negotiable only on foot or
horseback—are suspicious of *all* strangers. Tourism, they see, will mean changing
their way of life: their conservative and fundamental type of religion does not
approve of drinking or smoking nor the styles of dress worn by many tourists.
Moreover, tourism, as in Africa, hardly benefits the locals. Many families have
been forced to move to make room for national parks, as they have been forced to
move for the new dams. Farmers are not allowed to cut down trees in their
meadows. The Appalachian community sees vulgar, self-interested tourism; and
the tourist sees discourteous, hostile and mean locals—'primitives!'.

Appalachian life is 'primitive' in a technological sense and because they live in
small-scale, traditionalist communities. There is a strong division of labour,
between men and women's work. Socialization in the family is strongly seen in
terms of sex, boys and girls beginning their male- or female-oriented lives at six or
seven. The father rules the household patriarchally, he and his sons clearing land,
fencing, grubbing, ploughing, planting, cutting wood and working off the farm to
get cash. Communities are close-knit, bound not so much by ceremonies and
religion as by visiting, dancing and co-operative work. Their language, religious
beliefs, values and occupational interests, style of clothes and sense of being
mountain-people give them an intricate mesh of kin-shared experiences. As among
the Amish, the old are respected and given an important role. In a family-oriented
society, old people are not allowed to feel useless and unwanted; even if their roles
are rather negative ones they usually serve as symbolic focuses for the family as a
whole and thereby play an important part in the intricate family network.

As in other homogeneous culture groups—primitive societies—it is possible to
single out some basic value patterns or themes in Appalachian life. On the whole,
they contrast deeply with the values of the modern American organization-man.

A couple in their tobacco patch in Hinton, West Virginia. Self-sufficiency is the aim here.

The mountain farmers are self-reliant and individualists, each household in its hollow, living its own life under its provider and protector, who is the law-maker, the patriarch. Self-help, independent action are duties, not prerogatives. However, this kind of independence is 'inefficient' and the people are almost inevitably going to lose against the competition of factories and new ways: in an industrial economy, purchasing-power not self-sufficiency is the mark of success. It is because of the changing standards of the American nation, rather than any real deterioration of living conditions in the Appalachians, that the region has become an economic problem. The same can be said of half of Africa, where the self-sufficient farming communities have been forced to join a world economy and produce more and more, in order to provide raw materials for world markets and buy the consumer products of industrialized nations. As in Africa, the Appalachian peasant sees the government as 'them' and not 'us'.

The Appalachian is a traditionalist and a fatalist. Fatalism is a feature of his or her religion based on the idea that life is governed by external forces over which humans have little, or no, control—an outlook which seems peculiar only when advanced technology has given men the confidence (right or wrong) in their own ability to master nature. Like the African, the mountain people never possessed the resources necessary to gain control over an environment that at times must have seemed merciless. Their fatalist philosophy therefore seems reasonable in the ecological circumstances, many turning to God to seek recompense, in a future life, for earthly misery. As in all primitive communities, religious values so thoroughly permeate the culture of the southern Appalachian regions, that no aspect of life is unaffected. Moreover, they are fundamentalists in that they believe that the Bible contains the literal and infallible word of God.

Today, the Appalachian Mountains are lonely zones; bottom lands which used to be cultivated and cropped are now in grass and weeds; trees and bush are creeping down the steep mountainside. Old paths are covered in briars and there are wild stretches between occupied homesteads. The people, who have resisted the blandishments of the administration, have become even more isolated from

A float in the fourth of July parade, West Virginia. The quilts behind the Appalachian woman are made by members of the non-profit-making co-operative organized by mountain artisans. Work is their motive, not money.

external contacts, living in near-abandoned hollows and coves. Half the families there receive welfare payments; one third have 'donated foods', receiving surplus U.S. commodities, like the drought-stricken or epidemic-ridden Africans. They still live in small wooden houses with outside toilets and no telephones. Most of them pump water from an outside well. It has become a rural poverty-area, with such features as malnutrition and mental illness frequent. As J. Galbraith has said, 'Poor people have poor ways and left to themselves, these poor ways tend to perpetuate themselves'. The tragic contrast between modern America and the mountain-culture comes out in the fact that if poor people do not have what the larger community regards as the minimum necessary for decency, they cannot wholly escape the judgement of the outside community that they are, in fact, 'indecent'.

Yet, it is in no way their fault. They have been as much victims of industrial colonialism as poor Africans. Thomas Wolfe in *The Hills Beyond* has recorded it. 'Some changes had occurred . . . , but for the most part they were tragic ones. The great mountain slopes and forests of the section had been ruinously detimbered; the farm soil on hillsides had eroded and washed down; high up, upon the hills, one saw the raw scars of old mica pits, the dump-heaps of deserted mines. Some vast, destructive 'Suck' had been at work here; and a visitor had he returned after a hundred years would have been compelled to note the ruin of the change. It was evident that a huge compulsive greed had been at work; the whole region had been sucked and gutted, milked dry, denuded of its rich, primeval treasures; something blind and ruthless had been here, grasped and gone'.

Epilogue

One of the purposes of this survey has been to show the great range of cultures that still flourish throughout the world, despite pressures towards conformity in a world which is gradually becoming dominated by Euro-American, Pan-Russian or Chinese values. Yet the danger that exotic communities of gypsies, 'montagnards', nomadic pastoralists or African hunters face is a serious one. Thousands of cultures have been wiped off the face of the earth, either absorbed by neighbouring, monolithic groups or wiped out by physical aggression on the part of intolerant, invading powers hungry for land, resources and labour. Even today the anthropologist writes in the present tense but in many cases by the time his field material is published 'what the Bumulu do' has already become 'what the Bumulu did'. Most of the groups we commonly call 'primitive' or 'tribal', bands of hunters and gatherers, simple farming communities in isolated corners of the world, will have disappeared by the end of the century unless positive measures are taken to arrest this tragic process.

Some change is inevitable, and almost always desired by the people concerned. Is it, in fact, feasible to help these groups survive as such in the modern world? Or must all minority peoples become assimilated into the prevailing cultural norm? The Brazilian government, for example, plans to assimilate the Indian groups of the Amazon and Mato Grosso, settling them in reserves where settlers have taken root or beside towns and outposts where they can get what work they can. In enforced settlement some tribes have got into an appalling state, suffering from fatal epidemics or an incurable apathy. This is the kind of situation which has resulted in ethnocide in Tasmania, Northern America and other parts of Latin America.

Most observers are aware that a total and rapid assimilation of marginal peoples into the dominant culture is not desirable. The best policy would seem to encourage respect for local cultural traditions and to increase the local pride and numbers of minority groups. It is clear that the human zoo approach is not the answer to the 'problem of the primitive'—shutting them away in order to protect them. The Xingu National Park in Brazil has been an unprecedented success in allowing isolated bands a gradual contact with a completely different way of life. The Villas Boas brothers who began these parks have struggled not to shut tribes away, but to protect unsophisticated people from epidemics, aggression, land speculators, tourists and bigoted missionaries whether they be Protestant Christians or bearers of political ideologies.

The Australian government has also come to realise the importance of the eventual integration—not assimilation—of Australian Aborigines, at the same time preventing their further decline through illness and protecting them from the evils of complete cultural degradation. In fact the aboriginal population has slowly begun to increase rather than decline and their culture has been given a new lease of life. The policy now is that Aborigines are to achieve full status as citizens within Australian society; and at the same time white Australians are being taught tolerance, and understanding of the 'Blackfellow'. The Australian government wants the Aborigine to continue to observe and practice his own customs, even to revive his ceremonial life if possible in order to regain a sense of cultural belonging.

This may be a mere pipe-dream for the Aborigines. Nevertheless for other communities around the globe there is still the possibility of learning not to reject their own history and culture but to develop their own art, music, poetry and ways of thought. Some cultures have survived western invasions and colonialism and rejected the assumption that the world of Western Europe and America is the best of all possible worlds. Hundreds of African peoples have retained their languages and way of life while adopting those aspects of industrial society, Christianity or Islam which are compatible with Africanity.

Ethnic differences should be recognised, tolerated and valued. Such a policy of integration—as opposed to assimilation—would mean that equal opportunity would be available to all, the people concerned being free to become fully involved in the wider community or state while practising their own customs. Fortunately people in many areas of what we have traditionally regarded as the 'civilized world' are realising that the sameness that results from a world-wide melting-pot policy is undesirable. The Maori have successfully discarded elements of their old culture and adopted some of the new. With this there seems a greater hope that we may achieve a society where different groups live side by side without persecution, prejudice or proselytization.

Glossary

aboriginal: original inhabitant of a country; native; indigenous person—primarily applied to the black inhabitants of Australia.

acculturation: process by which a group acquires the cultural characteristics of another.

autochtonous: native, indigenous or aboriginal.

cash crop: crop, e.g. cotton, coffee or cocoa, grown for sale in the market rather than for subsistence.

caste: hierarchy of hereditary, endogamous and occupational groups with social statuses protected by ritual taboos.

clan: group of people claiming descent, usually patrilineal or matrilineal, from a common ancestor.

class: mobile social group based on wealth and status distinctions, associated by Marx primarily with capitalism.

classical: referring to an ancient or ideal cultural style.

collectivize: to form local face-to-face groups of co-operating producers and consumers.

creole: originally used to denote people born of Spanish parents; now used for descendents of non-aboriginal persons born or settled in the West Indies.

descent group: group of people claiming descent from a common ancestor; clans and lineages are descent groups.

double descent: system which occurs in some societies where people belong to two descent groups, one through females (matrilineal) and the other through males (patrilineal).

duality: involving a system based on a double principle or a two-fold distinction (see moieties).

endogamy: practice of marrying within one's group.

epicanthic fold: extra fold of fatty tissue in the eyelid in Mongoloid peoples.

exogamy: practice of marrying outside one's group.

extended family: grouping of two or more elementary families of parents and children formed through polygamy or the cohabitation of brothers and parents and married children.

initiation: ritual which celebrates the achievement of adult status or membership of a special association or social group.

ladino: in northern Latin America and Mexico, person of mixed black and white and Indian descent; in Central America, person of non-Indian origin living in a town and speaking Spanish.

lineage: descent group smaller than a clan within which all relationships are known.

loanword: word borrowed from another language such as sputnik.

mana: a Polynesian word for a supernatural power which may impregnate certain objects; generally a characteristic quality of certain persons (mainly chiefs) and spirits.

marginal: living on the edges of a majority culture or type of economy.

matrilineal: tracing descent through mother and other females.

mestizo: Spanish word for person of mixed race.

miscegenation: sexual union between different races.

moiety: one of a pair of separate groups formed by descent which may have important social functions or merely a ceremonial one.

monogamy: marriage permitted with only one spouse.

neophyte: beginner or novice of religious group.

nomad: member of group or tribe which moves from place to place to seek resources, usually pasture.

pastoralist: herder of cattle, sheep, goats, or reindeer, usually living a nomadic existence.

polyandry: marriage with more than one man; fraternal polyandry involves marriage of a woman with two or more brothers.

polygamy: marriage permitted with more than one woman.

prognathous: with projecting jaws.

reserve: area of land set apart for the exclusive use of certain tribal groups.

sedentary: applied to populations which do not move from place to place to seek resources.

shaman: priest or healer who cures through possession and trance.

slash and burn: method of agriculture where the ashes from burnt trees and shrubs are used to fertilize land.

steatopygia: a physical characteristic found in women wherein excess fat is located in the buttocks.

symbiosis: union of organisms or groups each of which depends for its existence on the other.

taboo: Polynesian word meaning 'forbidden', implying a prohibition of a magico-religious nature, the breaking of which provokes supernatural punishment.

totemism: system whereby there is a close, ritual relationship between natural objects and plants and social groups which may become a cult.

vernacular: language of a country; mother tongue.

Languages and Races of the World

Linguistic and racial classifications are referred to at many points throughout the book. The reader may find the following notes helpful as a brief summary of these groupings. When the prefix 'proto-' is used in connexion with a language or a people, it denotes a hypothetical classification of a race or language immediately ancestral to all languages or peoples known of a certain group—proto-Germanic, proto-Indo-European, proto-Malay. 'Palaeo-' as a prefix, on the other hand, denotes known, but extinct—i.e. archaeological—populations.

Languages: Most of the languages of the world can be grouped together into large family groups or phylums such as Indo-European, Sino-Tibetan and Austronesian. Basque and Ainu are two obvious examples of language isolates, however.

In Europe, the majority of languages are Indo-European and Uralic: the former are divided into Romance, Germanic, Slavic, Celtic, Baltic, Albanian etc; the Uralic subgroup in Europe is known as Finno-Ugric and is spoken by Finns, Lapps, Estonians. Maltese is an Arabian dialect. Turkic languages are also spoken in Europe, particularly in Bulgaria.

In South Asia, including India, the major subgroups of the large Indo-European group include Indo-Aryan and Iranian; the former includes Bengali-Assamese, Hindi, and Sinhalese. The Dravidian languages, mostly of Southern India, form a separate grouping.

In North Asia most languages belong to the Uralic family or one of the three families of the Altaic language grouping—Turkic, Mongolian and Manchu-Tungus, or to Indo-European (Slav for example).

In South-west Asia, the languages spoken in the area from Iran westward to the Mediterranean are Semitic (Arabic and Hebrew), Indo-European (Persian) or Turkic (Turkish). In the Caucasus, the Caucasian languages are isolated groups.

In South-east Asia, virtually all the languages of the islands belong to a single family—the Austronesian or Malayo-Polynesian family, while the mainland has various representatives of the Austro-Asiatic, Thai and Sino-Tibetan (Mon Khmer) groups.

In Oceania, Austronesian languages are spoken in Polynesia, Micronesia and New Guinea. Non-Austronesian languages are spoken in some parts of Melanesia and through-out Australia, apart from the dead Tasmanian languages.

In Africa, languages are grouped into four major families: the Hamito-Semitic groups of Northern Africa, the most widespread being Hausa; Nilotic languages of central-interior Africa; the Niger-Congo languages spoken across Africa from Mauritania to Kenya (there are nine hundred of them and they include Bantu); and Khoisan which numbers about four dozen languages and is mainly spoken in southern Africa primarily by Bushman and Hottentot groups.

In the Americas, apart from six official European languages, there is a myriad of languages which have been barely classified. The northern and central American language family includes Eskimo-Aleut, Athabascan, Algonkian and Aztec, while in southern America the Andean-equatorial group includes the three languages with the greatest number of speakers (Quechua, Guarani and Aymara). Ge-Pano-Carib languages are spoken by smaller groups. Another important language group is the Macro-Chibchan.

Races: Various classifications have been proposed for the understanding of the world's racial groups, and many old ones have been abandoned. The older terms which once divided Europe's population, for example Alpine, Dinaric, Nordic, and Latin, have generally been abandoned. The *Encyclopaedia Britannica* lists nine different races: American Indian, Polynesian, Micronesian, Melanesian, Australoid, Asiatic, Indic, European and African. Other classifications separate out the Pygmies or Bushmen (Bushmanoid) groups and the dwarf populations of South-east Asia known as Negritoes. A much simpler classification divides the world into Caucasian (or European), Mongoloid, Negro and Australoid, the other groups being considered as hybrid groups of these four major subspecies; American Indians are Mongoloid and Melanesians Negroid while the Negritoes are considered as dwarf groups of the people among whom they live.

Acknowledgements and Bibliography

The following works have guided the author and editors in enumerating the geographical, racial and cultural groups presented in this volume and also in the drawing up of the maps.

Abbie, A. A. (1969). *The Original Australians.* London: Frederick Muller; New York: American Elsevier.

Alkure, Q. H. (1972). *An Introduction to the Peoples and Cultures of Micronesia.* Reading, Massachussetts.

Anderson, R. T. (1972). *Modern Europe: an anthropological perspective.* California: Goodyear.

Bacon, Elizabeth E. (1966). *Central Asians under Russian Rule.* New York and Maidenhead: Cornell University Press.

Bellwood, P. (1975). 'The Prehistory of Oceania', *Current Anthropology*, March 1975.

Berndt, R. M. and Catherine, H. (1964). *The World of the First Australians.* London: Angus and Robertson.

Birket-Smith, K. (1959, 2nd ed.). *The Eskimoes.* London: Methuen.

Brain, R. and Pollock, A. (1971). *Bangwa Funerary Sculpture.* London: Gerald Duckworth.

Chagnon, N. (1968). *Yanomamo: The Fierce People.* New York and London: Holt, Rinehart and Winston.

Chen, Ta (1946). *Population in Modern China.* Chicago: University of Chicago Press.

Chowning, Anne (1973). *An Introduction to the Peoples and Cultures of Melanesia.* Reading, Massachusetts: Addison Wesley.

Cohn, B. (1971). *India: the social anthropology of a civilization.* New Jersey: Prentice-Hall.

Coon, C. S. with Hunt, E. E. Jr. (1966). *The Living Races of Man.* London: Jonathan Cape; New York: Alfred A. Knopf.

Coon, C. S. and Andrews, J. M. (eds.) (1943). *Studies in the Anthropology of Oceania and Asia.* Cambridge, Massachussetts: The Peabody Museum.

Cranstone, B. A. L. (1961). *Melanesia: a short ethnography.* London: The British Museum.

Farb, P. (1969). *Man's Rise to Civilization.* London: Secker and Warburg; New York: Avon.

Ford, T. (1962). *The Southern Appalachian Regions.* Lexington: University Press of Kentucky.

Garn, S. (1961). *Human Races.* Illinois: C. C. Thomas.

Geertz, H. and C. (1975). *Kinship in Bali.* Chicago and London: University of Chicago Press.

Gilpin, Laura (1969). *The Enduring Navaho.* Texas and London: University of Texas Press.

Graburn, N. H. and Strong, B. (1973). *Circumpolar Peoples: an anthropological perspective.* California and Hemel Hempstead: Goodyear.

Griaule, M. (1965). *Conversations with Ogotemmeli.* London and New Jersey: Oxford University Press.

Holmberg, A. R. (1950). *Nomads of the Long Bow.* New York and London: Natural History Press.

Horowitz, M. (1971). *Peoples and Cultures of the Caribbean.* New York: Natural History Press.

Hostetler, J. A. (1963). *Amish Society.* Baltimore and Maidenhead: Johns Hopkins.

Howells, W. W. (1973). *The Pacific Islanders.* London: Weidenfeld and Nicolson; New York: Charles Scriber's Sons.

Hunter, G. (1971). *South-East Asia: Race, Culture and Nation.* London and New Jersey: Oxford University Press.

Kennedy, R. (1943). *Islands and Peoples of the Indies.* Washington.

Kluckhohn, C. and Leighton, Dorothea (1973). *The Navaho.* Massachussetts: Harvard University Press.

Kunstadter, P. (1967). *Southeast Asian Tribes, Minorities and Nations* (2 vols.). New Jersey and London: Princeton University Press.

LeBar, F. (ed.) (1964). *Ethnic Groups of Mainland Southeast Asia.* New Haven: Human Relations Area File Press.

LeBar, F. *et al.* (1973). *Ethnic Groups of Insular Southeast Asia.* New Haven: Human Relations Area File Press.

Levin, M. G. and Potapov, L. P. (eds.) (1964). *The The Peoples of Siberia*. Chicago and London: University of Chicago Press.

McVey, Ruth (ed.) (1967). *Indonesia*. New Haven: Human Relations Area File Press.

Majumdar, Dhirenda, N. (ed.) (1958). *Races and Cultures of India*. Bombay: Asia Publishing House.

Malinowski, B. (1966). *Argonauts of the Western Pacific*. London: Routledge and Kegan Paul; New York: E. P. Dutton.

Maloney, C. (1974). *Peoples of South Asia*. New York: Holt, Rinehart and Winston.

Metge, Joan (1967). *The Maoris of New Zealand*. London: Routledge and Kegan Paul; New Jersey, Humanities Press.

Michael, H. N. (ed.) (1962). *Studies in Siberian Ethnogenesis*. Toronto: University of Toronto Press.

Murdock, G. P. (1959). *Africa: its Peoples and their Cultural History*. New York: McGraw.

Newcomb, W. W. Jr. (1974). *North American Indians: an anthropological perspective*. California: Goodyear.

Ohnuki-Tierney, E. (1974). *The Ainu of the North-West Coast of Southern Sakhalin*. New York: Holt, Rinehart and Winston.

Oliver, D. L. (1961, rev. ed.). *The Pacific Islands*. Cambridge, Massachussetts and London: Harvard University Press.

Owen, R. *et al.* (1967). *North American Indians*. London and New York: Macmillan.

Reina, R. E. (1971). *The Law of the Saints*. New York: Bobbs-Merrill.

Salim, S. M. (1961). *Marsh Dwellers of the Euphrates Delta*. London: Athlone Press of the University of London.

Schwarzweller, H. K. *et al.* (1971). *Mountain Families in Transition*. London and Pennsylvania: Pennsylvania State University Press.

Spencer, R. (1958, 3rd printing). *An Ethno-Atlas*. Iowa: William C. Brown.

Spencer, R. F. *et al.* (1955). *The Native Americans*. New York: Harper and Row.

Steward, J. H. (1946-1959). *Handbook of South American Indians* (7 vols.). Reprinted, Michigan: Scholarly Press.

Suggs, R. C. (1960). *The Island Civilizations of Polynesia*. New York: New American Library.

Sweet, Louise (ed.) (1971). *The Central Middle East*. New Haven: Human Relations Area File Press.

Tyler, S. A. (1972). *India: an anthropological perspective*. California and Hemel Hempstead: Goodyear.

Underhill, Ruth, M. (1958). *The Navajos*. Oklahoma and London: University of Oklahoma Press.

Vayda, A. P. (1968). *Peoples and Cultures of the Pacific*. New York: Natural History Press.

Vos, G. A. de (1971). *Japan's Outcastes: Problem of the Burakumin*. London: Minority Rights Group.

Wolfe, T. (1941). *The Hills Beyond*. New York: Harper and Row.

Yoors, J. (1967). *The Gypsies*. London: George Allen and Unwin.

Picture Credits

Permission to reproduce photographs has kindly been given by the following. (The picture numbers in italics refer to colour illustrations.)

AAA Photo, Paris: Picou: 82. Photo Almasy, Neuilly, France: 84. Courtesy of the American Museum of Natural History, New York: 261. Mike Andrews: 229, 231, 247. Australian Information Service, London: 22, 23, 26, 40, 45, 47, *53*. Anne Bolt: 234, 246. Douglas Botting: 155. Trustees of the British Museum, London: 99, 100. British Tourist Authority, London: 163. Fred Bruemmer, Montreal: 142, 143, 144, 145. Camera and Pen/J. Allan Cash Limited, London: 14, 31, 44, 77, 83, *90*, 92, 94, 95, 104, *119*, 125, 126, 127 (right), 152, 159, 164, 186, 193, 206, 244. Camera Press Limited, London: 171; Paul Almasy: 42; R. Harrington: 28, 32, 34, 51; Leon Herschritt: 169; Ken Lambert: 183; Rolf D. Schurch: 175; Randall Slaughter: 78. Bruce Coleman Limited, Uxbridge: Brian J. Coates: *18*; Nicholas de Vore: *35*, *36*, 38; M. P. L. Fogden: *218*; Charles Henneghien: *199*; Jaroslav Poncar: 178; Simon Trevor: 212. Colorific! London: Linda Bartlett: 270, 273, 274; Trevor le Goubin: 266. Douglas Dickins, F.R.P.S.: *54*, 60, 61, 65, 66, 68, *71*, 73, 96, 97, *107*, 192. Les Etudes Tsiganes, Paris: 172. Werner Forman Archive, London: 72, 79, 110, 114, 116, *130*, 198, *200*, 201, 202. Foto Fass, London: *89*, 187. Fox Photos Limited, London: 158. Peter Fraenkel: 88, 180, 196, 205, 207. Granada Television Limited, London, Disappearing World Series: Brian Moser: 76; Charlie Nairn: 21; André Singer: *120*. Susan Griggs Agency, London: Victor Engelbert: *17*, *217*; Jehangir Gazdar: 86; Adam Wolfitt: *148*, 264, *271*. Robert Harding Associates, London: Richard Ashworth: *253*; Robert Cundy: 249; Robin Hanbury-Tenison: 16, 19, 62; Peter Ibbotson: *235*; Bill and Clare Leimbach: 64; Aubrey Singer, B.B.C.: *118*; Times Newspapers Limited: *117*. John Hemming: 230, 237, 238, 239, *254*. Photo Hoa-Qui, Paris: 216, 219, 221, 223, 224, 225, *236*. Rosalind Howell: 188. Alan Hutchison Library, London:

181, 204, 214. Katja Klatt: 173. Photo Knudsen, Oslo: *147*. Steve McCutcheon, Alaska Pictorial Service, Anchorage: 146, 150 (left and right). Middle East Archive, London: 185. Tony Morrison: 232, 233. Novosti Press Agency, London: 124, 127 (left), 161, 167. Observer/ Transworld, London: *108*, 111. Photo Researchers Inc., New York: James Amos: 257, 267, 268; Thomas B. Hollyman: *272*; John Lewis Sage: 263. Professor Ruben E. Reina: 250, 251, 252. A. Robillard, Paris: 109, *182*, 220. S.C.R., London: 132. Novosti from Sovfoto, New York: 138, 154; Tass from Sovfoto, New York: *129*, 131. Western Americana Picture Library, Brentwood, Essex: 256.

The stipple line drawings are by Eddie Armer. Permission to reproduce objects from photographs has kindly been given by the following:

Australian Information Service, London: 46. Trustees of the British Museum, London: contents page, ivory mask representing an Oba of the Benin, 15, 20, 58, 67, 98, 101, 215. Werner Forman Archive, London: 29, 30. Robert Harding Associates, London, Chris Bryan: endpaper, village in Dahomey.

The wash and tone drawings are by John Norton from photographs from the following:

Australian Information Service, London: 12. Camera Press Limited, London, R. Harrington: 27. Werner Forman Archive, London: 74, 103. Granada Television Limited, Disappearing World Series, London, Charlie Nairn: 190. Robert Harding Associates, London, Robert Cundy: 243; Jon Gardey: 85; Robin Hanbury-Tenison: 226; Robert Harding: 177; Bill and Clare Leimbach: 56; Russell Polden: 140. Alan Hutchison Library, London: 208. Photo Researchers Inc., N.Y.C., David Hiser: 255. Tass from Sovfoto, New York: 122.

The maps are by Peter Pendrill.

Index

Page numbers in italic refer to captions to illustrations; those in bold type refer to maps.

283